Material Culture in Transi

Material Culture in Transit: Theory and Practice constellates curators and scholars actively working with material culture within academic and museal institutions through theory and practice. The rich collection of essays critically addresses the multivalent ways in which mobility reshapes the characteristics of artefacts, specifically under prevailing issues of representation and colonial liabilities. The volume attests to material culture as central to understanding the repercussions of problematic histories and proposes novel ways to address them. It offers valuable reading for scholars of anthropology, museum studies, history and others with an interest in material culture.

Zainabu Jallo is Post-Doctoral Researcher and lecturer in Anthropology at the Universities of Basel and Bern, Switzerland. Her PhD in Anthropology is from the Institute for Social Anthropology, University of Bern. She is also a Visiting Researcher in the Department of Anthropology at USP – Universidade de São Paulo, Brazil. Jallo is one of the Principal Investigators of the "Sacral Architecture Africa" Project. She is a Fellow of the Royal Society of Arts England and a member of the UNESCO Coalition of Artists for the General History of Africa. Her scholarly interests include museum anthropology, diaspora studies, iconic criticism, and material culture.

Routledge Studies in Anthropology and Museums

Material Culture in Transit
Theory and Practice
Edited by Zainabu Jallo

www.routledge.com/Routledge-Studies-in-Anthropology-and-Museums/book-series/RSANMU

Material Culture in Transit
Theory and Practice

Edited by Zainabu Jallo

LONDON AND NEW YORK

First published 2023
by Routledge
4 Park Square, Milton Park, Abingdon, Oxon OX14 4RN

and by Routledge
605 Third Avenue, New York, NY 10158

Routledge is an imprint of the Taylor & Francis Group, an informa business

© 2023 selection and editorial matter, Zainabu Jallo; individual chapters, the contributors

The right of Zainabu Jallo to be identified as the author of the editorial material, and of the authors for their individual chapters, has been asserted in accordance with sections 77 and 78 of the Copyright, Designs and Patents Act 1988.

All rights reserved. No part of this book may be reprinted or reproduced or utilised in any form or by any electronic, mechanical, or other means, now known or hereafter invented, including photocopying and recording, or in any information storage or retrieval system, without permission in writing from the publishers.

Trademark notice: Product or corporate names may be trademarks or registered trademarks, and are used only for identification and explanation without intent to infringe.

British Library Cataloguing-in-Publication Data
A catalogue record for this book is available from the British Library

ISBN: 978-1-032-22387-2 (hbk)
ISBN: 978-1-032-25257-5 (pbk)
ISBN: 978-1-003-28233-4 (ebk)

DOI: 10.4324/9781003282334

Typeset in Sabon
by Newgen Publishing UK

Contents

List of Figures   vii
List of Contributors   ix
Preface   xi
Acknowledgements   xiii

Moving Matter: Worlds of Material Culture   1
ZAINABU JALLO

PART I
Museology: Representation and Colonial Liabilities   17

1 After Interpretive Dominance   19
  ANNA SCHMID

2 "*Wo Ist Afrika?*": Of Reflexive Museography, and Other (Productive?) Disappointments   41
  SANDRA FERRACUTI

3 "Out of Context" – Translocation of West African Artefacts to European Museums: The Case of the Leo Frobenius Collection from Mali   60
  CÉCILE BRÜNDLMAYER

4 The Museum as a Colonial Archive: The Collection of Victor and Marie Solioz and Its Role in Forgetting the Colonial Past   78
  SAMUEL B. BACHMANN

5 Museum Collections in Transit: Towards a History of the Artefacts of the *Endeavour* Voyage 98
NICHOLAS THOMAS

PART II
Heuristic Materiality Meanings and Transformations 117

6 "To Give Away My Collection for Free Would Be Nonsense": Decorations and the Emergence of Ethnology in Imperial Germany 119
CARL DEUSSEN

7 Discourse on Objectification and Personification: Modern Forms of Material Cultural Identity in the Touareg Society 139
DJOUROUKORO DIALLO

8 The Material Culture of Vodun: Case Studies from Ghana, Togo, Germany and In-Between 150
NIKLAS WOLF

9 Ndambirkus and Ndaokus: Asmat Skulls in Transit 171
JAN JORIS VISSER

10 On the Art of Forging Gods: Techniques, Forces and Materials in an Afro-Brazilian Religion 185
LUCAS MARQUES

Index 201

Figures

0.1 Beans wrapped in leaves from the Hans Paasche Collection of the Ethnographic Museum at the University of Zurich. Inv.Nr.06051a,c,d, Photo: Kathrin Leuenberger — 11
1.1 A glimpse into the exhibition shows a part of the section on human remains. 2019 © MKB, photographer Omar Lemke — 25
1.2 The installation "Voices of the Ancestors" by Deneth Piumakshi Wedaarachchige integrated into the exhibition "Thirst for Knowledge meets Collecting Mania". 2020 © MKB, photographer Omar Lemke — 32
2.1 Detail of a Palù textile cut from my private collection. Image: Sandra Ferracuti — 46
2.2 *Wo ist Afrika?* permanent exhibition at the Linden-Museum Stuttgart (2019). Detail of section 1 — 49
2.3 *Wo ist Afrika?* permanent exhibition at the Linden-Museum Stuttgart (2019). Detail of section 2 — 50
2.4 *Wo ist Afrika?* permanent exhibition at the Linden-Museum Stuttgart (2019). Detail of section 3 — 53
3.1 Portrait of Leo Frobenius, around 1908, Frobenius-Institut Frankfurt — 61
3.2 Sogoni Koun Headdress, unknown artist, Mali, before 1908, Museum am Rothenbaum, Hamburg (MARKK) — 63
3.3 Setting up the research station in Bamako, Mali, around 1908, Frobenius-Institute, Frankfurt — 66
3.4 Nege Traoré and Karimacha Djaora, Mali, around 1908, Frobenius-Institute, Frankfurt — 67
4.1 Victor Solioz (second from the right) at work on the Otavi Railroad in Central Namibia — 83
4.2 "Hairdress No. 23" from Namibia in the Solioz collection. Inv. Nr. E/1906.342.0023 — 86
4.3 "Apron No. 73" from Namibia in the Solioz collection. Inv. Nr. E/1906.342.0073 — 86

viii List of Figures

5.1	Collections made during the voyage of the *Endeavour*, 1768–1771, illustrating the likely proportions of artefacts collected during encounters in the places shown	102
5.2	The movements and destinations of the artefacts brought back on the *Endeavour*: a selective illustration of the movements of objects between collections and institutions. Those museums underlined hold *Endeavour* voyage artefacts today	104
5.3	The *hoe* collected in October 1769 in the collection of the Museum of Archaeology and Anthropology, Cambridge; on display in the 'Oceania' exhibition, Royal Academy of Arts, London, September–December 2018	112
5.4	*Hoe* from Cambridge, the British Museum and other UK institutions in Gisborne, Aotearoa, New Zealand. In late September 2019, community collections-study events took place prior to the installation of artefacts for the 'Tū te Whaihanga' exhibition (September 2019–May 2022)	115
6.1	Letter sent to Lindor Serrurier by Wilhelm Joest. © Collection Nationaal Museum van Wereldculturen. Coll.no. NL-LdnRMV_A01_010_00417	120
6.2	Order of Albrecht, Knight's Cross First Class. © Münzkabinett Dresden / SKD	124
6.3	Wilhelm Joest in June of 1896, wearing his uniform as a *Rittmeister* and all his medals	126
8.1	Ištar, Mamishie Rasta shrine, Volta (Ghana), Photo: Niklas Wolf, 2019	153
8.2	Mural, Hahotoe (Togo), Photo: Niklas Wolf, 2019	156
8.3	Mami Wata Altar, installation view, *Voodoo*, Roemer- und Pelizaeus Museum Hildesheim (Germany) Photo: Niklas Wolf 2020	164
9.1	Dr. Visser Md. "Receiving a Ndambirkus ancestral skull", © Visser family photo, 1957	172
9.2	"Checking confiscated skulls". Photographer: Cees van Kessel (msc) Object code BD/216/199 © Stichting Papua Erfgoed	173
10.1	Zé Diabo in his workshop welding agogôs. Source: author, 2013	188
10.2	Exus and Ogum in Zé Diabo's workshop. Source: author, 2013	193

Contributors

Samuel B. Bachmann is Curator of the ethnographic collections from Africa at Bernisches Historisches Museum since 2017 and PhD candidate at the Center for African Studies in Basel.

Cécile Bründlmayer is PhD candidate at the Institute of Art History in the Department of African Art at the Free University of Berlin. Junior Fellow at the IFK International Research Center for Cultural Studies in Vienna.

Carl Deussen is PhD candidate at the University of Amsterdam's School of Historical Studies. Research Fellow at the Rautenstrauch-Joest-Museum, Cologne.

Djouroukoro Diallo is Post-Doctoral Researcher at the Center of the Study of Language and Society (CSLS) and lecturer for Applied Linguistics at the University of Bamako.

Sandra Ferracuti is Researcher in Cultural Anthropology at the University of Basilicata, Italy and co-editor of *Antropologia Museale* journal since 2002. Member of the scientific committee of the *Simbdea – Società Italiana per la Museografia e i Beni DemoEtnoAntropologici* (Italian society for museums and heritages anthropology).

Zainabu Jallo is Post-Doctoral Fellow, lecturer in Anthropology at the University of Basel and Research Fellow at the Center for Global Studies, University of Bern.

Lucas Marques has PhD in Social Anthropology from the National Museum of the Federal University of Rio de Janeiro. Researcher at the Laboratory of Symmetric Anthropology (NAnSi).

Anna Schmid is Director, Museum der Kulturen Basel, Switzerland, since 2006.

Nicholas Thomas is Professor of Historical Anthropology, and Director, Museum of Archaeology and Anthropology, University of Cambridge since 2006.

List of Contributors

Jan Joris Visser is Independent expert on Material Culture. Recent projects include reports on dealing with Colonial History. Member, advisory committee for the Dutch government, Repatriation of Human remains, restitution and legal ownership of material Culture.

Niklas Wolf is PhD Candidate and Research Associate, University of Zurich. Co-editor of *Colophon Magazine für Kunst und Wissenschaft*.

Preface

This volume is inspired by Material Culture in Transit, a virtual conference held in September 2020. Curators and scholars working actively within academic and museal institutions convened to discuss spatiotemporal movements of material culture from diverse disciplinary standpoints. The organisers, Samuel Bachmann and I, saw the necessity to bring academic research and museum practice closer at a time material culture had ignited weighty debates in the areas of acquisition, restitution and representation, among other topics. To a greater degree, questions of moral and political implications linger at the forefront of these debates. Our discussions acknowledged the value of a remarkably varied materialist orientation towards studying the mobility of cultural artefacts, either within museum collections or as a flow of things that generate ideas and significations within the spaces they traverse.

While the conference accommodated 26 speakers in engaging and thought-provoking interdisciplinary interchange, this volume is shrunk into two parts comprising five essays each.

Part I, Museology: Representation and Colonial Liabilities, addresses museum entanglements with colonial histories. Even more so today, museums risk being accomplices of "the colonial" schema by hosting collections linked to colonial practices. The museum world has been rife with discussions around the restitution of collections acquired in colonial contexts. Only recently has this rather sectoral debate on colonial heritage received the attention of a broader and global public. Contributions in this section offer critical explorations of the responsibilities of the museum and the archive in creating narratives and establishing collections histories, demonstrating that museums have institutional authority over the representation of collections and play a critical role in the "politics of display".

In Part II, Heuristic Materiality: Meanings and Transformations, material culture is seen as constantly subject to redefinition through relational interactions and reactions. While objects are not necessarily (and should not be) reducible to their operative functions, this section investigates the ways in which people actively engage in the transformation of narratives and meanings through objects. This, however, does not indicate that material culture is largely achromatic, upon which connotations are inscribed. The essays show the transformative power of materiality as constituent parts or symbols of dynamic ideas and mutable practices, from raw material to finished product. They reveal how objects augment social standings, catalytically impact upon cultural politics and serve as important symbols of religiosity.

Reflections on the core concerns of this publication advanced from different field sites until its final draft. This volume is, therefore, the outcome of a genuinely collective process, accentuating the importance of an interdisciplinary approach to studying material culture.

Zainabu Jallo
Bern, November 2022

Acknowledgements

Deep appreciation goes to the contributors for their commitment to this volume, especially to Samuel Bachmann, who was co-organiser of the conference, Material Culture in Transit, in Bern, Switzerland. Profound appreciation also goes to the Center for Global Studies at the Graduate School of the Arts and Humanities, Walter Benjamin Kolleg, Interdisziplinäres Forschungs- und Nachwuchsnetzwerk (IFN) at the University of Bern, Switzerland. The Swiss National Science Foundation, Burgergemainde Bern and the Bernishes Historisches Museum.

I would also like to thank Katherine Ong for her support in putting this volume together. I owe a considerable debt to Prof. Dr. Thomas Claviez, Prof. Dr. Michaela Schäuble, Lady Hajara Adah and Ar. Vivienne Harvey, with whom I shared ideas about this volume as it developed.

Moving Matter
Worlds of Material Culture

Zainabu Jallo

Studying Material Culture Across Disciplines

Studies within the humanities and social sciences hold a long tradition of thinking primarily about human intention, meaning, and consequences of human deeds upon their immediate societies. Through material culture – tangible realities of our physical world – investigating these same concerns bares humankind and things as indivisible in a series of dynamic and dialectical relationships.

The study of artefacts, objects, and things – or in whichever term the material world is described – is not only restricted to their physical attributes but engages in an interplay between people and things. As it were, the growing prominence of material culture, emerging from practices of critical antiquarianism,[1] views things as propellants of social networks. Various explanations for the reemerging attentiveness to material culture transcend the efficiency of things in facilitating multiform understandings of tangible traces of the past, for example, in archaeological investigations. Material culture is also imperative to understanding continuous processes and skills in the present. Accordingly, the material worlds of things, fashioned or natural, mediate different relations: social, political, religious, and so on.

As a scholarly term, material culture was first described as "outward signs and symbols of ideas in the mind".[2] The purported ideas of the mind remain instrumental in organising these realities into more comprehensible ideas. Hence, studies of material culture, which have been resuscitated in a series of turns, comprise examinations of situated narratives concerning the formation of material worlds, parallel to how human (and non-human) experiences are shaped. One of such recent turns is interpreted as the non-human turn, "understood as a continuation of earlier attempts to depict the world populated not by active subjects and passive objects but by lively and essentially interactive materials, by bodies human and nonhuman".[3]

While cultural studies focused more on nonmaterial features of cultures, such as dogmas, value systems, rules, traditional lore and mores, materiality and the beliefs connected with them remained largely unexplored. Therefore, the cultural turn that developed diversely within different disciplines tended more towards linguistic than material components of culture. Beginning in the 1970s, the cultural turn departed from a positivistic, unitary framework of analysis, valuing culture as constitutive of social relations, affiliations and identifications, wherein quotidian life is duly recognised for its meaning and significance in a bigger picture of contingencies. Bachmann-Medick (2016) takes account of the spectra of *cultural turns* as valuable means of analysing conceptual, theoretical and methodological developments within the humanities and social sciences. The cultural turns remained deeply associated with the linguistic turn, with a conviction that "all human knowledge, including scientific knowledge, is structured by language" (22).

Spinning off the cultural turns, the early twenty-first century is marked by renewed attention towards the importance of materiality.[4] Materiality, as I would loosely define it in the context of this volume, is the ontological status of matter through which human and non-human worlds are intricately cultivated. One could then conceive of materiality as, the matter, in itself, and the way that matter is operational as a means to various human ends.[5] Accordingly, materiality comprises symbolic expressions of human bearings and social patterns. Thus, the study of material culture is approached in multiple ways. From a structuralist approach, nineteenth-century anthropologists like Claude Lévi-Strauss, Mary Douglas and Marcel Mauss illustrated that objects have an intrinsic yet often overlooked role in shaping the ways in which we make sense of the world. Additional entry points offer ways we might better grasp the significance of material culture with proposals of "thinking through" them (Lévi-Strauss 1966; Henare et al. 2007) or approaching them as "material metaphors [that] differ from linguistic metaphors in their relative density of metaphorical compression (because material forms are synaesthetic, making them inherently ambiguous and polysemic in nature)".[6] Further envisaged as imbibables or consumables, Bennett approaches materiality as "the non-humanity that flows around but also through humans" (349). And as agents of social mediation, Gell (1998) dismisses the idea of objects as symbols and instead draws critical attention to how objects of art perform by mediating social agency.[7]

Hicks (2010), in "The Material-Cultural Turn: Event and Effect",[8] indicates a "Material-cultural turn" that "reinforced earlier divisions between archaeological and anthropological thinking-between the 'material' and 'cultural'" (28). Hicks argues that material culture studies developed as an attempt from the 1970s onwards to "reconcile structuralism and semiotics" (29). While the use of both structuralist and semiotic approaches has engendered queries pertaining to the degrees to which cultural understandings are consistent, one also takes into consideration that the semiotic redefinition of those materialities aids in guaranteeing their interpretation and re-appropriation across cultures.

A look towards more recent contributions from political theory and New Materialism (Bennett 2010; Braidotti 2013; Grusin 2015) suggest post-structuralist materialist ontologies that point out the constraints induced by the prominence accorded language, to the detriment of material realities. Tilley (2007) argues that objects connect to "far wider perceptual functions than words, they have multi-dimensional qualities relating to sight, sound, smell, taste, and touch, enabling remarkably subtle distinctions to be made".[9] This stresses that Ontology, unlike semiotics, is geared towards being and experiencing. Shankar and Cavanaugh (2017), however, proffer a "materiality of language" that may serve to overcome the material versus semiotic distinction.[10] A concept through which "explicit focus on materiality furthers understandings of language use and vice versa".[11] As pointed out by Hicks, within the re-emergent material culture studies, the problematic system of binary oppositions, for example, is being surmounted through more nuanced introspection of things studied. At this rate, the comeback of material culture is clearly augmented by collapsing divides with evolving disciplinary theories that depart from anthropocentric approaches. Decades of anthropological research in material culture studies verify the need to acknowledge objects – materiality – as heavily influencing our way of being.

Already over three decades ago, Daniel Miller's seminal work *Material Culture and Mass Consumption* (1987) expressed concerns about the dismissal of the efficacy of our material world to evoke emotions, holding that "the relation of persons to objects is in some way vicarious, fetishistic or wrong; that primary concern should lie with direct social relations and 'real people'".[12] Nowadays, scholars consider these features through phenomenological approaches (Brown 2003; Morgan 2010; Olsen 2013; Henare et al. 2007)[13] and sensory ethnography (Brown 2003; Edwards et al. 2006; Pink 2015; Howes and Classen 2013; Stoller 2010), revealing that things and the senses conjointly build social meaning. As a frame of inquiry, sensuous, phenomenological concepts integrate experiential knowledge into accounts of interaction with people and things. This is taken further with embodied material culture, explored along culinary, religious and medical lines of inquiry (Alaimo 2010; Crossland 2010; Csordas 2005; Pitts-Taylor 2016).

Expanding the strand of phenomenology initiated by Martin Heidegger, Bruno Latour's relational ontology through Actor-Network Theory[14] decentres humanism to contemplate active networks of humans and non-humans. On another spectrum, Graham Harman's "Object-Oriented Ontology" calls for a "flat ontology", that is, a commitment to understanding reality beyond the human experience. Harman contends that objects cannot be "undermined" by reducing them to what they are made of, nor "overmined" by reducing them to their network of relations. Harman's flat ontology has been widely criticised as radically reductionist in itself. A contraction of human relations with materiality means material worlds are left unreachable.[15]

The revival of material culture across disciplines recognises "distinct forms of agency and effectivity".[16] It embraces newer dimensions that also pay attention to ecological concerns (Bennet 2004; 2010; Ingold 2017) and technological advancement (Vannini 2009). Digital material culture here essay "*Wo ist Afrika?*, or of Storytelling and (Productive?) Disappointments" questions the notion of museums as reliable storytellers of humankind, demonstrating the colonial empire's grandeur. It explains the strategies and difficulties of working with specific actors in Europe and Africa directly connected to the objects. While navigating problematic acquisitions, Ferracuti's post-exhibition stance focuses on understanding various concepts linked with knowledge production. The essay reveals how the author sought to disrupt the perception of imagined, far-flung Others circulated through essentialist ethnological portrayals.

Meanwhile, through fieldwork carried out between Germany and Mali, Cécile Bründlemayer follows the upshots of the historical collection of Malian artefacts by Leo Frobenius and their entries into German museums from the late nineteenth and early twentieth centuries. In the essay "Out of Context – Translocation of West African Artefacts to European Museums", Brundlmeyer calls for more critical ways to manage colonial collections. Beginning with discarding obsolete forms of representation amidst calls for restituting colonial collections, the essay proffers a redirection of focus on the interests of Malian communities in building trust and transparency of the objects' provenances.

Samuel Bachmann presents the idea of the museum as a colonial archive in examining the material and immaterial legacies of the ethnographic collection of Victor Solioz at the Bernisches Historisches Museum. The essay uncovers the acquisition methods of the Swiss railway engineer who was very much implicated in and benefitted immensely from the German colonial territory based in German Southwest Africa between 1903 and 1906. Bachmann works actively with the Solioz collection. Some of the findings are presented in "The Museum as a Colonial Archive", advocating for the consideration of ethnographic museums as places of memory for the several ways institutions and collectors such as Solioz were enmeshed with European colonial expansion.

In what is considered the foremost "ethnographic" collection, artefacts of the *Endeavour* voyage were received in European educational institutions and museums directly acquired from the field. Nicholas Thomas' essay begins by pointing out the methodical gaps of provenance research that fail to consider the topics and questions arising from an object's mutability in transit. Next, the chapter cites the convoluted routes of artefacts collected during Captain James Cook's first voyage on the British Naval ship, the *Endeavour*. "Seized or stolen? Willingly and fairly exchanged?" Thomas analyses who is authorised to speak for the artefacts while tracing the different stages of the voyage and contacts with indigenous peoples of the South Pacific. "Museum Collections in Transit: Towards a History of the Artefacts of the *Endeavour* Voyage" attempts to follow the dispersion of artefacts of the voyage from 1768 to 1771 to various institutions. While asking if such investigative work of tracing objects is a "form of antiquarianism", Thomas also inquires if such research adds value to social, cultural and historical analysis in the age of digital humanities and contemporary theory.

Heuristic Materiality and Meaning-making

Material culture travelling in time and traversing newer spatial configurations is transformed in many ways. Meanings and use are altered in the face of new cultural or institutional horizons. This section takes into cognisance the weaknesses and dangers of limiting objects to their functions.[34] Materiality is seen as constantly subject to redefinition through relational interactions and reactions. Objects assume a polyphony of meanings in continual flux, leaving vestiges of their usage and adopting new definitions in some cases, as their previous lives decline.

While objects are not necessarily reducible to their operative functions, this section investigates the ways in which groups actively engage with the transformation of narratives and meanings of their material worlds. This, however, does not indicate that material culture is largely achromatic, upon which connotations are inscribed. Instead, the essays show the transformative power of materiality as constituent parts or symbols of dynamic ideas and mutable practices, from raw material to finished product, from originals to imitations. Moreover, they reveal how objects augment social standings, spur cultural politics and serve as crucial symbols of religiosity.

Carl Deussen's essay reveals how material possessions, such as a decorative medal, become a way through which status is negotiated. "To give away my collection for free would be nonsense" discloses how decorations and ethnographic objects banded together into a new hierarchy of value in the German empire. Deussen trails the collection and donation history of German collector and ethnologist Wilhelm Joest who expected medals as compensation for his donations to several European museums. The chapter investigates Joest's clamour for social and academic standing, which motivated his collecting. It emphasises how material transformation disrupts the history of ethnographic collecting while proposing new long-term approaches to the demands of representing such collections.

Within the Touareg societies of sub-Saharan Africa, Djouroukoro Diallo investigates the substitution of pre-existing cultural objects for Western apparatus, such as the Kalashnikov rifle and the four-wheel drive vehicle that still fulfil older traditional functions. The essay discloses how economic and social factors have contributed to the disruption of nomadic life and offers a two-fold analysis of transfers of culture and social identification. The admission of Western objects into Touareg societies also sees Western adoptions of expressions of Touareg cultural identification, such as the naming of a Volkswagen all-terrain SUV model "Touareg". In contexts of objectification and personification, Diallo reveals a phenomenon of an emergent social class made up of exilic Touareg men called the *Ishumar*. The essay questions the processes of transfer in Touareg identification, as well as discursive constructions of the term "Touareg" in a postcolonial heterogeneous transcultural third space.

In probing various representations of Vodoun objects within European museums, cyberspace and other non-religious domains, Niklas Wolf scrutinises the agencies of West African Vodun objects in the political contexts of migration and globalisation. The "Material Culture of Vodun" offers some indications of the meanings and instrumentality of a contemporary and globalised Vodun. Wolf raises questions on issues of "(im)mobilisation, appropriation, and continuous actualisation" while introducing aspects of steadfast connections between Vodun's display and material culture in West African shrines.

A dated tradition among the Asmat of New Guinea involved the headhunting of enemy groups. Human skulls were either revered in honour of ancestors or, in the case of headhunted enemy skulls, displayed as evidence of a warrior's valour. In Chapter 1, Anna Schmid briefly touches upon the current debates on the ethics of trading or displaying human remains. In "Ndambirkus and Ndaokus Asmat skulls in Transit", Jan Joris Visser follows the different entry points of Asmat Skulls in the Netherlands as part of ethnographic collections and tackles the ethical conundrum in the continued trading of Asmat skulls both online and in auction houses. Visser presents the interpretation and functions of human remains in traditional cultures of New Guinea and interrogates why human remains are still in circulation when even the Asmat have substitute skulls carved in wood. The essay explores the various laws on human remains as well as their limitations.

Lucas Marques' essay takes on the transformation of raw material into a venerated deity. "On the Art of Forging Gods" addresses aspects of material religion by illustrating the process of fashioning gods from metal in the Afro-Brazilian religion of Candomblé. Relying on ethnographic research carried out in the workshop of José Adário dos Santos, a religious blacksmith located in Salvador de Bahia, the article traces the rudiments followed in the making of an Exu, the god of the crossroads. Marques focuses on the interchange among humans, things and gods and states that in Candomblé, the processes of "technique" and "ontology" cannot be conceived independently. The creation of a deity is a composition of forces and materials that inhabit it. Such materials also give in to natural electrochemical processes such as corrosion and are, therefore, in a state of constant apparent change. As proven by the essays in the volume, material culture, in its relational capacity in several contexts, is neither static in form nor meaning.

In conclusion, the narratives accompanying material culture, as shown in this book, are also narratives of intercultural allegiances, global displacements, asymmetric power structures, and the evolutions and extinctions of customs. The journeys of objects are incontrovertibly the stories of appropriations and re-appropriations, connections, as well as misunderstandings or misinterpretations. To understand the mediating role of material culture, attention needs to be paid to its relational role,

Moving Matter 11

its shifting connotations from place to place, and the different impressions and sentiments materiality induces. As an academic enquiry, material culture remains essential for understanding interactions with our material world, revealing unparalleled insights into what it means to be human and non-human. It offers the prospect of a better understanding of the entanglement of humankind and their material worlds, both historically and extant.

The accentuation of "theory and practice" in this volume may seem to go against what Tilley (1992) understands as a "separation of philosophical and

Figure 0.1 Beans wrapped in leaves from the Hans Paasche Collection of the Ethnographic Museum at the University of Zurich, Inv.Nr.06051a,c,d.
Photo: Kathrin Leuenberger.

theoretical questions from the business of research", insisting that "[t]heory *is* Practice and all Practice *is* theoretical".[35] What this book presents are progressions of concepts or ideas into implementation. It might then be useful to consider the two aspects as interleaved stages, from the formation of a premise to its operational status. This book examines different imperative perspectives on material things emerging from Anthropology, Art History, Museology and Linguistics, further indicating material culture studies' defiance of strict disciplinary allegiance.[36] In varying degrees, the following chapters ratify the impact of travelling and ever-transforming material culture on effective transmissions of complex social and political meanings amidst forging relationships. In contributing to current debates on travelling and travelled objects, the essays illuminate the sensitivities and complications of material culture in transit through a wide range of primary and secondary responses available to the contributors.

Notes

1 See Miller 2017.
2 Pitt-Rivers 1901, p. 23.
3 Bennett 2015, p. 224.
4 In Anthropology, the use of material culture as primary data has existed since the nineteenth- century through scholars like James Deetz, Lewis Henry Morgan, Marcel Mauss.
5 Cf. Ingold 2017.
6 Tilley 2007, p. 262. Also see, Miller 1998.
7 In *Art and Agency*, Gell does not consider the agency of art objects in terms of their aesthetic appeal or performance as systems of actions, nor as visual encryptions that require decoding.
8 In *The Oxford Handbook of Material Culture Studies* (2010), pp. 25–98.
9 p. 260 and p. 359.
10 A reconciliation mentioned by Hicks earlier.
11 "Toward a Theory of Language Materiality: An Introduction", p. 1.
12 Ibid., p. 11.
13 Phenomenology as a concept commenced as attentive to practical, lived experiences advocating for ways of "relearning to look at the world" (Merleau-Ponty 1967), concerned with "the things themselves" (Heidegger and Hofstadter 1975; Husserl 1931).
14 Latour 2005.
15 See, Graham Harman "Object-Oriented Ontology and Its Critics", 2019, pp. 592–598.
16 Bennett and Joyce 2010, p. 14.
17 Bennett 2011, p. 224.
18 Moreso as materiality often implies fixity.
19 Prominent in the field of Migration studies. Migration studies is also often subsumed under the fields of anthropology and archeology.
20 *Honeymoon? 5 Questions on the 'Hans Paasche Collection' from East Africa.*
21 *The Social Life of Things: Commodities in Cultural Perspective* (2017) p. 5.

22 Other exhibitions worth mentioning here are, *Caravans of Gold, Fragments in Time: Art, Culture, and Exchange across Medieval Saharan Africa* – "Matter in Motion", section three of the exhibition emphasises the influence of trans-Saharan trade on cultural relations and the various transformations of the objects of exchange. The travelling exhibition held at the Block Museum of Art at Northwestern University (2019), the Aga Khan Museum in Toronto (2019–20), and the National Museum of African Art in Washington, D.C. (2020).
23 See Hicks 2020; Phillips 2022.
24 Emmanuel Kasarhérou 2005.
25 See Thomas, Chapter 5.
26 Ingold evokes Gilbert Simondon's concept of individuation: "When we talk about organisms, including human beings, we say they grow; that is, they undergo a process of biological development, and the technical term for that is ontogenesis". Which replaces being with becoming. See Ingold 2017.
27 Ibid.
28 www.britishmuseum.org/about-us/british-museum-story/sir-hans-sloane (accessed June 29, 2022).
29 "Cultural haemorrhaging" among other forms of plundering includes the forced removal of objects from indigenous cultures to museums and private homes in the various territories of Christian missionaries and colonial administrators.
30 Basu 2011, p. 28.
31 While it is generally understood that Anthropology is a field of study and ethnography, an investigative method within Anthropology, that is, a detailed report of findings, both terms are sometimes used interchangeably as a field of study especially in German-speaking Europe.
32 Clifford 1997, p. 193.
33 Cf. Macdonald 2006.
34 See Pinney 2005.
35 Tilley 1992, p. vii.
36 Ibid.

References

Alaimo, Stacy. *Bodily Natures: Science, Environment, and the Material Self*. Bloomington: Indiana University Press, 2010.

Appadurai, Arjun. *The Social Life of Things: Commodities in Cultural Perspective*. Cambridge: Cambridge University Press, 2017.

Bachmann-Medick, Doris. *Cultural Turns: New Orientations in the Study of Culture*. Berlin: De Gruyter, 2016.

Basu, Paul. *The Inbetweenness of Things: Materializing Mediation and Movement between Worlds*. New York and London: Bloomsbury Academic, 2017.

Basu, Paul and Simon Coleman. "Introduction: Migrant Worlds, Material Cultures." *Mobilities*, vol. 3, no. 3, 2008, pp. 313–330.

———. "Object Diasporas, Resourcing Communities: Sierra Leonean Collections in the Global Museumscape." *Museum Anthropology*, vol. 34, no. 1, 2011, pp. 28–42.

Bennett, Jane. "The Force of Things." *Political Theory*, vol. 32, no. 3, 2004, pp. 347–372.

———. *Vibrant Matter: A Political Ecology of Things*. Durham: Duke University Press, 2010.

———. *Material Powers: Cultural Studies, History and the Material Turn*. Milton Park:Taylor and Francis, 2013.

———. "Systems and Things: On Vital Materialism." In: *The Nonhuman Turn*. Richard Grusin (ed.). Minneapolis: University of Minnesota Press. 2015. pp. 223–240.

Braidotti, Rosi. *The Posthuman*. Cambridge: Polity Press, 2013.

Brown, Bill. *A Sense of Things*. Chicago: University of Chicago Press, 2003.

Brown, Karen, and François Mairesse. "The Definition of the Museum through Its Social Role." *Curator: The Museum Journal*, vol. 61, no. 4, 2018, pp. 525–539.

Clifford, James. *Routes: Travel and Translation in the Late Twentieth Century*. Cambridge, MA; London: Harvard University Press, 1997.

———. "Museums as Contact Zones." In: *Routes: Travel and Translation in the Late Twentieth Century*. Cambridge, MA; London: Harvard University Press, 1997. pp. 188–219.

Coombes, Annie E. *Reinventing Africa: Museums, Material Culture and Popular Imagination in Late Victorian and Edwardian England*. New Haven: Yale University Press, 1997.

Crossland, Zoë. "Materiality and Embodiment." In: *The Oxford Handbook of Material Culture Studies*. Mary Carolyn Beaudry and Dan Hicks (eds.). Oxford: Oxford University Press, 2010. pp. 386–405.

Csordas, Thomas J. *Embodiment and Experience: The Existential Ground of Culture and Self*. Cambridge: Cambridge University Press, 2005.

De León, Jason. "Better to Be Hot than Caught": Excavating the Conflicting Roles of Migrant Material Culture. *American Anthropologist*, vol. 114, no. 3, 2012, pp. 477–495.

Douglas, Mary. "Why Do People Want Goods?" In: *Consumption: Theory and Issues in the Study of Consumption*. Daniel Miller (ed.). London: Routledge, 2001. pp. 262–271.

———. And Baron Isherwood. *The World of Goods: Towards an Anthropology of Consumption*. London: Basic Books, 1979.

Edwards, Elizabeth, Chris Godsen and Ruth Phillips (eds.). *Sensible Objects: Colonialism, Museums, and Material Culture*. Oxford: Berg Publishers, 2006.

Grusin, Richard. *The Nonhuman Turn*. Minnesota: University of Minnesota Press, 2015.

Harman, Graham. "Object-Oriented Ontology and Its Critics." *Open Philosophy*, vol. 2, no. 1, 2019, pp. 592–598.

Heal, Felicity. *The Power of Gifts: Gift-Exchange in Early Modern England*. Oxford: Oxford University Press, 2014.

Heidegger, Martin, and Albert Hofstadter. *Poetry, Language, Thought*. New York: Harper & Row, 1975.

Henare, Amiria, Martin Holbraad and Sari Wastell. *Thinking through Things: Theorizing Artefacts in Ethnographically*. London: Routledge, 2007.

Hicks, Dan, and Mary Carolyn Beaudry. "The Material-Cultural Turn: Event and Effect." In: *The Oxford Handbook of Material Culture Studies*. Mary Carolyn Beaudry and Dan Hicks (eds.). Oxford: Oxford University Press, 2010, pp. 25–98.

———. *The Oxford Handbook of Material Culture Studies*. Oxford: Oxford University Press, 2018

———. *The Brutish Museums: Benin Bronzes, Colonial Violence and Cultural Restitution*. London: Pluto Press, 2020.
Howes, David, and Constance Classen. *Ways of Sensing: Understanding the Senses in Society*. New York: Routledge, 2014.
Husserl, Edmund. *Ideas: General Introduction to Pure Phenomenology*. New York: Collier Books, 1931.
Ingold, Tim. "An Ecology of Materials." In: *Power of Material/Politics of Materiality*. Susanne Witzgall and Kerstin Stakemeier (eds.). Zurich: Diaphanes, 2017, pp. 59–65.
Jennings, Benjamin. *Travelling Objects: Changing Values: The Role of Northern Alpine Lake-Dwelling Communities in Exchange and Communication Networks during the Late Bronze Age*. Oxford: Archaeopress, 2014.
Kasarhérou, Emmanuel. 'L'ambassadeur du brouillard blanc'. In: *Cent ans d'ethnographie sur la colline de Saint-Nicolas*. Marc-Olivier Gonseth, Jacques Hainard and Roland Kaehr (eds.). Neuchâtel: Musée d'ethnographie de Neuchâtel, 2005, pp. 285–286.
Knowles, Chantal. "'Objects as Ambassadors': Representing Nation Through New York Museum Exhibitions." In: *Unpacking the Collection: Networks of Material and Social Agency in the Museum*. Sarah Byrne, Rodney Harrisson and Robin Torrence (eds.). New York: Springer, 2012, pp. 231–247.
Lévi-Strauss, Claude. *The Savage Mind*. Chicago: University of Chicago Press, 1966.
Olsen, Bjørnar. *In Defense of Things Archaeology and the Ontology of Objects*. Lanham, MD: AltaMira Press, 2013.
MacDonald, Sharon. "Expanding Museum Studies: An Introduction." In: *Companion to Museum Studies*. Sharon MacDonald (ed.). London: Blackwell, 2006, pp. 1–12.
Malefakis, Alexis (Curator). "Hochzeitsreise? 5 Fragen an Die Sammlung Hans Paasche' Aus Ostafrika." Zurich: Völkerkundemuseum Der Universität. 22 May 2022–21 January 2024.
Mauss, Marcel. *The Gift: The Form and Reason for Exchange in Archaic Societies*, Translated by W.D. Halls, New York & London: W.W. Norton, [1925]1990.
Merleau-Ponty, Maurice. *Phenomenology of Perception*: Colin Smith (Transl.). Routledge & Kegan Paul, 1967.
Morgan, David. *Religion and Material Culture: The Matter of Belief*. New York: Routledge, 2010.
Miller, Daniel. "Materiality: An Introduction." *Materiality*. Durham: Duke University Press, 2005.
Miller, Daniel. *Material Culture and Mass Consumption*. Oxford: Blackwell, 1987.
———. Why Some Things Matter. In: *Material Cultures. Why Some Things Matter*. London: University College London Press, 1998.
Miller, Peter N. *History and Its Objects: Antiquarianism and Material Culture since 1500*. New York: Cornell University Press, 2017.
Peffer, John. "Africa's Diasporas of Images." *Third Text*, vol. 19, no. 4, 2005, pp. 339–355.
Phillips, Barnaby. *Loot: Britain and the Benin Bronzes*. London: Oneworld Publications, 2022.
Pink, Sarah. *Doing Sensory Ethnography*. Los Angeles: SAGE, 2015.
———., Elisenda Ardèvol and Déborah Lanzeni *Digital Materialities: Design and Anthropology*. London: Routledge, 2016.

Pinney, Christopher. "Things Happen: Or from What Moment Does that Object Come?" In: *Materiality*. Daniel Miller (ed.). Durham, NC: Duke University Press, 2005, pp. 256–272.

Pitt-Rivers, Lane-Fox. "On the Evolution of Culture." In: *The Evolution of Culture and Other Essays*. Myers, J.L. (ed.). Oxford: Clarendon Press, 1906, pp. 20–44.

Pitts-Taylor, Victoria. *The Brain's Body: Neuroscience and Corporeal Politics*. Durham: Duke University Press, 2016.

Schorch, Philipp, Martin Saxer and Marlen Elders (eds.). *Exploring Materiality and Connectivity in Anthropology and Beyond*. London: UCL Press, 2020.

Shankar, Shalini, and Jillian R Cavanaugh. "Toward a Theory of Language Materiality: An Introduction." In: *Language and Materiality: Ethnographic and Theoretical Explorations*. Cambridge: Cambridge University Press, 2017, pp. 1–28.

Shyllon, Folarin. "Chapter Unraveling History: Return of African Cultural Objects Repatriated and Looted in Colonial Times." *Cultural Heritage Issues*, 2010, pp. 159–168.

Stoller, Paul. *Sensuous Scholarship*. Philadelphia: University of Pennsylvania Press, 2010.

Thomas, Nicholas. *Entangled Objects: Exchange, Material Culture, and Colonialism in the Pacific*. Cambridge: Harvard University Press, 1991.

Tilley, Christopher. "Ethnography and Material Culture." In: *Handbook of Ethnography*, Paul Atkinson(ed.). SAGE Publications, 2007, pp. 258–272.

———. *Reading Material Culture Structuralism, Hermeneutics and Post-Structuralism*. Cambridge: Basil Blackwell, 1992.

Trabert, Sarah. "Understanding the Significance of Migrants' Material Culture." *Journal of Social Archaeology*, vol. 20, no.1, 2020, pp. 95–115.

Tsing, Anna. *The Mushroom at the End of the World: On the Possibility of Life in Capitalist Ruins*. New Jersey: Princeton University Press, 2015.

Vannini, Phillip. *Material Culture and Technology in Everyday Life: Ethnographic Approaches*. New York: Peter Lang, 2009.

Waxman, Sharon. *Loot: The Battle over the Stolen Treasures of the Ancient World*. New York: Times Books, 2009.

Whitfield, Susan. *Silk, Slaves, and Stupas: Material Culture of the Silk Road*. Berkeley: University of California Press, 2018.

Part I

Museology

Representation and Colonial Liabilities

1 After Interpretive Dominance[1]

Anna Schmid

Introduction

Over the recent decades, a plethora of publications have discussed major problems and potentials of museums in general and the ethnographic museum in particular. Coombes and Phillipps (2015) highlight "the Western museum as a primary site for authoritative articulation, inscribing in its visitors the Eurocentric hierarchies of race, class and gender"[2] as one significant result of the research in/of museums. A vast array of exhibition projects around the globe have delivered new, albeit cautious, answers to the question of how to transcend the authoritative articulation or – as I prefer to call it – the interpretive dominance[3] fundamentally connected to museums' practices and outcomes. Thus, exhibition experiments have addressed this problem, for example, by recognising enduring imperial/colonial attitudes and positions, creating awareness of structural and institutional racism, probing institutional and social activism, collaborating with members of so-called source communities, activists or other stakeholders.[4] In this respect, the project "The Past is Now", which took place in 2017 at the Birmingham Museum and Art Gallery, is outstanding. Apart from the exhibition itself, various participants and observers published on the project, its procedures and many difficulties.[5] The museum seemed to be stuck in its modus operandi and thus unable to accommodate the external co-curators' alternative conceptions attempting at decolonisation and experimenting with decolonial curating. The spectrum of difficulties ranged from internal communication to the selection and placement of objects to the labelling and wording for marketing activities; repeatedly, expectations, as well as passed decisions, had to be negotiated and re-negotiated. Kassim (2017), one of the six co-curators, preceded her reflections on the project with Audre Lorde's dictum "The Master's Tools will never Dismantle the Master's House", not without pointing out that it had nevertheless become part of the exhibition: "I'll admit that there were tears. Even though the process was challenging, I couldn't help it: we got Audre [...] on those white museum walls". Despite this apparently difficult partial success, Kassim strongly questions the possibility to decolonise the museum and suspects that museums "will

DOI: 10.4324/9781003282334-3

only end up co-opting decoloniality" (ibid.).[6] Other projects in which participation was a distinctive part, too, reinforce her apprehensions. Thus, Elliott (2019) concludes that "an imbalance and an ambivalence" are inevitable: "a European white curator would retain interpretive authority over collections that were stored and documented within institutional and disciplinary structures that are profoundly European and colonial" (637). The exhibition "Take your Pick – 125 objects for 125 years" at the MKB (the Museum der Kulturen Basel, in short: MKB) was conceived as a participatory project on the occasion of the 125th anniversary of the MKB. This included leaving the object selection – "supposedly free from authoritative interpretation" (Kaufmann 2019, 90) – in the vast storerooms to the persons who by personal invitation and on a public appeal had agreed to a visit to the depot. Although this example was not a negotiation between former colonised and colonisers, the negotiation of interpretations under the unequal conditions of the parties reveals another facet of the problem of "interpretive dominance". Evaluating the project, Kaufmann concluded that free choices of objects from storerooms by persons who do not have a background in museum work do not necessarily result in decolonising knowledge production. They can even foster the opposite, reproducing or reinforcing clichés.

These experiences and projects raise many questions. They refer, inter alia, to local and other audiences, to the location of the respective museum, to its architecture, its organisation and structure, to its collections, and to categorisations that permeate the entire museum work – often unconsciously and deeply embedded in everyday practices. Should henceforth only "affected" persons voice their thoughts on topics, events and collections? Are there (still) intelligible, valid notions and a common language in terms of visual rhetoric – practices of showing, seeing, debating – in museums aiming at mutual understanding, naming incompatibilities and contradictions yet leaving them for the time being? If so, what notions could these be and with whom and on which basis are they to be negotiated? If not, can they be developed? What would be the basic requirements for this? For some of these questions, the positioning of the MKB as well as the basic facts of the museum, its assets, proportions and specifics can provide partial answers.

The MKB's Location

Basel has an extremely rich and top-class museum landscape. The MKB is one of five cantonal museums in the city and one of almost three dozen museums in and around Basel. In the midst of the old town, the MKB is located on the venerable Minster Square, the former religious and political centre of power; architecturally, the cathedral dominates the square. The usage of this tranquil, surficially unscathed place – by some declared the world's most beautiful public space – is controversial: one party wants to enliven and reactivate the prodigious space; others want to maintain the sublime tranquillity undiminished. Although the ideas about the square differ substantially,[7] it is undisputed that the Minster Square is not only the geographical and historical but also the ideational centre of the city: a historically shaped, urban space with extraordinary charisma.[8]

With the completion of the refurbishing and enlargement project in 2011, the entrance of the MKB was moved from the Augustinergasse, a side lane, to Minster Square. Passing through the gate, one enters an ample inner courtyard with an irregular stair landscape. To enter the museum, however, one strides *down* the stairs. This is quite unusual since, at almost all museums, people have to ascend the stairs to enter the building; few have ground-level access. This new basement entrance replaced the former ground-level, venerable, ceremonial portal of the first museum building from 1849. As "entrances to a museum constitute fundamental statements about the institution" (Bouquet 2015, 137), the new entrance not only testifies to the autonomy of the ethnographic museum (the former entrance led in a rather labyrinthine way through the Natural History Museum to the MKB; as if it were an appendage to the natural history) but also of a departure from the monumental, which is most often interpreted as an affirmation of significance, grandeur and dignity.

Since its establishment in 1893, the MKB has undergone several transformations. At first, integrated into the Universal Museum, the ethnographic collection received its own annex in 1917 – in the midst of the First World War. In the 1970s and 1980s, the building was renovated, which was followed by a reorganisation of the permanent exhibitions. In 1996, the "Museum of Ethnology and the Swiss Museum of Folklore"[9] was renamed "Museum of Cultures Basel"; the change in name was also meant to herald a paradigm shift. A thorough refurbishment and substantial expansion was the last major transformation: after several years of planning and after two years of construction carried out by the architects Herzog and de Meuron, the museum reopened in 2011. The architectural features of the new MKB include an irregularly folded, cantilevered roof; a clear spatial structure (with 3000 square metre of exhibition space on four levels); an inviting entrance area with front glazing; exhibition rooms with floor-to-ceiling windows guaranteeing, rather than suppressing, a connection to the outside. This last structural transformation went hand in hand with a radically new orientation in content (cf. Schmid 2011, 2021, Plankensteiner 2018, 30).

Audiences of the MKB

The MKB focuses on local and regional audiences. Basel is a city with more than 200,000 inhabitants, of whom about 75,000 are foreign nationals. The largest group – almost 17,000 people – are German immigrants, followed by Italian (approx. 8600), Turkish (approx. 6000) and Spanish (approx. 4000) nationals.¹⁰ In the small area of just under 37 square kilometres, which constitutes the canton of Basel City, more than 130 nationalities are represented. Basel citizens proudly consider this a sign of openness, cosmopolitan attitude and appreciation for other nationalities.¹¹ Moreover, it is also supposed to refer to the extremely high quality of life that Basel offers its inhabitants. A substantial part of this quality are the cultural institutions: in addition to theatres, conservatories and other music institutions, this includes, above all, the numerous museums. Furthermore, Basel conceives itself as the centre of the border triangle of Switzerland, Germany and France. This trinational area with the central places Basel (CH), Freiburg im Breisgau (D) and Mulhouse (F) and their respective hinterlands is a coherent living and economic area with rich opportunities for intensive exchange and circulation (of people and goods). The events and programmes of cultural institutions such as museums provide a substantial part of the exchange supply.

These few demographic data indicate the potential local and regional audiences. Although the MKB's activities are commented on locally and regionally until now, very few individuals have raised claims vis-à-vis the MKB or its presentations. Instead, MKB employees have approached potentially interested groups or persons with requests – such as in the exhibition project "Take your Pick" already mentioned, or on a city tour entitled "Have I arrived at last? Migrants show their Basel" in the educational programme for the exhibition "Migration".¹² Migrants from Afghanistan, Syria, Italy and other countries guided the tour. It was particularly popular with the people of Basel. Participants often emphasised that the guide's remarks enabled new perspectives on their own city, questioned common ideas about buildings or public spaces, the taken-for-granted familiarity with paths, routes, institutions such as the MKB, and even social and cultural conduct. A different glimpse or view on seemingly self-evident stances sometimes left behind a sense of shame and doubt but also provided intellectual and emotional enrichment. In any case, the guides had the potential for affecting people. Hence, this example provides different aspects of being affected on both sides, among the audience as well as the guides. The guides showed their bewilderment, confessed to loneliness or continuing incomprehension of rules and (over-)regulations. These expressions, however, focused on their experiences as migrants attached to the place where they are now living their lives and not on their competencies as members of different cultures. These many facets of experiences hint at a possible transference of affectivity and empathic concern into a new discourse in which interlocution and negotiation possibly lead to and convey mutual understanding. This new quality enables other perspectives and interpretations without having to efface contradictions that may arise and thereby partially leaves behind the interpretive dominance. The entries in the exhibition's guest book suggest a beginning of reflections in this direction.

Imperialism/Colonialism[13] on the Swiss agenda

A completely different kind of empathic concern raises the question of Swiss involvement in imperial/colonial enterprises and their consequences, which continue to this day. Meanwhile, the MKB houses over 340,000 objects from all over the world, including Europe. Initially, the collections were intended to reconstruct the cultural history of humankind and depict it in the museum – this required material culture products as primary sources, hence the rush to create extensive collections. Switzerland was not a colonial power and never had colonies of its own. Thus, the seemingly "easy way" of object acquisition, a direct access to all material from conquered or administered colonial regions, was not at the museum's disposal. However, the documentation of many objects substantiates that European colonial rule was also decisive for the collections of the MKB.

Occasionally, collectors had close contacts with representatives of the colonial authorities; at times, these contacts induced far-reaching, extensive, informal networks. Both could provide or facilitate access to objects. In these networks, Swiss nationals appeared in various places, engaged at economic and political levels of the colonial government and operated in many fields. Employees from trading companies, merchants, sailors, travellers, mercenaries, civil servants, missionaries, petrogeologists and scientists of all disciplines were enmeshed in colonial activities or simply served in colonial administrations. They went to colonised areas either under the protection or in the service of a colonial power and knew how to use this protection in the targeted or accidental acquisition of objects.[14] Undoubtedly, the collection of the MKB is permeated by the global colonial project and its implications – a circumstance that is only slowly being noticed by the public.[15] Subsequently, recent research has elucidated the switch from Switzerland's "colonial innocence" to its "colonial complicity" (Purtschert and Fischer 2015, 4).

However, the museum actors themselves were anxious to keep their distance from the "tragic process of colonization". Instead, they emphasised the urgency to collect. Staff members, as well as donors, had to rush "to collect as long as we still have daylight because the custodians of our collections in the future probably do not have the opportunity to purchase such authentic objects at such reasonable prices"[16] – as Rütimeyer, a physician turned anthropologist and leading staff member of the museum, put it in 1902. With this, Rütimeyer had joined an earlier, albeit differently accentuated, statement by Fritz:

> Meanwhile, the scarcity of space should not prevent us from augmenting the collections to the best of our ability, as we are convinced that, in a matter of a few decades, the tragic process of colonization will have reached even the most distant lands, and the abundance of stylish and

artistic objects produced by these foreign peoples will have disappeared forever.[17]

And augment the collection they did – not least through the active financial support and donation of artefacts from Basel citizens who

> migrated to the wide world and still wander; their strong patriotic feeling always drives them to commemorate the hometown and decorate it with treasures of all kinds. The ethnographic museum, like so many other collections in Basel, is shining proof of this touching attachment. With a small exception, almost everything mentioned here has been given by Baselers.[18]

However, staff members hardly ever mentioned, let alone commented on, the practices of object acquisition. Against this background of the suggested ambivalent attitude towards collecting – a tentatively critical stance towards colonialism and colonial events with simultaneous collective rage, superficially concealed with the salvage paradigm – it is paramount to elucidate the history of the institution itself and the implicit establishment of interpretive dominance. Reflection on historicity in all its aspects is an inevitable premise towards prospects of different modes of engagement with and interpretation of the collections.

Historicity

Drawing on the experiences of historical research and the exhibition *Thirst for Knowledge Meets Collecting Mania*, I want to elaborate on the issue of historicity. How to deal with the gap between the contradictions implicit in wanting to be relevant today while relying heavily on historic artefacts, collected under the most opaque circumstances? How, then, to address historicity? By historicity, I mean all historical dimensions of a given person, thing, or event, as well as the methods to research these dimensions. Applied to collections of the ethnographic museum, historicity includes, among other elements, the institution itself, the collectors, the collecting practices, the circumstances of collecting in imperial, colonial, post-colonial or global times with all people involved in the processes. In "Expeditions. The World in a Suitcase", staged in 2012, we started to deal explicitly with the institutional history in an exhibition (cf. MKB 2012); the research and disclosure continued in *Thirst for Knowledge meets Collecting Mania*.[19] The show dealt with conditions of collecting, insensitive collecting practices through time and in different places, as well as with forms of display. The written sources – letters, reports, publications etc. – tell us about competition between cities,[20] euphoric statements on the excessive enlargement of collections and about blank spots on the world's map filled in when substantial collections from any region had reached Basel.

After Interpretive Dominance 25

In sharp contrast to this feverish acquisitiveness, documentation is scarce: we are rarely in possession of documents that allow us to reconstruct how an object reached the museum; sometimes, not even the region of origin is mentioned. In most cases, there is no reference to the path of the object between production and purchase, and, in addition, the producers are barely ever named. What we almost invariably do know, however, is who gave a specific object to the museum, either as a gift, through sale, or in exchange.

This was the starting point for the "Collecting Mania" show,[21] in which we presented problematic object categories and objects whose acquisition is often incompatible with ethical guidelines. Interpretations, appraisals, sheer collectors' enthusiasm, recognition and ambitions were investigated as well. The exhibition had five sections: human remains and grave goods, weaponry, difficult materials, "imitation" as a mode of representation and "showable/unshowable".

The sections on human remains and grave goods dealt mostly with unauthorised excavations of graveyards and with the acquisition of grave goods and human remains. Although a highly sensitive issue, examples of these categories were put on display (cf. Figure 1.1). We contextualised the acquisition through information, with the intention to provoke reactions from those concerned and affected, which might lead to new questions or other dialogues and practices. This section included examples from all over the world, often bare of any indication regarding the purpose and significance of these items in the museum's collection. Why, then, did collectors

Figure 1.1 A glimpse into the exhibition shows a part of the section on human remains.
2019 © MKB, photographer Omar Lemke.

26 *Anna Schmid*

struggle so hard for their acquisition? Other entries read like excerpts from adventure novels in which victory was paramount – did object procurement advance to a ritual of (male) reassurance?

In 1928 Eugen Paravicini set out to the south-eastern Solomon Islands to collect artefacts on behalf of the museum. The approximately 900 objects (as well as numerous objects reserved for barter) included an ossuary with two skulls. Paravicini had gone to great lengths to obtain such a piece, although he was aware of the enormity of this undertaking: "The natives, full of suspicion and armed with clubs, followed us everywhere; they were afraid we might rob a skull or even an entire skull house" (Paravicini 1931, 97). After a missionary had alerted him to an "abandoned" ossuary, Paravicini took it without further ado; eventually, he had to return it and pay the deceased's son a reparation to restore his "father's disturbed death rest".[22] In the end, Paravicini obtained an ossuary from a different source.

When in 1949, Alfred Bühler, then curator at the museum, travelled to Sumba, he returned with more than 6000 objects, among them a headstone and two burial figures. Bühler attempted to justify the three acquisitions referring to the activities of the Japanese army, which had opened graves in Sumba during their occupation of the island in the Second World War and then left them to decay. However, on October 17, 1949, he wrote in his diary:

> One evening, schoolboys brought me two headstones from a grave and, the next day, fragments of the corresponding bodies. I felt that not all was right here but did not have the slightest reason to suspect evil play. [...] The next morning, after I had already packed all except two pieces, I received a visit by a few elders who claimed that the figures had been stolen and that they wanted them back. [...] The negotiations went on for two days. In the end, they agreed to allow me to keep the figures against an additional payment of a piece of cloth, 200 fl. [in those days, approx. CHF 325, MKB], and a kilogram of tobacco, claiming that these gifts were necessary to wash away the sin, to appease the Marapu (supernatural beings), and have new figures made.[23]

In the 1980s, a museum employee suspected mischief, travelled to Sumba to clarify the ownership and eventually offered to return the figures to their owners. However, the descendants declined; they preferred to have new figures made.

Instead of showing a skull from East Arnhem Land, an empty stele (cf. Figure 1.1 far left) was labelled indicating the fragmentary knowledge: In 1934, the MKB had purchased a painted skull from an Australian missionary. Recently, research in East Arnhem Land disclosed the skull's affiliation to a specific clan.[24] The cooperation with members of this clan might, hopefully, lead to its restitution and to further research on the circumstances of its acquisition. In the next stele, the cast of a preserved Maori head, *toi moko*, was shown. When a Maori attending the PAA conference in 2019 visited the exhibition, she firmly suggested that the cast should be withdrawn from the exhibition and restored since ancestors are also present in a cast. In 1992, the *toi moko* had gone on loan to the Te Papa Tongarewa Museum in Wellington and remained thereafter a consensual restitution procedure. Yet, before sending it, staff members of the MKB had produced casts of the head. The MKB has repeatedly approached the Te Papa Museum: the repatriation will take place as soon as an official New Zealand delegation travels to Europe.

In contrast, the procurement of two painted skulls from Hallstatt, Austria, seems to appear almost unproblematic, if somewhat bizarre. To this day, the skulls of deceased relatives are exhumed and painted in Hallstatt. They are marked with the deceased's name and life data and conferred to the local ossuary. In 1972, a museum employee wanted such a skull for the museum. However, the skull painter replied, "[…] unable to provide a skull from any old grave, only if relatives apply to the local church authority can a skull be painted and assigned to the ossuary, but you might consider using a skull of your own and sending it to me". The employee got two anonymous skulls from the Natural History Museum, sent them to Hallstatt, got them painted and returned to the MKB.

Scientific questions may have been decisive in the procurement of human remains and associated objects. However, considering the circumstances of acquisition and subsequent handling, the collectors prioritised probably other motives. Restitution of these objects is an important step but does not supersede examination of the acquisition proceedings and the attitudes and behaviour of the collectors. These range from passing exams in the field to recognising achievements as soon as the collections arrived at their destination to exposing other practices as curious – at best. Of course, there might have also been legitimate scientific interests, yet this is difficult to identify in the examples mentioned.

The section on weaponry contained an installation of nearly 300 arrows alongside spears, lances, an armour of Kiribati and other weapons. On the one hand, we marvelled why the collection – not only in Basel – is brimming with all kinds of weapons. On the other, we checked the collector's attributions of individual objects. The bulk of weaponry can partly be explained by its categorisation as comparative material. At least until the middle of the 20th century, weapons were considered significant for comparison and classification into an evolutionary scheme. Yet, the plethora of weapons is probably also due to male collecting behaviour and conquest experiences since disarming indigenous peoples was also considered to serve the pacification of newly won colonial territories.

At times, the male gaze might have played a trick on collectors: bows and arrows are important hunting tools among the Tuparí, with a distinction made between hunting arrows and arrows used in war and on ceremonial occasions. Obviously, the collector Franz Caspar (1975) did not

28 *Anna Schmid*

comprehend this distinction: "Carrying weapons is an expression of manliness and prowess. Women neither carry nor use weapons. In this sense, this arrow, allegedly from a tribe of Amazons living north of the Tuparí, is quite striking (*aramira-eköp-tsiru-eköp* = arrow of arrow-bearing women)" (58).

In the section on problematic materials, objects made of ivory, feathers and hide were on display. Among them were a feather cloak from Tupinambá in the Amazon delta, a Maori feather cloak (inter alia with feathers of the kiwi, *Apertyx sp.*), a robe of painted hide (bison or deer) from the United States, as well as a large number of ivory objects including pieces of jewellery, *netsuke*, small skill games, a baton and a piano key. The mass slaughter of elephants began in the 19th century when ivory became a coveted raw material. By the mid-20th century, strict controls and the establishment of reserves resulted in recovering populations, but in the 1960s, thousands of elephants were killed again to meet the demand for ivory in the countries of the north. Despite international restrictions and national legislation, the trade in ivory continues to flourish. Merely allowing museums the acquisition of objects made of ivory was certainly not a reason to kill elephants, yet it is surprising just how fervently such objects are described and how they appear to enhance the status of whole collections.

The ivory tusks from Benin City stand out in the collection of the MKB. The entry in the 1899 annual report describes the quite standard acquisition and dispersal practices of the era:

> As with most of the world's ethnographic collections, last year's acquisitions bore the stamp of Benin. Recall that on account of the destruction of Benin City by the British, there have emerged products of an ancient craft tradition of singular character unsurpassed in the workmanship of the Negro peoples. The spoils of Benin were cast upon the market this year, and we viewed it as our duty to secure for our collection at least some exemplars of a civilization that has now passed from sight for all time.[25]

The rich carvings also show Europeans discernible through their swords, weapon belts and a cross on the chest of one of the figures. The MKB bought the tusk from the company Umlauff in Hamburg, which, in turn, most likely had acquired it from William D. Webster, London. The object has traces of fire damage, which may bear witness to the pillage during the British punitive expedition of 1897. When the MKB had the opportunity to acquire an additional carved tusk in 1926, Rütimeyer enthused:

> By far the most valuable item among the African additions is a long elephant tusk from ancient Benin. This splendid item was acquired from an original private collection. [...] Carved in flat relief at intervals between the bands is seen a sword typical in the form of those from ancient Benin. Together with the other objects from Benin, this tusk now

represents one of the most distinguished ornaments within the African department.[26]

Probably, this tusk belongs as well to the prey from the British punitive expedition.

Unlike many other ethnographic artefacts, objects from the looting of Benin City were quickly and consensually recognised as works of art among European museum people and valued accordingly. The prices paid for individual works mirror the appreciation.[27] The appeals and restitution requests of various Nigerian governments since the 1950s to a number of museums – unsuccessful to this day – give a vivid idea of an enduring and potentially irreconcilable framing of historicity. In the meantime, however, several projects have been launched to critically review the objects – projects with European and Nigerian participation.[28]

As mentioned, Swiss nationals were often located at interfaces between European colonial powers and colonised peoples. The arrival of some 200 objects from Central Africa was hailed as "a superb collection".[29] The Swiss national Erwin Federspiel had collected them; he "has spent several years in the Congo, from where he has undertaken lengthy explorations" (ibid.). An employee in the military service of the Belgians in the euphemistically named Congo Free State, he had excellent access to objects of all kinds. On his inspection trips to various stations, he repeatedly received gifts from elders or chiefs. In his writing – a kind of statement of accounts for the colonial rule under the Belgian King Leopold II – he describes receptions at which gifts were presented to him (Federspiel 1909: 37). However, he never mentions transverse horns made of ivory as gifts. He mentions these only as a means of communication with a penetrating and sometimes frightening sound (ibid. 68). He donated the "official gifts"[30] to the museum, but objects such as these horns he sold to the museum.

What prompted Federspiel to give up his position in the Swiss army to enter the services of the Belgian king remains to be researched. He was one of about 200 Swiss who signed on as civil servants, tax collectors, army officers etc., under Leopold II.[31] With his writings, Federspiel wanted to put into perspective the shocking reports about the Congo atrocities in the European press. In an indictment published in the same year, however, his countryman Daniel Bersot from Neuchatel (cf. Minder 1994) denounced not only the cruel colonial conditions in Congo but also colonialism as such.

Another section dealt with the principle of imitation in ethnographic exhibitions. The urge to collect and display cultures in their alleged unity led to the development of a whole branch of trade: model figures – equipped with clothing, jewellery and weapons collected in their place of origin – were intended to provide a realistic insight into life elsewhere. From the end of the 19th century until the Second World War, model figures made of plaster, papier-mâché or synthetic materials were in great demand across Europe.

The Hamburg-based supplier of ethnographica Umlauff or Berlin's Replica Workshop produced catalogues with over one hundred different types of figures from all over the globe – ranging from a Mongolian princess to a Fiji Islander to a Masai warrior. The MKB also placed orders for such model figures or commissioned them from sculptors.

These figures were modelled on the descriptions, photographs, and measurements of people provided by researchers and travellers on their return home. Physical dimensions, hair colouring and suitable facial expressions conformed to the wishes of clients who wanted to show "typical" representatives of indigenous groups. Employees of the Basel museum, as well as their Berlin counterparts at the Royal Museum of Ethnology, were quite pragmatic in their approach to model figures: according to a note, ritual objects of the Marind-Anim people of New Guinea were "to be installed on a brown plaster figure".[32] Although the figure was not in the workshop's catalogue, it was ordered from Berlin in 1916. Eventually, a figure was cobbled together: a torso representing South East Asia was paired with a Western Pacific head. Apparently, the mixing of "different types" was common practice. What is astonishing, however, is that despite high scientific requirements – especially with regard to relevant data on physical anthropology – the Basel orders were kept unspecific if not completely indifferent. Then, the question arises as to what purpose the elaborate and costly imitation should serve, especially since, on other occasions, the faithfulness to reality had been emphasised. Some 125 years ago, Fritz and Paul Sarasin photographed a member of Sri Lanka's indigenous Vedda people, "Perikabalai from Danigala Mountain". They recorded his height, age, waist, chest size, facial as well as body skin colour. Using these data and his photograph, a commissioned sculptor produced a plaster figure of him. The Sarasins intended to get "an exact portrait of a true member of an aboriginal tribe prone to extinction".[33] Fritz Sarasin was extremely pleased with the sculptor's work, since

> this lifelike figure reproduces extraordinarily well the impression made by a living Vedda on a viewer; but not only that – the facial features and physical proportions of the body are grasped in such a way as to lend the figure great anthropological value.[34]

The same sculptor also produced the figures of a Vedda woman and child in plaster.

The two Sarasins undertook five expeditions to Sri Lanka between 1883 and 1925. Initially, they focussed on natural science research; later, they dedicated themselves exclusively to the group of the Vedda.[35] In addition to social and economic life, the Sarasins were interested in physical anthropology. They generated massive data on skull shape, physique, skin colour and hair – not just among the Vedda. To convey an idea of their meticulousness: out of nearly 600 fixed measuring points on the human skull, the Sarasins chose 20 to "uncover real differences in skull construction".[36] These included length, width, height of the skull, height and width of the face, yoke width, height and width of the eye socket, and width of the nasal bone. They transferred these measurements to indices and created skull curves to indulge in comparisons, for example, with skulls of Europeans and monkeys.[37] Most of the human skulls in the Sarasin collection from Sri Lanka were exhumed at graveyards with the consent of their relatives. Sometimes, however, relatives denied them access to the graves. If they could not be persuaded, for example, with gifts, the Sarasins went "in the hottest noon hours" to the gravesites "while everybody slept and no one bothered us at work".[38]

One reason to integrate the intervention of Deneth Piumakshi Wedaarachchige (cf. Figure 1.2), a Sri Lankan contemporary artist, into the exhibition was the overdue criticism of this approach and the associated ideas. In "Voices of the Ancestors",[39] Deneth presented herself, that is, a life-size replica of her own body with a skull likewise 3D-reproduced, which she holds in her hands in front of her. With this 3D sculpture, she confronted the museum, its practices of racialising in representation with the violence inherent in museum practices:

> I wanted to bring to light the objectification of (their) bodies as "exotic" and "primitive" during the colonial times in Sri Lanka in the 19th century. During the making of the sculpture, it was important for me to follow the same procedure that my ancestors had to go through 136 years ago, such as being measured, compared, photographed, and exhibited. The sculpture is part of a wider project. As part of the making of the sculpture, like my ancestors, I had to expose my half-naked body in front of two Swiss men, who scanned, measured, and photographed it before sending their work to a Swiss male artist who compared and selected exact skin colours according to a colour chart, which was then painted onto the 3D-printed figure. The sculpture is a representation of me as a contemporary Sri Lankan, brown skin, female, immigrant artist living in France. It is also a vision of me coming to Switzerland and discovering the forgotten, stolen past of the Sri Lankan Adivasi (Sri Lankan aboriginal people formally referred to as Vedda) then bringing their unethically removed remains back to Sri Lanka with my own hands.
> (Wedaarachchige 2020)

Clearly, the inclusion of this particular piece of contemporary art in the show is – as Geismar points out – "a form of institutional, and often indigenous, critique",[40] especially since the artist conducted intensive research in the MKB archives. This art genre "has significantly interfered with the representational and epistemological paradigms"[41] as in this case, by denouncing not only the practice of collecting but also categorisations *per se*. The artist has inscribed survey data and colour specifications on the torso, face

Figure 1.2 The installation "Voices of the Ancestors" by Deneth Piumakshi Wedaarachchige integrated into the exhibition "Thirst for Knowledge meets Collecting Mania".
2020 © MKB, photographer Omar Lemke.

and feet (cf. Figure 1.2) according to a skin-colour scale as the Sarasins had designed them – divided into 12 shades of colour.[42] The artistic work does not relieve the museum of continuing to seek ways out of the dilemma of the "historical contamination of the collections". However, it refers to category formations with which people were fixed, rendered passive and implicitly excluded from participation. Today, bodies are no longer measured and calibrated, and objects enter the collections in different ways; yet, this does not eliminate categorisation and fixing.

However, until the 1980s, the MKB refused queries and requests for restitution from Sri Lanka. The above-mentioned intervention might (hopefully) lead to a renewed dialogue to arrange the restitution of objects as well as photographs[43] and thus establish a different relation between the past, the present and the future, as well as between different places, institutions and individuals.

In a small in-between section, the question was raised: what should be shown and what should not be shown? Who is to decide? If artefacts are only accessible to certain members or segments of a community – is a museum then entitled to put them on display? Do objects retain their potential and power when relocated to a museum? Are objects with a discriminatory potential showable? We selected a lighter on which the logo of a Basel carnival clique was emblazoned: a black man with large lips wearing a grass skirt and adorned with a bone in his hair. In 2018, a fierce dispute erupted over the racism of the logo; finally, it was removed. Next to a Komo ceremonial mask from Mali and a wooden cabinet for storing sacrificial cakes from Tibet, we staged two Zuni objects, a deity statue and a mask, although representatives of the Zuni people have called for the return of all their deity figures and the masks. What was not physically present was a secret-sacred object from central Australia, a *tjurunga*. Instead, a caption explicated why others than the initiates should not be able to see it.

All sections of the exhibition were implicitly or explicitly a challenging debate on the institutional history as well as an engagement with a vast array of persons who have been important for the museum. It is crucial to emphasise that most of these persons simply followed the zeitgeist. The show was neither an indictment of those actors nor a reckoning with them. Instead, it was an invitation to the public to engage with differing perspectives on the world, facilitated by the show's devices like the open cubes (cf. Figure 1.2). These cubes, the eschewal of showcases or the use of colour communicated and reflected the attitude of the MKB – openness to any suggestion, appeal or request, from visitors and non-visitors alike. Other features of the exhibition process were – as always – the thematic approach in which the regional as a category is subordinate,[44] and the topical link with the "here and now" to stress connectivity.[45]

Conclusion

The sections, their themes and the examples mentioned address fundamental questions pertaining to the ethnographic museum, all of which require further elaboration. Here, I shall concentrate on relating the concepts of affectivity and historicity to interpretive dominance.

An initial question was: should henceforth only "affected" persons voice their thoughts on topics, events and collections? Certainly not. Affectivity and concern arise when things, an event, incident, interlocution, experience or people touch you. This empathy guarantees that the counterpart – be it a thing or a person – intervenes in your own life. In the sketched circumstances of acquisition, very different emotions resonate with the collectors: Paravicini described his defeat when he had to return the laboriously transported ossuary and, on top of it, had to pay a "penalty note". How did he feel when he finally acquired another ossuary? Federspiel was convinced that he had enriched the MKB with his gifts. He gave to the MKB what had been gifted to him. How did he obtain the other objects? How did he relate to them? Participants in the guided tour of the migration exhibition were concerned about the experiences that migrants have in Basel and how they process them. What questions did the participants ask themselves afterwards? A controversy among the staff of the MKB finally led to the Australian *tjurunga* not being shown, although the two objects of the Zuni were on display. Is this affectivity and concern in contradictions? Although the list of divergent emotions could be continued, the examples suffice to suggest that the empathic quality of encounters has to be transformed into an analytical comprehension of the collections – not just in terms of object acquisition – in order to uncover new potential in this vast depository of knowledge, memory and imagination. However, it is exactly this kind of affective response that hints at the agency of objects or their arrangements and which discloses the potential of connecting with objects – in whichever way possible. Dudley (2015) qualified this encounter: "The object's materiality and my sensibility, then, together can create powerful, albeit culturally, historically, and personally constituted effects" (56). It should thus not be a matter of – former or present – "owners" being entitled to talk about *their* objects. Ownership is but one of the many elements in this discourse. Totalising ownership – and the power attached to it – prevents us from scooping the potential of the objects.

As to historicity: when assembled, the objects were mostly contemporary. For the larger part of the collections, this means they are by now historical objects.[46] However, for the better part of ethnographical museums' history, the artefacts were not understood as being linked to time at all. We have seen, in part, the adventurous paths of objects to the museum, and that personal ambition, political circumstances, competition among museums and coincidences determined collecting. Subsequently, we can hardly assume systematic collecting or consistent academic interests. Should we, then, subject the collections to a single systematic approach *post factum* and pursue research along notions of Western academia? Should individual objects or entire collections not be open to various interpretations, in which former contexts, acquisition circumstances, detours and errors, arrival at and (possible or factual) retrieval from the museum can be used, but do not have to be – especially since "we have done with representation"?[47] Hence, a "politically correct" contextualisation might be counterproductive. Recently, James Clifford provided a different approach, drawing on examples of his fieldwork in several cultures on how to re-historicise resources: "A discursive linking of pasts and futures is integral to the positioning of collective subjects. Thus, to imagine a coherent future, people must selectively mobilize past resources – historical practices that take diverse forms and are expressed in unfamiliar idioms".[48] Possibly, artefacts in themselves are such an idiom of bygone days into which history and its relevance for today are inscribed. If the materialised past can be a source for the new, then we have to strengthen culturally specific topics like memory, mnemonics and contemporary processes of activating things to build presents and futures in our research and exhibition agendas.

The recourse to affectivity – encompassing a wide range of emotions from being touched, to concern, to an experience of intrusiveness, to a wide range of sensibilities and historicity while simultaneously including different perspectives – is a first careful step against interpretive dominance. The active, conscious abandonment of attitudes which include interpretive dominance, is a liberating empowerment of all involved to think, speak and act differently. The concomitant openness to new practises and research agendas – including unfamiliar idioms beyond moral guilt and juridical procedures – might not be the end of institutional restraints but an important move towards it.

The ethnographical museum's critical endeavour is no longer (only) to impart factual knowledge, to document or reconstruct other ways of life. The primary task of an ethnographical museum has shifted to generating and presenting offers of interpretation on burning issues and important topics. The interpretations have to include differing views, perspectives and categories allowing the connection to one's own life and world. Therein lies the promise of anthropology, as David Graeber has powerfully put it:

> [Anthropology] opens windows on other possible forms of human social existence; it served as a constant reminder that most of what we assume to be immutable has been, in other times and places, arranged quite differently, and therefore, that human possibilities are in almost every way greater than we ordinarily imagine.[49]

If Western sciences, with their methodologies and epistemologies, are no longer the gatekeepers of the *right* understanding but will have become "Western particulars",[50] then the alternative could be multi-voiced interpretations, nurtured by different arguments, modes of understanding, conceptions of time, cultures of remembrance and other dimensions inherent in the objects of ethnographic museums.

Notes

1 I would like to thank the organisers of the conference, Zainabu Jallo and Samuel Bachmann, for inviting me as a keynote speaker and to contribute to the publication.
2 Coombes and Phillipps 2015, p. xxxiii.
3 Preferring interpretive dominance strengthens the shift from the authority in knowledge production to arguments and the resulting possibilities of different interpretations. With this shift, the negotiation processes regarding interpretations is centre stage; it might replace merely power-ridden confrontations.

4 Cf., for example, Sharon McDonald, Witcomb and Message, von Zinnenburg Carroll, Van Broekhoven and the other authors who published a paper on "Decolonizing the Museum in Practice" in the *Journal of Museum Ethnography*, 2019, vol. 32.
5 Cf. Kassim 2017, Minott 2019, Giblin et al. 2019.
6 Cf. also Tuck and Yang 2012.
7 Cf. MKB 2011, pp. 54–89; in this publication, 15 statements on the question "To Whom does the Minster Hill Belong?" highlight the diversity of stakeholder positions.
8 cf. Kriemler 2011.
9 In German: "Museum für Völkerkunde und Schweizerisches Museum für Volkskunde"; for three changes in naming cf. Schmid 2021.
10 Statistical Office; Number of foreigners by country 2019. www.basleratlas.ch/#c=indicator&i=bevheim.anzahl_al_heim&p=1&s=2019&view=map2 (accessed 2.3.2021).
11 Cf., for example, the city's website of the www.bs.ch/Portrait/einleitung-weltstadt/Geschichte-von-Basel.html (accessed 2.3.2021).
12 For the exhibition "Migration" and a multi-voiced installation, see Glass 2017, Schmid 2019, 2021.
13 For discussions on imperialism and colonialism, cf., for example, Osterhammel 2015, 16f. The focus on the colonial period may suffice for the discussion of the issues at stake. Thus, the following text will talk about colonialism only.
14 A telling example is the acquisition of a tomb *waruga/timbukar* from Minahasa, Sulawesi. With this object, the Sarasins succeeded in a brazen coup: although the Dutch colonial government had issued an export ban "for such objects", Fritz and Paul Sarasin were able to have a grave monument removed *with the support of a colonial official*. Cf. Kunz 2011.
15 Only recently, this subject has become a topic for research in a number of disciplines; cf. Purtschert et al. 2012, Schär 2015, Purtschert and Fischer 2015, Étienne et al. 2020.
16 Annual Report 1902, p. 7.
17 Sarasin, Annual Report 1897, p. 27.
18 Kollmann and Rütimeyer 1894, p. 4.
19 March 2019–November 2020.
20 Competition between cities was also a major stimulation in the development of German ethnographical museums; cf. Penny 2002, p. 10, 41ff.
21 Beatrice Voirol was project leader and main curator of the show. Nine staff members wrote the captions and labels. These texts are available at www.mkb.ch/en/programm/events/2019/wissensdrang-trifft-sammelwut (accessed 3.3.2021). The descriptions which follow are in parts extracted from this script, cf. MKB 2020.
22 Paravicini 1931, p. 168.
23 Bühler 1949, p. 178.
24 For a detailed account of the research, cf. Voirol 2019.
25 Annual Report 1899, p. 284.
26 Annual Report 1926, p. 5f.
27 Initially, prices for ivory carvings were considerably higher than for the so-called bronzes. This ratio reversed slowly from the 1920s onwards. For the second tusk, however, the MKB still had to pay the then high price of 1750 Reichsmark (equivalent to about 500 euros today).

28 Between the submission of the essay and its publication, this has changed: Germany and other nations have since restituted objects to the Nigerian state.
29 Annual Report 1901, p. 639.
30 Federspiel 1909, p. 48.
31 Cf. www.swissinfo.ch/ger/philanthropie-und-kolonialherrschaft_schweizer-im-dienst-von-leopold-ii-spurensuche-im-kongo-freistaat/43337402 (accessed 4.3.2021).
32 MKB Archive, 04-0079; Correspondence and Documentation 1901–1920.
33 Annual Report 1908, p. 22.
34 Ibid.
35 (cf. Kunz 2012).
36 Sarasin 1892/93a, p. 163.
37 Cf. Sarasin 1892/93b.
38 1892/93a, p. 164.
39 The work was part of a larger exhibition project: "Voices from a silenced archive" (cf. Ryser and Schonfeldt 2019); it was exhibited in the foyer of the Theater Basel. During the research for her work the idea arose to integrate her part of the project – after the performance in the theatre – into the exhibition at the MKB.
40 Geismar 2015, p. 185.
41 Ibid., p. 192.
42 Sarasin 1892/93b, Panel II.
43 Deneth Piumakshi Wedaarachchige had taken photographs from the MKB on her trip to Sri Lanka and shown them there to talk to the descendants of the pictured about what they know about the production of the pictures. A surprising reaction to this was that the people addressed were incensed that the photographs were in Basel – a place where they would never have suspected them. Deneth reported that no person involved was interested in restitution or provision of the photographs.
44 To this day, ethnographic museums – their departments, their storage facilities, their exhibitions – are mostly organised along geographic axes. I have dealt with this categorisation repeatedly to finally reject it as a principle of our exhibitions (cf. Schmid 2011, 2019). Concisely, to say it with Fardon (1990, 24), who certainly did not oppose the regional as a basic ethnographic category: "Regionalization is another strategy with its own effects upon power and knowledge in terms of authoritative presentation […] and the sustenance of regional stereotypes".
45 cf. Schmid 2021.
46 cf. Penny 2018.
47 The article of Koyuncu (2019) discusses the impossibility to represent the Holocaust. Meanwhile, the impossibility of representing cultures or groups (cf. Belting 2005) has reached the ethnographic Museum as well.
48 Clifford 2013, p. 23.
49 2007, p. 1.
50 Cf. Singh 2013, p. 5:

> The museum questions the universal validity of Western science, and seeks to give space to the affective […] The "scientific" and "rational" values ultimately derived from the Enlightenment become displaced within the ethnographic museum. No longer a universal, the Enlightenment itself becomes the relic of a cultural particular.

References

Annual reports cf. Bericht.
Belting, Hans. "Gibt es eine Ausstellung von Kulturen?" In: *Hans Belting. Szenarien der Moderne. Kunst und ihre offenen Grenzen.* Hamburg: Philo. 2005. pp. 222–240.
Bennett, Tony. "Introduction: Museums, Power, Knowledge." In: *Museum Worlds: Advances in Research.* Vol. 6, 2018. pp. 1–16.
Bericht über das Basler Museum für Völkerkunde für das Jahr 1897.
Bericht über das Basler Museum für Völkerkunde für das Jahr 1899.
Bericht über das Basler Museum für Völkerkunde für das Jahr 1901.
Bericht über das Basler Museum für Völkerkunde für das Jahr 1902.
Bericht über das Basler Museum für Völkerkunde für das Jahr 1908.
Bericht über das Basler Museum für Völkerkunde für das Jahr 1926.
Bouquet, Mary. "Reactivating the Colonial Collection. Exhibition Making as Creative Process at the Tropenmuseum, Amsterdam." In: Coombes, Annie E. and Ruth Phillips (eds.). *Museum Transformations: Decolonization and Democratization.* Chichester: Wiley, 2015. pp. 133–155.
Bühler, Alfred. Tagebuch-Notizen: Sumba 1949. Dokumentenarchiv MKB: 08-0022.1949.
Caspar, Franz. *Die Tuparí. Ein Indianerstamm in Westbrasilien.* Berlin, NY: Walter de Gruyter, 1975.
Clifford, James. *Returns: Becoming Indigenous in the Twenty-First Century.* Cambridge, MA: Harvard University Press, 2013.
Coombes, Annie E. and Ruth B. Phillips. "Introduction: Museums in Transformation. Dynamics of Democratization and Decolonization." In: Coombes, Annie E. and Ruth B. Phillips (eds.) *Museum Transformations: Decolonization and Democratization.* Chichester: Wiley Blackwell, 2015. pp. xxxiii–lxiii.
Dudley, Sandra. What, or Where, Is the (Museum) Object? Colonial Encounters in Displayed Worlds of Things. In: Andrea Witcomb and Kylie Message (eds.) *Museum Theory.* Chichester: Wiley, 2015. pp. 41–62.
Elliott, Mark. Decolonial Re-enactments? Facing and Retracing Colonial Histories in Collecting' Another India. In: *Third Text*, vol. 33, no. 4–5, 2019. pp. 631–650.
Étiennne, Noémie; Claire Brizon, Chonja Lee and Étienne Wismer (eds.). *Exotic Switzerland? Looking Outward in the Age of Enlightenment.* Zürich: Diaphanes. 2020.
Fardon, Richard. "General Introduction – Localizing Strategies: The Regionalization of Ethnographic Accounts." In: Richard Fardon (ed.) *Localizing Strategies. Regional Traditions of Ethnographic Writing.* Edinburgh: Scottish Academic Press, 1990. pp. 1–36.
Federspiel, Erwin. *Wie es im Congostaat zugeht: Skizzen.* Zürich: Art Institut Orell Füssli. 1909.
Geismar, Haidy. The Art of Anthropology: Questioning Contemporary Art in Ethnographic Display. In: Andrea Witcomb and Kylie Message (eds.). *Museum Theory.* Chichester: Wiley, 2015. pp. 183–210.
Giblin, John; Imma Ramos and Nikki Grout. "Dismantling the Master's House: Thoughts on Representing Empire and Decolonising Museums and Public Spaces in Practice. An Introduction." In: *Third Text*, vol. 33, no. 4–5, 2019. pp. 471–486.

Glass, Claudia. Migration – Bewegte Welt. Eine Ausstellung im Museum der Kulturen Basel. In: *Museum Aktuell*, no. 244, 2017. pp. 9–14.
Graeber, David 2007. *Possibilities: Essays on Hierarchy, Rebellion, and Desire.* Edinburgh: AK Press, 2007.
Hoffmann, Anette. "Of Storying and Storing: Reading Lichtenecker's Voice Recordings." In: Jeremy Silvester (ed.). *Re-Viewing Resistance in Namibian History*. Windhoek: University of Namibia Press, 2015. pp. 89–104.
Kassim, Sumaya. "The Museum Will not be Decolonised." *Media Diversified*, 2017 https://mediadiversified.org/2017/11/15/the-museum-will-not-be-decolonised/ (accessed 23.2.2021).
Kaufmann, Karin. "Open for Interpretation: An Experimental Exhibition Project in an Ethnographic Collection." In: *Tsantsa*, vol. 24, 2019. pp. 89–98.
Kollmann, Julius and Leopold Rütimeyer. "Bericht über die ethnographische Sammlung der Universität Basel." In: *Mitteilungen der ethnographischen Kommission Basel*, vol. 1, no. 1, 1894.
Koyuncu, Emre. "To Have Done with Representation. Resnais and Tarantino on the Holocaust." In: *Third Text*, vol. 33, no. 2, 2019. pp. 247–255.
Kriemler, Daniel. "The Minster Square as a Museum." In: Museum der Kulturen Basel (ed.) *Intrinsic Perspectives* vol. 2: From Miss Kumbuk to Herzog & de Meuron. Basel: MKB, 2011. pp. 115–123.
Kunz, Richard. "Primäres Ziel ethnografischer Museumssammlungen." In: *Museum der Kulturen Basel* (ed.) EigenSinn, Bd. 1. Basel: MKB, 2011. pp. 183–184.
Kunz, Richard. "The Five Sri Lanka (Ceylon) Expeditions, 1883–1925, Paul and Fritz Sarasin. Measuring, Collecting, and Doing Research." In: Museum der Kulturen Basel (ed.) *Expeditions. The World in a Suitcase*. Basel: MKB, 2012. pp. 4–9.
MacDonald, Sharon; Paul Basu (eds.). *Exhibition Experiments*. Malden, MA: Blackwell Publisher, 2007.
Minder, Patrick. *D'Helvétie en Congolie: les pionniers suisses au service de l'Etat indépendant du Congo et du Congo belge (1885–1914)*. Fribourg, 1994.
Minott, Rachael. "The Past Is Now. Confronting Museum's Complicity in Imperial Celebration." In: *Third Text*, vol. 33, no. 4–5, 2019. pp. 559–574.
Museum der Kulturen Basel (MKB) (ed.). *EigenSinn* Bd. 2. Basel: MKB, 2011.
Museum der Kulturen Basel (MKB) (ed.). *Expeditions*. Basel: MKB, 2012.
Museum der Kulturen Basel (MKB) (ed.). *Thirst for Knowledge Meets Collecting Mania*, 2020 .www.mkb.ch/en/programm/events/2019/wissensdrang-trifft-sammelwut.html (accessed 27.2.2021).
Osterhammel, Jürgen. *Die Verwandlung der Welt. Eine Geschichte des 19. Jahrhunderts*. München: C.H. Beck, 2015.
Paravicini, Eugen. *Reisen in den Britischen Salomonen*. Frauenfeld Leipzig: Verlag Huber, 1931.
Penny, Glenn. *Objects of Culture: Ethnology and Ethnographic Museums in Imperial Germany*. Chapel Hill: University of North Carolina Press, 2002.
Penny, Glenn. The Ethnographic Museum: "A Lot of Possibilities". Conversation between Glenn Penny and Anna Schmid. 2018. www.mkb.ch/de/blog/2018/q1/glenn-penny.html (accessed 26.2.2021).
Plankensteiner, Barbara. "Being a World Culture Museum Today." In: Barbara Plankensteiner (ed.) *The Art of Being a World Culture Museum. Futures and Lifeways of Ethnographic Museums in Contemporary Europe*. Bielefeld/Berlin: Kerber Culture, 2018. pp. 25–42.

Purtschert, Patricia; Barbara Lüthi and Francesca Falk (eds.). *Postkoloniale Schweiz. Formen und Folgen eines Kolonialismus ohne Kolonien.* Bielefeld: Transcript, 2012.

Purtschert, Patricia and Harald Fischer-Tiné (eds.). *Colonial Switzerland: Rethinking Colonialism from the Margins.* Basingstoke: Palgrave Macmillan, 2015.

Ryser, Vera and Sally Schonfeldt. *Voices from an Archived Silence. A Research and Exhibition Project on Basel's Colonial History.* Basel: Theater Basel, 2020. http://veraryser.ch/10/Stimmen%20aus%20einer%20archivierten%20Stille_Publikation.pdf (accessed 4.3.2021).

Sarasin, Fritz. *Bericht an E. E. Regenz über die Ethnographische Sammlung des Museums für das Jahr 1897.* Basel, 1897.

Sarasin, Paul und Fritz. Ergebnisse naturwissenschaftlicher Forschung aus Ceylon. Vol.3: Die Weddas von Ceylon und die Umgebenden Völkerschaften. Textband. Wiesbaden: Kreidel's Verlag, 1892–1893a.

Sarasin, Paul und Fritz. Ergebnisse naturwissenschaftlicher Forschung aus Ceylon. Vol. 3 Die Weddas von Ceylon und die Umgebenden Völkerschaften. Atlas. Wiesbaden: Kreidel's Verlag, 1892–1893b.

Schär, Bernhard. *Tropenliebe: Schweizer Naturforscher und Niederländischer Imperialismus in Südostasien um 1900.* Frankfurt a.M.: Campus, 2015.

Schmid, Anna. "The Ethnographical Museum: Another Crises and Possible Consequences." In: *Forum for Anthropology and Culture,* no. 4, 2007. pp. 217–220.

Schmid, Anna. "Das Ethnologische Museum: Ort der Reflexion – Ort des Verweilens." In: *Museum der Kulturen Basel* (ed.) EigenSinn, Bd.1. Basel: Museum der Kulturen Basel, 2011. pp. 13–23.

Schmid, Anna. "The Ethnographic Museum: Connectedness and Entanglements." In: *Nuova Museologia,* vol. 41, 2019. pp. 30–36. www.nuovamuseologia.it/2019/12/21/the-ethnographic-museum-connectedness-and-entanglements/ (accessed 26.2.2021).

Schmid, Anna. "Europe as Blind Spot. Struggling for Connectivity." In: Iris Edenheiser; Elisabeth Tietmeyer and Susanne Boersma (eds.). *What's Missing? Collecting and Exhibiting Europe.* Berlin: Reimer Verlag, 2021. pp. 186–195.

Singh, Kavita. "The Future of the Museum Is Ethnographic". 2013. https://leading-edge.iac.gatech.edu/aaproceedings/files/2015/10/The-Future-of-the-Museum-is-Ethnographic.pdf. (accessed 26.2.2021).

Stoler, Ann Laura. "Epistemic Politics: Ontologies of Colonial Common Sense." In: *The Philosophical Forum Inc.*, vol 39, no. 3, 2008. pp. 349–361.

Tuck, Eve and K. Wayne Yang. "Decolonization Is Not a Metaphor." In: *Decolonization: Indigeneity, Education & Society*, vol. 1, no. 1, 2012. pp. 1–40.

Van Broekhoven, Laura. "On Decolonizing the Museum in Practice." In: *Journal of Museum Ethnography*, no. 32, 2019. pp. 1–8.

Voirol, Beatrice. "Decolonization in the Field? Basel – Milingimbi back and forth." In: *Tsantsa*, vol. 24, 2019. pp. 48–57.

Von Zinnenburg Carroll, Khadija. "Museopiracy: Redressing the Commemoration of the Endeavour's Voyage to the Pacific in Processions for Tupaia." In: *Third Text*, vol. 33, no. 4–5. 2019, pp. 541–558.

Wedaarachchige, Deneth Piumakshi. "Voices from the Ancestors." In: Museum der Kulturen Basel (ed.). *Thirst for Knowledge meets Collecting Mania.* 2020. www.mkb.ch/en/programm/events/2019/wissensdrang-trifft-sammelwut.html (accessed 27.2.2021).

2 "Wo Ist Afrika?"
Of Reflexive Museography, and Other (Productive?) Disappointments

Sandra Ferracuti

Introduction

Estamos Juntos: We Are Together

At the time of my research in Mozambique (2006–2010; see Ferracuti, 2020), the Portuguese expression "*Estamos juntos/as*" was especially used by residents when bidding farewell to someone who was based in another country and was about to go back to where she came from. It was also used under difficult or unsure circumstances, such as between research partners who were discussing their chances to acquire the necessary funds for further collaborations or the acquisition of specific artifacts for private or museum collections. Interestingly enough, some years later, when I visited the anglophone regions of Cameroon (2017–2018; see Ferracuti 2019), the English expression "We are together" was used under the same circumstances.

Stone Karim Mohamad, a member of the *ABRAC – Advisory Board for the Representation of African Collections at the Linden-Museum Stuttgart*[1] born in Cameroon and based in Stuttgart with whom I travelled to the North-western kingdom of Oku and shared all the activities planned for the collaborative research and interpretation project *Sharing Heritage: The Cameroon Project, Oku, Stuttgart, Foumban* (Ferracuti 2019), made me aware that this expression is likely to be rooted in (post)colonial relations. The languages in which it is expressed – Portuguese and English – are, in fact, the ones that were imposed by the European governments that once occupied the two country's territories, and the contexts of its occurrences at the time of our joint research in Cameroon did still point to the unstable, unequal, and ambivalent character of relations entertained with someone based in the European continent. She appears to be perceived as someone who needs to be explicitly "reminded" of the pact of loyalty on which human relationships better be based. In both countries, moreover, our ancestors play highly relevant roles in our lives, and the features of each specific human relation will also have significant, tangible effects on the future generations of all parties involved. Hence, the special care that is put onto the quality of our interactions.

DOI: 10.4324/9781003282334-4

I started working with Stone in 2016, when I was assigned the responsibility to direct the "Afrika" department at the Linden-Museum Stuttgart and stepped into the *Volkerkunde* ("Ethnology") museum curator persona for the first time. At that time, the debate concerning the colonial soul of (European) Ethnology museums was already, yes, a longstanding, heated, and crucial one, but it was still mostly relegated to the realm of "expert" discussions and quite removed from the public arena. I had been taking part in these debates, especially since 2009, thanks to a series of European projects[2] that called museum studies scholars and professionals to reassess the predicament of ethnographic museums with a view to develop new strategies that could, in brief, turn these institutions and their mythologies on their heads so as to put their colonial history at the service of awareness-raising programs on the contemporary legacies of European imperialisms.

By late 2016, especially prompted by the disputes surrounding Berlin's *Humboldt Forum* project (von Bose 2016) and by the opening of the first exhibition on the history of German colonialism at Berlin's *Deutsches Historisches Museum* (October 2016–May 2017),[3] the issue of European (post)colonialism had instead fully "exploded' in Germany's public arena, and the breadth and intensity of this debate reminded me of those associated to "total social facts". I was far from not welcoming this new wave of public interest in these museums and their collections. Still, at times I had the impression that in Germany, the voice was out to go and "solve" colonialism as if it were something merely concerning Europe, anthropology, museums, and exhibitions, and not something (Euro-centrism and its mythologies of modernity) that had ended up shaping worlds and worldviews far beyond the physical borders of Europe. As a European curator who was working to deliver the concept for a new permanent exhibition based on historical (colonial) collections[4] from the African continent, I was scared to the bone that the expectations about it would simply be too high. Still, if it was not already too late, those seemed to be fertile times in which to drop a thread of (permanent) critical, deconstructive, and reflexive "breadcrumbs" addressing the past and present role of ethnology museums themselves in this far-reaching predicament. If, for some, that is, the more "conservative" members of Stuttgart's society, this might have been annoying or disappointing,[5] it might have provided others with at least more ground to (re)build upon.

The main aim of the exhibition *Wo ist Afrika? Storytelling a European Collection*,[6] which opened in 2019, is to contribute to dismantling the vision of imaginary, faraway "Others" that had been distributed by essentialist ethno-logical narratives. Its main strategy is to rely on exhibiting *relationships* between specific actors based in both continents who connected directly to the objects and the stories on display: historical, contemporary, and future (imaginations of) relationships. Along this path, I was especially encouraged by the motto of the Museum Association of Namibia ("Museums make connections") and by an essay by Ruth Phillips (2009). More specifically, by an appeal that she makes in one of her abstracts of that essay: "Drawing on Bruno Latour's notion of the 'imbroglio', I urge the necessity of incorporating an awareness of hybridity and networks of interconnection into museum representation".[7] With a view to not only nourish and engage in stable and durable research and interpretation-based relationships, but also include them in museum representations, reflexivity inevitably comes into play, and to include this process in museum displays may also contribute to deconstruct the vision of the all-knowing, impersonal curator and substitute it with that of a maker/translator/mediator of partial, intersubjective, and positioned truths.

Sharing the Ride

Wo ist Afrika? came to be in constant dialogue with a group of ten research and interpretation partners who live "in-between" Germany, Cameroon, the Democratic Republic of Congo, Mozambique, and Nigeria.[8] In July 2016, a few months after I was appointed curator, with the encouragement and the support of the Linden-Museum Stuttgart's director, Inés de Castro, we had founded the ABRAC. In advocating for this project, de Castro was especially inspired by the long-term work of the COMRAF, the *Advisory Board for the Africa Museum and the African Associations*, which had been founded in Tervuren, Belgium, almost 20 years before, in 2003.

Much similarly to the COMRAF, the ABRAC was not merely meant as a way to collaborate to inspire and share ideas about a new exhibition of the African collections held in the Linden-Museum, but rather as a structure and a channel for opening and granting durability to a dialogue between the museum and a highly relevant part of its contemporary publics and taxpayers, that is, representatives of civil society organizations of the African diaspora who have been active in the field of Afro-European cultural, social, and political dialogue in the region of Stuttgart for many years before I even appeared on the scene.

In their exchange with the museum, I believe that the members of the ABRAC are exercising the role of a "heritage community" as defined by the *Framework Convention on the Value of Cultural Heritage for Society* drafted in 2005 by the Council of Europe. What identifies the members of "heritage communities" in this legal document is not merely the fact that their members were born or are choosing to live in a specific nation, but the fact that they are actively attributing "social value" to "specific aspects of cultural heritage" (Council of Europe 2005, 2). That is to say that they recognize cultural heritages as highly relevant to contemporary democratic dialogue.

I cannot take the space here that would be needed to really delve into our path together. I can say that for me, it simply is a *continuously* fertile experience in itself: that of *keeping* an open exchange going along its "natural" upside-downs, and that is not "notwithstanding problems or issues that *might* arise", but rather experiencing a path together *right within* the inherently problematic, pain- and inequality-ridden field of a postcolonial relationship based on colonial collections in a colonized world. I am not entitled to speak about it also on behalf of the ten different members of the ABRAC, and I would also need to clarify that we did not write the exhibition concept together, the responsibility of which lies with me. Still, my own socialization process as a recent immigrant to Germany from Italy with no previous personal ties to the city of Stuttgart was accompanied especially by them, and our exchanges during these years not only had an impact on me as a person, but certainly also on the development of the very "soul" of the exhibition concept, in ways that are difficult for me to pinpoint.

Individual contributions in this process are impossible to summarize here without sacrificing too much in terms of richness and complexity.[9] Each one of the members of the ABRAC also contributed something very precious and very concrete to the exhibition at hand, depending on their professional experience and on each one's specific politics and poetics: from researching, interpreting, and documenting with me the history of the "Afrika" department, to co-collecting, reviewing, and commenting the exhibition texts in their making, to sharing audio-visual messages with the museum's publics, all the way to coauthoring an original site-specific performance that has been impacting not only the exhibition, but the entire museum (Zobel 2018).

Glimpses into the Professional Disappointer's Persona

> "To become aware of the relativity – and hence of the arbitrariness – of an element that is characteristic of our culture already means to shift it a little".
>
> (Tzvetan Todorov qtd. in Marcus and Fischer 1986, 95)

Back to my specific responsibilities as curator for the new exhibition: I did not approach the Linden-Museum and the projects for its Africa Department as an "Africanist" or as an "ethnologist", but with a background in museum studies and the anthropology of heritage-making processes, which is what I have been focusing on for some years now, especially since 2002, when I entered the Board of *Simbdea*, the Italian national association for the anthropology of museums and cultural heritages, and the editorial team of the journal *Antropologia Museale*.[10] Along this tradition and line of enquiry, I have been exploring actors and structures within and from the standpoint of a variety of locations and events where (tangible and intangible) objects were being turned into – and spoken to as – legacies in the present and were participating, as such, in storytelling and history-making movements. Mine is a multi-sited field that, to date, has come to encompass heritage and "art-culture systems" (Clifford 1998, 223) active in a number of cities and villages in Italy, in the city of Maputo, Mozambique, at the Biennale of Venice (Ferracuti 2020), and at the Linden-Museum Stuttgart.

"Wo Ist Afrika?" 45

When an ethnographer chooses heritages and museums as research fields, she quite naturally incorporates reflexivity into her habitus, given the meta-cultural and meta-historical nature of the actions and reflections of the actors that she encounters in these fields. This also quite naturally characterizes as a research-action field, and my position as curator only made it more evident that I am one of the actors in the field itself. The subtitle of the exhibition that I conceived for the Linden-Museum is "Storytelling a European Collection", and as curator, I clearly was one of its main storytellers. Its texts are written so as to make those exploring the exhibition aware of the presence of specific collectors and authors, both as professionals and as persons, including myself. Throughout the exhibition, objects and topics are quite consistently presented as often deriving from and more broadly as having pertained to specific relationships through time: during the actual European colonial occupations of the African continent, after the independence of African States, and up until the times, prior to the opening of the exhibition, when the Linden-Museum's staff and the members of the ABRAC have been engaging in dialogue with each other and with the collections and histories of the museum.

As a way to address my use of reflexivity in the display, I will recall a specific example concerning my time. It is an installation included in the second section of the exhibition that focuses on two cuts of textiles (two *capulana*, for those reading who are familiar with Mozambique) called *Palù*[11] and *Anjo da Guarda*,[12] which in Maputo are used in therapy. They come from my personal property: I bought them in 2010 on the advice of Samson Makamo (ca. 1945), a prominent sculptor and healer in Maputo, in the medicine section of Maputo's largest open-air market, *Xipamanine*.

On the advice and with the professional guidance of Makamo, cuddling with the *Palù* (Figure 2.1), in particular, allows me (I only donated a cut from my textile to the museum) to maintain a functioning connection with Gianni, one of my ancestors who is especially relevant to my life path (Ferracuti 2020). The presence of this ancestor in my life has resurfaced since then, when Makamo helped me figure out that I was part of his legacy and that meant that we were comakers of a possible future that we needed to dream toward together (Ferracuti 2016). In the exhibition, these two textiles are not presented, described, or explained only in abstract terms as signs from the vocabulary of the wider knowledge system which these textile-signs spell into the domain of actual psychological and physical experiences, but they are also directly connected to one actual occurrence of their use by a concrete actor whose body is situated in the close vicinities of those of the museum's publics: the exhibition curator.

I used biographical accounts of my own and those of others as a way to translate cosmologies, legacies, histories, and practices, which were embedded into artifacts on display, into the lived experience of individuals, thus pulling them "closer" to visitors and pointing to their potential to

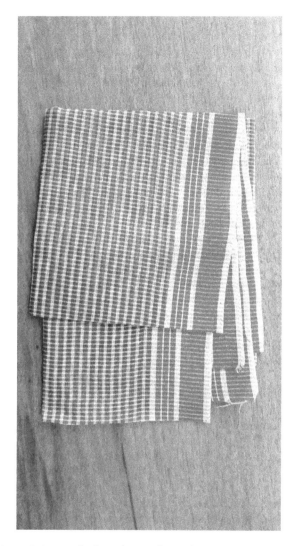

Figure 2.1 Detail of a Palù textile cut from my private collection.
Image: Sandra Ferracuti.

inform and move the life of anyone, wherever they were born or lived. This hopefully collaborates with our shared efforts to counteract the discriminating effects produced by images of "Otherness" that are still distributed within and without museums.

By exhibiting reflexivity, the author of a museum text herself is turned into *a person* and one may further experiment with the use and distribution of "anthropology as cultural critique" (Marcus and Fischer 1986). The writer can then be seen by the museum's publics in the act of performing as one of the "characters" of the stories that are being told and this character, as we usually do, is not only delivering "information" but also sharing a perspective, a positioning, and at times even something that may come out as incongruent or unexpected (i.e., "disappointing") in a museum. In our case, for example, the curator (who in the German ethnology museum context is often referred to as "a scientist": "*eine Wissenschaftlerin*") quite openly declares possessing and assigning value to "emotions" and exhibits a manifest tendency to experience the presence of ancestors in her own life. Is this even allowed in a "scientific" European museum? Why is she doing that? Does that also make her "irrational"? And what does that mean?

Hints such as these might lead to the very notions of "museum", "culture", "history", and "knowledge" that become available for critical reflection on the part of readers when we are reminded that, for as much as we might like for it not to be so, history, society, knowledge, and culture are all human movements of which we are all inevitably not only testimonies to, heirs, or consumers of but also coproducers and a part of. Not only in the past were museum information and knowledge *selected* and *performed* within an interpretative narrative – a storyline, that is – but the same applies today. And no matter how detailed, or how large, not one photograph will be the world itself, while, at the same time, each one is. And I do not mean at all to say that *knowledges* and *expertise* do not exist or that they should not be respected and recognized when cultivated and exercised by specific individuals who are also held responsible for them within a given social system. Quite on the contrary, it is in respect of knowledges, experiences, and expertise themselves that it may be preferable that cultural workers are not asked to limit themselves to deliver (or feed) "information", but also be transparent and inform as to how knowledges and expertise are built, selected, and proceed. This not only honors and keeps these ongoing processes healthy and alive, but it may also allow for museums to further socialize the same knowledges and methodologies, and thus have a better chance to contribute to actual social realities, such as de-colonizing processes; borrowing a quite fertile expression distributed by Ivan Karp and Corinne Kratz's volume on "museum frictions": to reach into the potential of the museum as a "social technology" (Karp and Kratz 2006, 4). If one knows something, that does not mean that she knows (or should be expected to know) everything, and for knowledges to really be such and progress, it is always better if we keep a check on each other, if not even manage to acquire the habit to proceed together. Together, I do not mean only within a specific "scientific, or academic, community" but within the public arena, into which the museum is a precious threshold. It might be one of the sites from where to contribute to "deparochialise the idea of research and make it more available to young people with a wide range of interests and aspirations" and to explore "the relevance of the right to research, as a human right" as proposed by Arjun Appadurai some years past (1986, 176, 177).

This "proceeding together" does happen somewhere else. For example, it happens on the occasion of periodical public performances of cultural heritage and history through "the dancing of masks" hosted by the *Mfon* of Oku in Northwest Cameroon.[13] On these occasions, all members of the kingdom, its entire social body, including its political, religious, and scientific authorities (often appearing bare-chested, thus expressing their availability to public scrutiny), actively participate in the representation or, better, concur to the "presentification" of the cosmology of which they are a part of. These public actions of presentification of a cosmology that happen in the heart of the public arena – the main front courtyard of, and threshold to the royal palace – both allow and require that each member of the social body, each for their own part, remain actively vigilant of and exercise a quite imperceptible but steady influence on how such cosmology is moving along the flow of its constant tension between past and future, between the ancestors of the past and the ancestors of the future. This is something quite different from experts crafting a portrait of the king or from making an illustrious artist, or a supposedly "perfect hero", available to the body of society as visitors, spectators, or even consumers, if one wants to take seriously poet Pier Paolo Pasolini's quite early warnings of the signs of a process where consumption was taking the place of culture itself in many societies (Pasolini [1975] 2008).

So, more than working to "share" or "pass on" the kind of "authority" that I was consigned when I became curator in Stuttgart, I tried to make certain elements of a certain social organization of the authority on knowledge, art, and culture available to public scrutiny within the museum arena, where "traditionally" an allegedly all-knowing, infallible, neutral, authority is relegated behind the scenes of a stage where its "products" are distributed.

Take One: The Colonial Matrix of the Present

> The war was lost – The treaty signed […] – The story's told – With facts and lies – I have a name – But nevermind […] – Your victory – Was so complete – Some among you – Thought to keep – A record of – Our little lives – The clothes we wore – Our spoons, our knives – The games of luck – Our soldiers played – The stones we cut – The songs we made […] But we had names – More intimate – Names so deep and – Names so true – They're blood to me -They're dust to you […] – The story's told – With facts and lies – You own the world – So nevermind.[14]

The storyline of the exhibition is organized into three main sections. The first is titled *Things to Collect, or of a Deafening Silence* (Figure 2.2) and it is meant to make the museum's publics aware that the first and very core of the museum's acquisitions in the African continent (ca. 90 %; see Grimme

"Wo Ist Afrika?" 49

Figure 2.2 Wo ist Afrika? permanent exhibition at the Linden-Museum Stuttgart (2019). Detail of section 1.
Copyright Linden-Museum Stuttgart. Foto Harald Völkl.

2018) was directly occasioned by and occurred at the time of the actual European colonial occupation of African territories. The Age of European imperialisms that these objects were direct testimonies to is presented here as one of the main social and cultural contexts of the historical collections on display.

This section discloses how collecting in that context had little to nothing to do with a "scientific" or academic endeavor, given that neither Count von Linden nor the vast majority of his networks in the colonies (colonial administrators, soldiers, and businessmen) had an academic background in the then young discipline of "ethnology" and that they could not be further away from what cultural anthropology is meant to be today. Visitors may here come to know that the colonial collecting endeavor had instead much to do with the interest of Count von Linden and his peers around Europe to acquire social recognition based on the quantity of artifacts they were able to acquire and the recognition and value that was being assigned to them as "specimen" by the "armchair anthropologists" who were also using them to establish their own authority and that of the new "science" of ethnology on the rise throughout Europe.

Here, the exhibition shares with its publics that the archival documents in the museum clearly mirror the lack of knowledge that the artifacts came to Germany with and the actual overall interests of "collectors" at the time. The standard entry would not, in fact, ever do without an "ethnic" attribution and the name of a so-called (European) donor, while at the same time, it virtually always lacked any reference to individual names, personalities, specific political and social organizations and positions, and the knowledges and views of the person(s) who had made, used, owned, and/or exchanged the artifacts. The thick, deafening silence that was imposed on knowledges, histories, and personalities on the continent (all shoveled under a patchwork carpet of "ethnic attributions") can still be heard in this room, in stark contrast with the abundance of material possessions that were taken from them and turned into "tokens of value" to be used in "tournaments of value"[15] organized and held within European, and Euro-centric, "art-culture systems".[16]

This room addresses European imperialism as a moment in the history of globalization that has given a most significant push to the way that the world is organized today. The Euro-centric complex that produced colonialism is presented as a crucial matrix of our present, with its component roots of academic racism, a myth of "modernity" conceived as a positive, pointed, one-way arrow of speed moving from novelty to novelty and from progress to progress, ever-growing industrialization, construction and consumption, and a quite provincial, centralized knowledge system.

Figure 2.3 Wo ist Afrika? permanent exhibition at the Linden-Museum Stuttgart (2019). Detail of section 2.
Copyright Linden-Museum Stuttgart. Foto Dominik Drasdow.

"Wo Ist Afrika?" 51

This room also contains a memorial section that recognizes the objects on display as "testimonies of a crime", as Ciraj Rassool would put it,[17] and a clear reference to them being present in a holocaust. However, this is not the only story that the exhibition liked to tell.

Take Two: Performing S(O)bjects

The title of section 2, *Performing S(O)bjects*[18] *or of Cultural* Creativity (Figure 2.3)[19], refers to one of the main "lessons" that the objects from Africa held at the Linden-Museum could offer to its publics. One thing that all the objects on display in the three sections of the exhibition have in common is that none of them was either only meant to achieve an aesthetic effect or to merely function as a tool. None of them can be encaged within one of the two options allowed by the museum-made dichotomy between "objects of daily use" and "objects of art" or by the distinction, created in the same context, between artifacts connected to "lay", or "political" contexts and ones pertaining to a "sacred" realm.

One can say that all of the artifacts on display – from the early 20th century's arrows from Namibia and the containers from Tanzania on display in the first section to their coeval *songo* game boards from Cameroon in the third one – have been pertaining to all of these museum-made categories/realms, but especially that they have been more. With them, specific human beings in specific moments in time, *performed* (*presentified*, one might say) their presence in the world. In their company, human beings would both address everyday issues and needs *and* make an aesthetic and often also spiritual impact on the world that they inhabited, thus quietly but persistently contributing to shaping it.

When I have had the chance to story-tell the exhibition in person, I have usually chosen to use the example of the motorcycle that Stone Karim Mohamad and I acquired in Yaoundé, Cameroon in 2018, which is on display in this second section. I often choose this object to refer to the focus of this section with a view to contrast the idea that its role within the exhibition is to act as a specific reference to Cameroon's present times as opposed to its historical (or, worse, "traditional"), or to "contemporary art" as opposed to "objects of daily use" or to "sacred art", and so on. I argue that the motorcycle speaks a quite similar object-language as, for example, the wooden mask that Stone Karim Mohamad and I acquired from notable and master sculptor Fai Mankoh in the Oku kingdom during the same year. Similar to the mask, it also challenges these classifications, speaking instead of something more. The bike was made in China, but the designs that were added to it (in this case, following the directions of Mohamad, who wished to have inscribed on it, parts of the history of the ABRAC itself) transformed it not only into a "quite typically Cameroonian" motorcycle, but also into the motorcycle that is traveling with a specific person.

The decorations and writing that this person asked a professional customizer to be applied to it produce a specific aesthetic effect on the landscape (moving within it, the motorbike changes, ephemerally and pervasively at the same time, the way that the world through which it travels "looks" and "means"). It not only projects a certain color and shape composition onto the landscape, but it also distributes values, advise, and beliefs through the sentences and icons that are inscribed in its body. I use the expression "aesthetic effect" because the concept of aesthetics in the European tradition is not limited to the formal domain or to that of "beauty", but it inheres to philosophy, cosmology, and values.

We might be tempted to equate these public actions performed with a motorbike to the work of "street (or graffiti) artists" as they are defined within the institutionalized art system (to that of Banksy, for example), but these motorbikes originally ride in a context where the need for this label does not apply. Here, in fact, the right and the responsibility to contribute to shape the world's aesthetics does not only pertain to those who would call themselves or have been labelled as "artists", or "street artists" by and within the bounded, exclusive, and highly stratified "art system".

While developing the exhibition concept, and as we keep on reconsidering the destination and scope of the agency of the "objects" that we tried to bring on the exhibition stage, the actions that we saw being performed with the bikes in 2018 in the North-western regions of Cameroon come together with the heritage performances of masks being danced at the kingdom of Oku during the same year. They also resonate with a case of re-appropriation of "heritage" that I followed some years earlier in Satriano di Lucania, a small village counting ca. 2,000 residents located in Italy's southern region of Basilicata. Here, starting around 2012, a group belonging to the generation of those born in the 1980s carried out a process of re-appropriation of a historical "carnival mask" that mimics a walking tree (a human figure covered head-to-toe by ivy shoots). Through the years preceding their movement, this protagonist of the local historical carnival had been turned from a ritual device into no more than one of the characters of a "folk spectacle and parade". This group of persons reclaimed for themselves and their generation the authority and responsibility for the interpretation of this heritage from the local authorities by wearing it and walking it as a means for collective symbolic actions relevant to the present life of the village and amplified its capacity to embody their own eco-system.[20] These associations lead me back to the concept of "presence", presentification (or lack thereof), introduced by Ernesto de Martino in the late 1940s.

De Martino introduced the concept of "presence" in negative terms, as he reported episodes of a "crisis of presence" experienced by individuals that were being addressed in the south of Italy through collective therapeutic rituals. He referred to these crises as moments where the sense of being present in one's own history and shared meaning had become lost in the face of impactful events such as illness or forced migration. Here, however, I am

Figure 2.4 Wo ist Afrika? permanent exhibition at the Linden-Museum Stuttgart (2019). Detail of section 3.
Copyright Linden-Museum Stuttgart. Foto Dominik Drasdow.

tempted to use it to refer to what I believe to be an important lesson that the artifacts on display might teach us, when I have a feeling that De Martino's "crisis of presence" might resonate with more than a few citizens of what has been called a "liquid modernity".[21] And that lesson resides in how the *objects* on display have conjured with *subjects* – not within a bounded art or heritage system, but in dialogue with *the whole* – to achieve the performance of meaningful acts of "relational presence", where members of society exercise the right and the responsibility to *presentify* a cosmology, and thus to participate in shaping the aesthetics of the world that they inhabited. Under this light, might also the difference be seen between riding the unmodified "newest model" of a motorcycle brand and riding one that has been made "our own".

Karingana Karingana

The third section of the exhibition, titled *Things to Connect, or of Joint Histories* (Figure 2.4), focuses on the contemporary circulation of objects, ideas, and persons between Africa and Europe. Inspired by such performances of presence as the ones that the "s(o)bjects" on display have been part of before entering the museum – creative in its fullest sense – this section calls each one to consider our own presence in a hopefully empowered way. A large image of Stuttgart is printed on the wall in this section, and a market stand installation recalls the ones that many museum visitors are likely to have encountered in their daily lives, be it at an "Afro-festival" in Frankfurt or at a tourist craft shop in Yaoundé: among the most common sites of Euro-Africa encounters in the days of "tolerance" and consumption of "cultures", or tokens thereof. Museum publics will here hopefully feel they have been personally called into question and sense an invitation to reconquer and exercise their own "presence" (De Martino 1948) within the social arenas that we are part of, starting with the museum halls and the city of Stuttgart. To be in the presence of a shared history of colonial relations may not only exert a scandal within, but also empower us to reposition ourselves within history, which would, in turn, enable us to exercise the right to creatively participate in shaping the relationships of the future.

This section more clearly characterizes the *Wo ist Afrika?* exhibition project not as an end in itself, but as a potential new starting point. Here is where the most important storytelling performances can happen, among visitors, between visitors and members of the museum staff, members of the ABRAC, and the hall guards, who are also citizens of Stuttgart and often have a so-called migrant background, including in African countries. One or the other might, for example, possess the knowledge and be willing to teach to those who do not know it one of the many variants of the '*ntxuva* game of strategy (a Mozambican version of the *mancala*) and play across the gameboard that is installed in the centre of the room.

The text of the main panel for this section ends with the expression: *Karingana wa karingana*. This specific Shangana expression from southern Mozambique signals that something special is about to happen. When it is pronounced, important stories are about to be told; stories with a long breath, crossing time and space. They are the stories that we tell about ourselves. To share stories is a powerful creative act and while playing '*ntxuva* in the middle of the room, which might be used as an excuse to "talk to strangers", maybe some new stories will be born and shared that might even one day become strong enough shared "performances of presence" to build a safe bridge between Tripoli and Lampedusa, where Europe, from the perspective of many persons, begins.

Museums of Possible Worlds[22]

> Every epoch, in fact, not only dreams the one to follow but, in dreaming, precipitates its awakening.
>
> (Benjamin 1999, 13)

In their concept, the curators of the *Material Culture in Transit* conference (the seed of this publication) associated the production of "self-critical" exhibitions in "Ethnographic Museums" with "potentially remedial dialogues". I let this optimistic reference inspire my paper as well, even though, when I moved from reflecting upon museums and heritages to acting within one of them, I did not want to let myself be caressed by the overwhelming ambition to be able to "decolonize" them. To do "something" (or, better, as Stone Karim Mohamad put it in a poem that he spoke during the exhibition opening events, to "*keep moving*") already felt (and feels) like a daring enough move for a European museum curator responsible for historical (colonial) African collections. Yet, it felt relieving to read the conference curators lucidly articulate the dream that actually, many of those working in museums still hope to be dreaming toward. That is a dream that my colleagues at the Linden-Museum Stuttgart also share, and the director's welcoming of such a concept for a permanent exhibition, points in the same direction.

The dream "to decolonize": goes something like "to change the world", but some illustrious insights such as Walter Benjamin's and those of the "dancers of cosmologies" who are recalled in the second section of *Wo ist Afrika?* seem to have been suggesting that that is actually how it works. The idea of "The Museum" as the most authoritative (at the same time indeterminate, singular, collective, universal, in a word, somewhat "godlike") storyteller of humanity has been widely distributed from Europe in its imperialistic spree and has long been creatively "localized" and 'naturalized' in most regions of the world. What kind of a storyteller is she now? What future is she dreaming of? Is she even still a storyteller after all, or did Pier Paolo Pasolini foresee her full transformation, within a regime of "tolerance", into one of the cogs of an even more efficient system for the centralized control of cultures and bodies: a department store?

> No fascist centralism ever managed to do what the centralism of consumer civilization has successfully accomplished. [...] A neo-secular hedonism, blindly oblivious to every humanistic value and blindly alien to human knowledge.[23]

Notes

1 See paragraph 2.
2 *READ-ME – Réseau Européen des Associations de Diasporas et Musées Ethnographiques* (2007–2012); *RIME – Ethnography Museums and World Cultures* (2008–2013); *SWICH – Sharing a World of Inclusion, Creativity, and Heritage* (2014–2018). Concerning these projects, see Bouttiaux and Seiderer; Ferracuti et al.; Modest et al.; Munapé. The ongoing project *TAKING CARE – Ethnographic and World Cultures Museums as Spaces of Care* (Creative Europe Programme, 2019–2023) is the most recent development in this process.
3 This exhibition also included an object on loan from the Linden-Museum Stuttgart: Captain Hendrick Witbooi's (1834–1905) family copy of the New Testament, which was later repatriated (February 2019) together with a whip that also used to belong to him (see Deutsches Historisches Museum 2016; Linden-Museum Stuttgart 2019; Ferracuti 2018, 63–64).

4 In 2018, Gesa Grimme published the results of the first systematic provenance research concerning two historical collections from the African continent (Cameroon and Namibia) held in the Linden-Museum Stuttgart, which she carried out between 2016 and 2018 (Grimme 2018). Her work contributed to highlight how the large majority of these artifacts were included in the collection during the German colonial occupation of these African territories (1900–1920), and how the vast majority of its "collectors" were not scholars or researchers but members of the occupying troops, German colonial administrators, or traders.
5 The previous permanent exhibition of African collections at the Linden-Museum Stuttgart had been conceived by Hans-Joaquim Koloss between the late 1970s and the early 1980s and had been later reviewed by Hermann Forkl, who as early as the late 1980s had already included reflexive mechanisms as well as explicit, direct references to the violent context of many of the historical (colonial) acquisitions and its postcolonial legacies. The "Afrika" exhibition, however, remained coherent with a specific, longstanding tradition at that department of Stuttgart's Museum: that of an "ethnographic realism" that made large use of dioramas and 1:1 "mimetic" installations that responded to a positivist epistemology and contributed to distribute the illusion of being in the presence of "Africa" and not in that of an author's specific interpretation of elements of a particular collection. Under these circumstances, a postmodern, deconstructivist, interpretive approach is very likely to have taken "by surprise" many local visitors. After the opening of the new exhibition, even one of the members of the team of Stuttgart's architect Raimund Docmac's, who inscribed its concept into the display, confirmed this unsettling effect: he mentioned that the new exhibition had an effect that reminded him of someone who's tapping *quietly but persistently* at your shoulder.
6 I "encountered" what was to become the main title of the exhibition, *Wo ist Afrika?*, on the internet in 2017 by chance, while I was developing its concept. Since then, this expression stuck to my head until I chose it as most appropriate to the core aim of the exhibition: to contribute to deconstruct the image of a continent "far away" in time and space, "Other", which anthropology contributed to produce and distribute throughout Europe (Fabian 1983). It originally was the title of a three-year (2010–2013) teaching-learning project directed by Annette Bühler-Dietrich and Françoise Joly for the University of Stuttgart (Bühler-Dietrich and Joly 2015).
7 Phillips 2009 (preface).
8 Felix Abayomi Saka, Olimpio Alberto (President of the Board of *Bazaruto e.V.* and member of the Board of *Forum der Kulturen Stuttgart e.V.*), Pierre Bayangane Mpama (Member of the Board of *Ndwenga e.V.*), Loic Steve Lefang (President of the Board of *Eyes on Cameroon e.V.*), Afonso Manguele (Member of the Board of *Bazaruto e.V.*), Stone Karim Mohamad, Cathy Nzimbu Mpanu-Mpanu-Plato (President of the Board of *Ndwenga e.V.* and member of the Board of *Forum der Kulturen Stuttgart e.V.*), Samuel Ekarika Nanna Obot, Djenneba Obot, and Natacha Tchoumi Pettie (see Ferracuti 2015/2016, 2017).
9 Having landed in Stuttgart in 2016 and opened the exhibition in the early 2019, I have not yet had the breath to publish a catalogue or produce a broad enough text to account for all the lessons that these racing and intense years have been teaching me. For now, for more insights into the path toward the exhibition, see Ferracuti 2016, 2019; and the brief yearly reports that I published in the Linden-Museum's journal, *Tribus*, between 2016 and 2019.

10 In order to shed light on the specific perspective interpreted by the director, Vincenzo Padiglione (2002) and the editors of this journal, it is here sufficient to mention that the cover of its first issue (2002) paid homage to the reflexive exhibition *Le musée cannibale*, installed between 2002 and 2003 at the MEN – *Musée d'ethnographie de Neuchâtel*.
11 Inv. F 56417.
12 Inv. F 56418.
13 The kingdom of Oku, from the perspective of the Linden-Museum Stuttgart, is what Berardino Palumbo would call an "*antropoluogo*" ["anthropo-place"] (Palumbo 2006), where Margaret Mead's Samoa and Bronislaw Malinowski's Trobriand Islands would be examples of most renown "*antropoluoghi*". Oku was the site, for decades, of most of the research and acquisition activities of this museum's former curator of the "Afrika" department, Hans-Joaquim Koloss. It also was the main site of the activities carried for the collaborative research and interpretation project *Sharing Heritage: The Cameroon Project, Oku, Stuttgart, Foumban* (2017–2019), which I and the current director of the Linden-Museum Stuttgart, Inés de Castro, shared with one of the Cameroon-born members of the ABRAC, Stone Karim Mohamad. Both the previous and the current permanent exhibition of African collections at the Linden-Museum Stuttgart have a strong focus on stories, relationships, installations, and artifacts produced between Oku and Stuttgart (Ferracuti 2019; Forkl 1989; Koloss 2000).
14 Cohen and Leonard 2014.
15 Appadurai 1986.
16 Clifford 1988.
17 Unpublished paper presented at the international conference titled *Schwieriges Erbe: Koloniale Objekte – Postkoloniales Wissen* [*A difficult legacy. Colonial objects and postcolonial insights*], Linden-Museum Stuttgart, April 24, 2017.
18 The title of this section, which is focused on the concepts of performance and *presentification*, was inspired by that of the collaborative exhibition *S[o]ggetti migranti. Dietro le cose le persone* (Munapé 2012), and intended so as to reconnect the plane of "museum artifacts" with that of the human relationships within which they have been and are exercising agency.
19 The concept of "cultural creativity" was introduced by Adriano Favole (2010) as a way to contribute to dispel the dichotomy between a conceptualization of "modernity" that was associated to "progress" and "development" and an idea of "tradition" that was associated to the passive and stale reproduction of a-historical beliefs and practices. This dichotomy and its elements are famously rooted in unilinear evolutionist anthropology and the Euro-centric definition of modernity.
20 Ferracuti 2016.
21 Bauman 2000.
22 See Lattanzi 2013.
23 Pier Paolo Pasolini [1975] 2008.

References

Appadurai, Arjun. *Introduction. The Social Life of Things. Commodities in Cultural Perspective*. Ed. Arjun Appadurai. Cambridge: Cambridge University Press, 1986. pp.1–72.

———. "The Right to Research". *Globalisation, Societies and Education* vol. 4, 2006. pp. 167–177. https://docs.ufpr.br/~clarissa/pdfs/Research_AppaduraiA.pdf (accessed 27.01.2022).

Benjamin, Walter. *The Arcades Project*. Cambridge: Harvard University Press, 1999.

Bauman, Zygmunt. *Liquid Modernity*. Cambridge: Polity Press, 2000.

Bouttiaux, Anne-Marie, and Anna Seiderer (Eds.). *Fetish Modernity*. Tervuren: Musée Royal de l'Afrique Centrale, 2011.

Bühler-Dietrich, Annette, and Françoise Joly, eds. *Kulturelle Kartographien: Schüler, Lehrer und Wissenschaftler erkunden Westafrika*. Baltmannsweiler: Schneider Hohengehren, 2015.

Clifford, James. On Collecting Art and Culture. *The Predicament of Culture. Twentieth-Century Ethnography, Literature, and Art*. Cambridge: Harvard University Press, 1988. pp. 215–251.

Cohen, Leonard and Patrick Leonard. "Nevermind". *Popular Problems*. Sony, 2014. CD.

Council of Europe, *Framework Convention on the Value of Cultural Heritage for Society*. Faro: Council of Europe, 2005. www.coe.int/en/web/conventions/full-list/-/conventions/rms/0900001680083746. (accessed 5.04.2021).

De Martino, Ernesto. *Il mondo magico. Prolegomeni a una storia del magismo*. Torino: Einaudi, 1948.

Deutsches Historisches Museum (Ed.). *German Colonialism: Fragments Past and Present*. Berlin: Theiss, 2016.

Fabian, Johannes. *Time and the Other. How Anthropology Makes Its Object*. New York: Columbia University Press, 1983.

Favole, Adriano. *Oceania. Isole di creatività culturale*. Bari: Laterza, 2010.

Ferracuti, Sandra. "Autorità". *Antropologia Museale*, no. 37–39 (2015/2016). pp. 38–42.

———. "Nuova linfa per (il Rumìt di) Satriano di Lucania: eredità culturali e ritualità contemporanee in un paese della Basilicata." *Etnografia e processi di patrimonializzazione*. Ed. Roberta Bonetti and Alessandro Simonicca. Rome: CISU, 2016. pp. 81–107.

———. "Heads and Hands: The Lives and Work of Makamo, Sculptor and Healer in Maputo." *Tribus*, vol. 65, 2016. pp. 88–125.

———. "Yearly Scientific and Acquisitions Report for Year 2016". *Tribus*. vol. 66, 2017. pp. 36–37; pp. 50–53.

———. "Yearly Scientific Report for Year 2017". *Tribus*. vol. 67, 2018. pp. 52–55.

———. "Yearly Scientific and Acquisitions Report for Year 2018". *Tribus*. vol. 68, 2019. pp.38–39; pp.62–65.

———. Our House Is Made of Thin, Burning Ice. Let's Dance." *Matters of Belonging. Ethnographic Museums in a Changing Europe*. Wayne Modest, Nicholas Thomas, Dorsi Prlić, and Claudia Augustat (Eds.). Leiden: Sidestones Press, 2019. pp. 68–85.

———. *Não consigo ser moçambicana. Arti, antropologie e patrimoni culturali a partire da Maputo*. Palermo: Edizioni Museo Pasqualino, 2020.

Ferracuti, Sandra, Elisabetta Frasca, and Vito Lattanzi, eds. *Beyond Modernity. Do Ethnography Museums Need Ethnography?* Rome: Espera, 2013.

Forkl, Hermann. *Linden-Museum Stuttgart. Abteilungsführer Afrika. Von Hermann Forkl mit einem Beitrag von Petra Konerding*. Stuttgart: Linden-Museum, 1989.

Grimme, Gesa. *Provenienzforschung im Projekt "Schwieriges Erbe: Zum Umgang mit kolonialzeitlichen Objekten in ethnologischen Museen" –Abschlussbericht–*. Linden-Museum Stuttgart, 2018. www.lindenmuseum.de/fileadmin/Dokumente/SchwierigesErbe_Provenienzforschung_Abschlussbericht.pdf. (accessed 5.04.2021).
Karp, Ivan and Corinne A. Kratz. Introduction. *Museum Frictions. Public Cultures/Global Transformations*. Ed. Ivan Karp et al. Durham: Duke University Press, 2006. pp. 1–31.
Koloss, Hans-Joachim. *World-View and Society in Oku (Cameroon)*. Berlin: Reimer, 2000.
Koloss, Hans-Joachim: *Cameroon: Thoughts and Memories. Ethnological Research in Oku and Kembong 1975-2005*. Berlin: Reimer, 2012.
Lattanzi, Vito. "Towards a Museum of Possible Worlds". *Beyond Modernity. Do Ethnography Museums Need Ethnography?*. Ed. Ferracuti, Sandra, Elisabetta Frasca, and Vito Lattanzi. Rome: Espera, 2013. pp. 3–20.
Les séquelles de la colonisation Patrimoine africain en Europe et ses conflits. Dir. Raoul Tejeutsa Zobel, Stone Karim Mohamad and Joachim Wossidlo. Feat. Stone Karim Mohamad. Robert Bosch Foundation. Linden-Museum Stuttgart. Wossidlofilm, 2019. Film.
Le musée cannibale. 9 March 2002–2 March 2003. Musée d'ethnographie de Neuchâtel. Dir. Jacques Hainard and Marc-Olivier Gonseth. Concept Jacques Hainard, Marc-Olivier Gonseth, and Nicolas Yazgi, Neuchâtel.
Linden-Museum Stuttgart. "Die Familienbibel und Peitsche von Hendrik Witbooi". *Tribus*, vol. 68, 2019. p. 27.
Marcus, George E., and Michael M. J. Fischer. *Anthropology as Cultural Critique: An Experimental Moment in the Human Sciences*. Chicago: The University of Chicago Press, 1986.
Modest, Wayne, Nicholas Thomas, Doris Prlić, and Claudia Augustat, eds. *Matters of Belonging. Ethnographic Museums in a Changing Europe*. Leiden: Sidestone Press, 2019.
Munapé, Kublai, ed. *S[o]ggetti migranti. Dietro le cose le persone*. Rome: Espera, 2012.
Padiglione, Vincenzo. "Editoriale: Casaa". *Antropologia Museale*, no.1, 2002. p. 5.
Palumbo, Berardino. "Iperluogo." *Antropologia Museale*, no. 14, 2006. pp. 45–47. www.edizionimuseopasqualino.it/product/nao-consigo-ser-mocambicana-arti-antropologie-e-patrimoni-culturali-a-partire-da-maputo/
Pasolini, Pier Paolo. *Corsair Writings*. Libcom, [1975] 2008. Web. 5 April 2021. libcom.org/files/Corsair Writings – Pier Paolo Pasolini.pdf.
Phillips, Ruth. Résumé. *The Mask Stripped Bare by Its Curators: The Work of Hybridity in the Twenty-First Century*. OpenEdition, 2009. Web. 5 April 2021. journals.openedition.org/actesbranly/336.
von Bose, Friedrich. *Das Humboldt-Forum. Eine Ethnografie seiner Planung*. Berlin: Kulturverlag Kadmos, 2016.
Zobel, Raoul Tejeutsa. *Les séquelles de la colonisation 2. Patrimoine africain en Europe et ses conflits*. Site Specific Performance. Feat. Stone Karim Mohamad. Linden-Museum Stuttgart, 19 February 2018.

3 "Out of Context" – Translocation of West African Artefacts to European Museums

The Case of the Leo Frobenius Collection from Mali

Cécile Bründlmayer

Introduction

In 2018 Felwine Sarr and Bénédicte Savoy published their ground-breaking report on the restitution of African artefacts, commissioned by French President Emmanuel Macron (Sarr/Savoy 2018). Since then, discussions about the proper treatment of ethnographic artefacts deriving from colonial contexts have gained significant momentum. Sarr and Savoy's demand to repatriate large parts of African collections from former French colonies resulted in polarized, emotionally charged debates among museum professionals, academics, activists, politicians, and art dealers in Africa and Europe.

In order to exact a dissection of these discussions, this article focuses on a hitherto unexplored collection from West Africa, acquired between 1907 and 1909 by the well-known German anthropologist Leo Frobenius (1873–1938) during his second expedition to the African continent. To this end, I will first present a short overview of the collection, expounding specifically on an array of headdresses from Mali. I will then proffer the political and structural implications of Frobenius' journey by examining the historical collection from the time of its original use to the present, to develop an understanding of its polysemous and protean nature. Finally, I will reflect upon strategies of dealing with ethnographic museum collections today in light of current restitution debates.

In September 1907, the young German anthropologist Leo Frobenius entered a steamship in Hamburg heading towards Dakar (now the capital of Senegal) in order to start his second expedition to the African continent. He was accompanied by the geodesist Reinhard Hugershoff and the painter Fritz Nansen who produced nearly a thousand drawings of objects, landscapes, people, and festivities that are archived today at the Frobenius-Institut in Frankfurt. For over two years, they travelled through the former French colonial territories of "French West Africa," or what is currently

Translocation of West African Artefacts to European Museums 61

Figure 3.1 Portrait of Leo Frobenius, around 1908, Frobenius-Institut Frankfurt.

referred to as Senegal, Mali, Guinea and Burkina Faso, as well as the former German colony Togo, where their expedition ended.

Leo Frobenius was one of the most influential German-speaking ethnologists and researchers in Africa in the 20th century. Subsequently, there is a proliferation of publications pertaining to his life and work (e.g. Haberland 1973; Jahn 1974; Heinrichs 1998; Streck 2014). Of his 12 expeditions to Africa, his first to the Congo was the most thoroughly examined (cf. Ackermann/Röschenthaler/Steigerwald 2005; Fabian 1998). His second research expedition has only been partially investigated thus far (Oberhofer 2016; Hahn 1995; Zwernemann 1987).

The material outcome of this journey is predominantly distributed among three German museums: The Museum am Rothenbaum in Hamburg, the GRASSI Museum für Völkerkunde in Leipzig and, to a lesser extent, the Ethnological Museum in Berlin. In addition, there are numerous objects from the collection in other European museums which have been exchanged over time as nominal "doublets." Due to the magnitude of the collection, it is impossible to examine every facet in this article. For example, Leo

Frobenius' interest in collecting a vast series of similar objects, or his theory of cultural morphology, will be the focus of future articles. Here the focus lies on the collection in Hamburg, where the museum director offered me free access to the repositories.

During my research at the Museum am Rothenbaum in Hamburg, I found that the largest part of the collection comes from areas in present-day Guinea and Mali. Most frequently represented in the collection are quotidian objects, followed by numerous masks and sculptures carved from wood, used by initiation societies. Among these objects, a significant assortment of finely carved "Ci Wara" headdresses stand out. These will be examined more closely in the following section.

Ci Wara – From "Ethnographic Stuff" to "Works of Art"

Ci Wara headdresses are ritual objects used by the Bamana in Mali. They are zoomorphic in shape and carved from wood in male and female pairs, each tied to a woven basket that adorns the head of a dancer. The fine, linear design of the sculptural elements is silhouette-like and mostly inspired by an antelope's form, but also features other symbolically significant animals, such as the aardvark and the pangolin, occasionally combined abstractly in one object. Depending on their origin and context, appellations such as Wara Koun, Waraba Koun, or Sogoni Koun are used to describe the headdresses. Often interpreted as a monolithic tradition in ethnographic accounts, they are instead representative of a heterogeneous set of regional traditions and individual interpretations reflecting an overarching agricultural ideal. Therefore, the term "Ci Wara" encompasses several distinct yet related performative genres. At the beginning of the 20th century, initiation societies ritualistically used these masks to teach young men social values as well as agricultural techniques. The form of Ci Wara headdresses is widely recognized, as they are among the most famous collectibles of African art in Europe, even maintaining a kind of iconic status within African art history due to their abstract nature.

One example is a Sogoni Koun headdress from the collection in Hamburg (Figure 3.2). It combines the horns of an antelope with the physical characteristics of twoother animals. The lower part resembles an aardvark, and the middle part represents a pangolin with a large bow and spikes on its back. Together they embody balance and harmonic symmetry. Although it is possible to read the composition as semantically stratified, their characteristics are so gracefully integrated that the impression of a single zoomorphic being dominates when perceiving the object. Curves are found throughout the composition – a gentle sickle-shaped arch at the bottom, a vertically serrated arch of the back, and a gracefully extended crowning horn at the top. The narrow-pointed snout completes the arch of the back. It is decorated with a few cowrie shells, fine carvings, and pieces of metal

Figure 3.2 Sogoni Koun Headdress, unknown artist, Mali, before 1908, Museum am Rothenbaum, Hamburg (MARKK).
Image: Cécile Bründlmayer.

that could be melted bullets and screws. The small ears are thrown into relief as they merge with a perpendicular curved line, perhaps representing an abstract neck connecting to the lower body. According to James Pascal Imperato, such objects were made in the Bougouni region in response to the popular Sogoni Koun dance introduced by Wassoulou communities from the South (Imperato 1981). He states that before 1940, the Sogoni Koun dances took place in December, at the end of the harvest season. This also coincides with the period of Frobenius' ethnographic account of the Sogoni Koun dances in late December 1907, as mentioned previously.

Once all artefacts arrived in Germany, they went through a contentious process of distribution between the museums in Hamburg and Leipzig. The museum directors, Georg Thilenius and Karl Weule, decided to split the collection according to regional and ethnic affiliation. Both directors praised the quality of the masks and headdresses, but also complained about the disorganized and chaotic condition of the collection, which lacked basic information about the objects' provenance and meaning (cf. Oberhofer 2016). Nevertheless, once the objects arrived in Germany, they were incorporated into the museum collections. Each object was numbered, measured, and replicated as an image on a file card. Thus, ritual objects,

objects of utility, and objects representative of social status went through the same standardized process of musealization. They were transformed into museum artefacts to be stored in the museums' repositories and further studied or displayed behind glass cases.

With the influx of African artefacts into European museums from the late 19th and early 20th century onwards and subsequent increased recognition of their formal characteristics, African sculptural forms became fashionable amongst European artists, collectors, and art dealers (cf. Biro 2018). Some of the sculptures from ethnographic collections today regarded as African masterpieces were once disparaged by their former collectors. Ci Wara headdresses, especially in their more abstract forms, quickly became popular and inspirational objects for modern artists in Europe, who praised them as a veritable artistic discovery. André Derain, a Fauvist painter and pioneer in collecting African art, featured Ci Wara masks in his collection, as did Constantin Brancusi, George Braque, and Fernand Leger. The masks' form validated the Cubist experiments in France, while the emotions they expressed paralleled the primitivism of the Brücke and Blauer Reiter art collections in Germany. In 1917, artist Guillaume Apollinaire and collector Paul Guillaume finally published images of the Ci Wara in their "Sculptures nègres." The Ci Wara mask thus transformed from ritual object to museum artefact indicative of "primitive art."

Evidently, the meaning and utility of material objects shift depending on their spatio-temporal context. These "objects in diaspora," to borrow John Peffer's coinage, not only move through time and between institutions, but also from one socio-cultural context to another. In this sense, Ethnographic museums and their collections perpetuate a process of constant and complicated reinterpretation. Echoing Igor Kopytoff's understanding of the "social life of things," John Peffer positions art objects as surrogate bodies or persons with biographies. He, therefore, suggests one should refrain from searching for the "original social, cultural, and aesthetic contexts of African art objects as a means to uncover their true, local relevance" (Peffer 2005: 339). Peffer continues that we should "move beyond the colonial categories based on a false sense of fixed ethnicities and static geographies" and argues that "objects are thus themselves diasporic in the sense that they may hybridize their subjects, and their beholders, in differing configurations of meaning and affect, according to historical and cultural context" (340). It is therefore appropriate to focus on the objects' successive iterations of meaning, or, as Jacques Maquet articulated, the "metamorphosis" from functional object to artwork (Maquet 1979).

Leo Frobenius' collection practice reveals that the process of transformation and reinterpretation did not begin in museums, but much earlier. I will subsequently turn to the structural and historical context of Frobenius' expedition to examine in more detail how these objects were collected and commodified.

Colonial Context

Leo Frobenius was a typical autodidact. During his first expeditions, he was still an academic outsider. Standard funded research opportunities were not available to him, and he, therefore, sought out alternative means of acquiring funds to realize his travels and research agenda. Early in his career, his travels were often funded by the ethnographic museums that bought the objects he collected during his research trips. To this end, he negotiated nuanced agreements with the Ethnological Museums in Hamburg and Leipzig. They determined how much the museums would contribute to the trip, which instalments were to be paid out at what time, and how objects were to be distributed between the two museums (Oberhofer 2016: 224). In addition to funding from museums, Frobenius received small amounts of money from private donors, the Rudolf-Virchow and the Carl-Ritter-Stiftung, and a payment of 5000 marks from the German Imperial Colonial Office. While 5000 marks was not a large sum of money, it still indicated German imperial interest in Frobenius' expedition. Frobenius was, after Heinrich Barth, one of the first Germans to travel to the French colonial territory in West Africa with such notable purpose. He understood the commitment of the German Imperial Colonial Office as an invitation to deliver, "as usefully as possible, results for concrete colonial policy" (Kuba 2020). Indeed, after his return to Germany, Frobenius handed a 60-page report to the Imperial Colonial Office in which he described in detail his impressions of French colonial rule.

These preliminary agreements highlight the colonial entanglements of Frobenius' endeavour, although they are constitutive of the first steps towards transforming venerated ritual objects into commodities.[1] In an act of patriotic reverence, Frobenius raised the flags of Germany and France over his newly established research station in Bamako as soon as he arrived in Mali.

From this research station in Bamako, Frobenius organized most of his expeditions. Here he also stored large parts of his collections, as well as dozens of boxes containing commodities such as weapons, fabrics, knives, salt, and cowrie shells.

Building upon preliminary agreements in Germany concerning the purchase of objects, the process of commodification thus continued in Africa. Objects that had previously been used in ritual or quotidian contexts were transformed into merchandise through barter and purchase. The local Africans Frobenius hired for his expedition played a central role in this process. Contributors from territories under European colonial rule generally played a subaltern role in early Western travel accounts, even though the role of local carriers, guides, and translators was integral to the composition of ethnographic collections and thus essential to European museums. They bridged the linguistic and cultural gaps that separated European colonial

Figure 3.3 Setting up the research station in Bamako, Mali, around 1908, Frobenius-Institute, Frankfurt.

officials from the local, colonized population, controlling the generation of knowledge and the interactions of distinct local groups. Translators were crucial to the success of colonial administration because, aside from a few rare exceptions,[2] Europeans were not interested in learning African languages. Subsequently, they were unable to confirm or control what the interpreters conveyed, which gave the local translators the ability to negotiate in their own interest, especially during the early phase of colonial rule until the 1920s. Single travellers, such as Frobenius, who did not speak any African languages (Kuba 111), were especially dependent on the mediation of their African employees when it came to the generation and translation of knowledge. Thus, local cultural brokers also had great influence on what was or was not collected, who could collect, and under what conditions. In this way, they controlled the process of commodification and the generation of knowledge pertaining to the objects. The task of translating was never an "innocent act" (Álvarez/Vidal 1996).

During his expedition to Mali, Frobenius' most important contributor was Nege Traoré, whom he met in the city of Kayes after French colonial administrators recommended Traoré as a trustworthy guide and translator. According to Frobenius' travel report, Nege Traoré was then about 40 years old and locally very highly regarded.

Figure 3.4 Nege Traoré and Karimacha Djaora, Mali, around 1908, Frobenius-Institute, Frankfurt.

In the following passage, Frobenius describes Nege Traoré's and other staff members' personal interests and individual approaches when choosing which objects to collect.

> Not only did they have no interest in the matter, but they looked down with great contempt on this "miserable" peasant device, considered it a damage to my property if I bought such stuff expensively, and were ashamed to broker such a deal at all. (...) it is significant and instructive to observe with what contempt those who had grown up in urban interests looked down on this commercial nonsense that I wanted to carry out there. Miraculously, they were far more interested in the even more difficult and delicate matter of purchasing masks, and it was very noticeable how diligently and even sacrificially Nege undertook this matter. Yes, sacrificially, for he sacrificed half his night's rest. When late in the evening, during the "coffee hour," the drummers were rewarded, he immediately inquired in detail about the "address" of the mask dancers. Since he justified this with the intention of bringing a gift, it was not concealed. He went and fetched the people and then began the proceedings in front of our door. Until morning, I usually heard the back and forth and the familiar phrases of the haggling trade.
> (Frobenius 1911: 40–41)[3]

This passage demonstrates the important role Frobenius' employees played in the compilation of the collection. They had their own vision and interests concerning what should be collected and what should not, which sometimes opposed Frobenius' own interests.

As several publications demonstrate, African colonial employees were not simply passive enablers of the colonial state, but used the available possibilities created by colonial rule to pursue their own agendas. "Among the tools available to African clerks was their control over the timing and flow of information" (Lawrance, Osborn and Roberts 2015: 20). Today, with some exceptions, there are hardly any traces of African intermediaries left, even though they played a crucial role in European travellers' and collectors' endeavours. The significant scope of action of Frobenius' local staff also becomes visible when looking at their particular modes of collecting. Frobenius sent his staff on independent sub-expeditions to collect manufactured goods, masks, tools, and jewellery. He sent, for example, Nege Traoré, accompanied by 30 carriers, to the Bougouni and Wasoulou region, southwest of Bamako, from where he brought back goods and informants. The latter also operated as Frobenius' entryway into the secret society of the Komma in the Beledougou region. Because Nege Traoré was a member of the society, he managed to convince the local authorities to accept Leo Frobenius and his assistant Fritz Nansen into their midst.

It is impossible to say what Nege Traoré's intentions were, or what he hoped to achieve when he granted Frobenius access to the Komma-society.

It is, however, safe to say that he was not merely subordinate to Frobenius. Traoré certainly followed his own agenda and pursued his own interests. It is therefore important to continue the search for original accounts and sources that uncover the obscure African agendas latent within the collection. As Cheick Anta Diop emphasized in the 1950s, recovering the voices and perspectives of the oppressed, their bodies and mutilated traditions continue to be one of the most important tasks for historians and anthropologists alike.[4]

Besides uncovering historical sources that reflect the hidden perspectives of colonized communities, cooperating with their descendants in the present has been the most effective means of moving beyond Eurocentric colonial assumptions and narratives.

Challenging Colonial Narratives

Beyond the specific history of the collection, the general discursive framework within which museum ethnographic collections are analysed has undergone significant changes in recent decades. During the reflexive turn within the anthropological discipline, and the emergence of postcolonial approaches beginning in the 1980s, diverse debates developed about the legitimacy of the burgeoning self-consciousness of ethnological museums as a response to changing socio-cultural conditions. The revision of colonially influenced collections is essential to counteract an uncritical reproduction of outdated scientific paradigms in the description, classification, and representation of collection objects (Förster et al. 2018). A central method in this context is the cooperation with representatives of the countries of origin (cf. Peers/Brown 2003) in the processing and interpretation of the collections from a contemporary, postcolonial perspective (cf. Clifford 1997). What significance do the objects in the collections have for communities who understand themselves as legitimate descendants? How are they contextualised today? Through international cooperation and conversation, Eurocentric narratives are challenged, and the opportunity for an exchange of knowledge emerges (cf. Basu 2011; Clifford 1997; Laely et al. 2018).

In order to further familiarize myself with current perspectives in Mali on the Frobenius collection, I travelled to Bamako in 2019. There, I conducted interviews with different stakeholders and experts in the museum field. Most notably, my interview partners were Dr. Daouda Keita, archaeologist and the new Director of the National Museum of Mali, Dr. Salia Malé, anthropologist and Vice Director of the National Museum, Dr. Samuel Sidibé, art historian, and Keita's predecessor, who led the museum for over 30 years. Initially, we discussed the historical context of the Frobenius expedition to Mali. I recorded their thoughts on how to treat ethnographic collections that were assembled in the former French colony and were then stored in Europe, and in particular, the Frobenius collection. What role does the collection play for present-day Mali, and what meaning do these objects have today?

What are the inherent potentials of such a collection for the Malian public? Throughout the interviews, three main topics emerged: cultural heritage, current museum practice, and restitution. At the heart of all these issues was the colonial context in which the objects travelled from Mali to Germany, as well as questions surrounding the practice of using such a collection today, both in Africa and in Europe.

As mentioned at the beginning of this article, the themes of colonial context and contemporary practice comprise Keita's assertion that the Frobenius collection in Germany lives an existence outside of its original context. Keita states:

> (...) these objects, for us, are not only art objects (...). These objects contain information. They are useful and belong to societies that know why they have produced them. (...) They are very important and show the difference between my look at an object from Mali and your look at the same object. Since this object is in Germany, it is not in its context. It is out of context. And when it is out of context, it loses a lot of its cultural and functional value (...). [5]

According to Keita, African objects stored in European museums embody an existence separate from their original purpose, as they are suddenly "out of context." However, he further emphasized that these objects, often exhibited as "art objects" in Europe, need to be brought out of their repositories, as they carry the potential to be reconnected with their communities of origin. They can subsequently be re-contextualized or even re-sacralized if the objects used to have ritual functions. Communities that might have suffered the loss of valuable cultural objects could be afforded the chance to re-appropriate and endow them with new meaning. Material objects are inevitably embedded in human practices, and therefore take on new semantic and symbolic meaning in differing contexts. When objects move into new cultural spheres, their symbolic attributes change. Temporality must also be considered, given that over time objects can experience de-contextualization and reconfiguration. In this vein, Keita stated that from today's perspective, most of the objects in the Frobenius collection have likely already lost their ritual significance and subsequently cannot be re-sacralized. Because they were collected over 100 years ago, the knowledge pertaining to the power and proper treatment of these particular objects has been forgotten. Salia Malé, who spent many years doing field research as an anthropologist among Bamana communities, stated that many of the rituals from the time of Frobenius' travels in the early 20th century have also disappeared due to the expansion of Islam. He explains that ritual objects act as vehicles of belief systems and initiation practices. When the initiation practice disappears, so does the object or carrier of that faith. This is especially the case when certain practices are forbidden, such as blood sacrifices or initiation rituals, due to their reference to other belief systems. According to Malé many of the villages where Frobenius collected later converted to Islam and therefore, its inhabitants ceased to endow historic ritual objects with any importance. They might evoke memories in the elder generation, but nothing more.

However, Malé continues that even though many objects may have lost their original religious or spiritual purpose, they still facilitate a connection to the past. Similarly, Keita emphasizes the value of such objects in this contemporary role, stating,

> (...) I think that such objects can be a means of reminiscence and for the population to know where they come from. I think that's very important because each of us needs to have some kind of reference point to guide our lives.
>
> (Keita 2019)

Ci Wara headdresses, for example, still play an important role in Mali today, even though they are rarely used as ritual objects anymore. They can be seen everywhere in Bamako: on banknotes or tea packages, as logos for big enterprises or cultural institutions, and as popular commodities in the tourism industry. Ci Wara, the brave and diligent cultivator, serves today as a symbol of national identity. Objects that were once ritualistic transformed into symbols of national identity within European museums and within their countries of origin.

In this vein, Samuel Sidibé has emphasized the importance of collections as cultural heritage for Malian citizens and communities, even if their religious purpose has vanished. According to him, heritage is the possibility for current generations to be rooted in their history. The loss of your material heritage means, as for Sidibé, a deep and ongoing rupture of cultural identity.

Both Keita and his predecessor emphasize the importance of cultural heritage as an *aide de mémoire* and powerful tool for the construction of national identity. However, as it pertains to art, their points of view diverge. Samuel Sidibé believes art is the perfect vessel through which the meaning of objects can be communicated, especially to a younger, urban generation that has lost its connection to historical ritual objects. Daouda Keita, however, rejects this notion due to the conflicting nature of a modern artistic interpretation of an object versus its original function and meaning. Yet Sidibé articulates the importance of museums to arouse the curiosity of its younger visitors. According to him, if you want the younger generation to be interested in their own heritage, you need to deploy the artistic qualities of an object to reach them through their senses.

Of course, given Samuel Sidibé's background as an art historian, it is hardly surprising that he lauds the power of aesthetic perception. However, Keita's scepticism towards the notion of art is legitimate, especially when in communication with the communities from which these objects originate.

Their contradicting viewpoints illuminate a long-lasting debate surrounding aesthetics and anthropology. Formal versus contextual presentation in museum displays, as well as the well-known challenge of presenting adequate contextual information without overwhelming the visual and emotional presence of objects, is strongly contested and often difficult to resolve. The new permanent exhibition at the Musée du Quai Branly in Paris, which was the source of intense debate regarding whether it is better to emphasize the aesthetic or the historical and ethnographic context of the exhibited artefacts from overseas, is certainly germane (cf. Price 2007). Whether objects should be presented as art objects or as evidence of cultural history has been debated since the "discovery" of so-called primitive art by Western avant-garde artists in the early 20th century, as mentioned previously. The attention to formal, aesthetic qualities of objects of African or Native American provenance, inspired by the interest of artists such as Braque or Picasso, and canonized by an emerging art market, compelled a range of museums to showcase artistic quality and expertise as an integral aspect of presenting the ethnographic object. Today, it is common practice to combine contextualising representational strategies such as the incorporation of elaborate texts, images, films, and, more recently, multimedia stations, with aesthetic strategies characteristic of art museums, such as strategic lighting, spacing, and placement. This hybrid practice ostensibly serves a common purpose: to enable a full appreciation of the formal qualities of the objects displayed and to convey their historical context and original meaning at the same time.

However, Keita's statement about returning these "out of context" ethnographic objects to their originating communities in order to re-contextualize and thus re-establish their status as ritual objects goes beyond this primarily museological debate. It also evokes the widespread notion that ritual objects possess a monolithic identity that was disrupted by colonialism and subsequently transformed into commodities and works of art. In this vein, political activists, academics, and museum experts frequently demand the repatriation of objects in order to restore their original purpose and meaning. However, as Stephen Greenblatt articulates:

> (…) cultural artefacts never stand still, they are never inert. Their existence is always embedded in a multitude of contexts, with tensions surrounding their roles, usages and meanings. Objects are meaningful only in relation to conflicts, negotiations and appropriations. Things shift in a wide range of modes, and very often it is through these particular alterations that they assume a specific meaning.
> (Greenblatt 2009: 250)

Daouda Keita's and Samuel Sidibé's different approaches to the ethnographic collection illustrate that it would be overly simplistic to claim that ethnographic objects are works of art in a European context and ritual objects in a Malian context. In fact, the meaning of these objects has always been embedded in a web of complex social practices which cannot be neatly mapped onto discrete geographical regions, nor onto linear progressions of symbolic significance. Similarly, Arjun Appadurai states that "things have no meanings apart from those human transactions, attributions, and motivations endow them with," and that we must "follow the things themselves" in order to grasp the meanings that are "inscribed in their forms, their uses, their trajectories" (Appadurai 1986: 5). Drawing inspiration from Georg Simmel and acknowledging that value is not an inherent property to objects but rather emerges reciprocally through exchange, Appadurai traces the circulation of objects as they pass through different spatio-temporal "regimes of value." These regimes may or may not equate with other cultural hierarchies. The circulation of objects may involve different kinds of pathways, diversions, and trajectories, perhaps involving multiple processes of commoditization and decommoditization. In this sense, objects are almost afforded "life histories." Subsequently, methodologically, Appadurai and his colleagues promote a "biographical" approach to studying objects' various translations and transformations.[6] However, the agenda the term "biography" infers can also be misleading. A biography refers to a linear lifespan, which fails to capture the complexity of the iterations of the existence of ethnographic objects. Following this critique, Hoskins expands on this notion by referring to the image of a network that has knots constitutive of the intersections of things and people. Instead of the suggested linearity of a biography, the network of these nodes better represents the reciprocal transformations caused by the interaction between people and things. (Küchler 2001 in Hahn/Weiss 2013: 4) Furthermore, as the ethnographic focus of anthropologists has shifted to embrace what Appadurai (1990) has characterized as the "new global cultural economy," the metaphor of "entanglement" becomes more appropriate than the straightforwardly balanced notion of "exchange." Indeed, an increasing number of anthropologists have recognized that transcultural complexity at a global scale is not novel, criticizing anthropological discourses that have constructed "unitary conceptions" such as "gift economies," arguing instead that indigenous economies have long been entangled in other systems beyond colonial trade (cf. Thomas 1991).

In order to develop strategies of ethically engaging the Frobenius collection, it is important to apply these theoretical insights to concrete museum practice. In doing so, one should acknowledge the hybrid, polysemous character of ethnographic artefacts while avoiding a parochial approach to the notion of exchange within an entangled system of meaning. In this regard, Keita's statement that most of the visitors of the National Museum of Mali are foreigners is germane. According to him, Malian citizens rarely visit, as they do not feel the same Western reverence for museums. As a museum director, he aims to change this by ceasing to focus solely on a "Western" approach to museum collections. Instead, he intends to engage the cultural practices inherent in ethnographic objects to better reflect the interests of local communities. He wants to turn the museum into a "living" institution by presenting ethnographic objects in ways that traffic in local methods of perception and comprehension. Keita wants to show the Malian people that the museum is not merely made for international tourists, but for them as well. Local communities should be able to take ownership of the museum and feel that it is "their" institution.

To engage such a new approach, museums need to critically deconstruct colonial categories such as "art" and "ethnographica" and focus instead on the needs and interests of the communities to which these objects belong.

But what about the traces of Mali's cultural heritage that extend beyond Africa, such as the Frobenius collection? How can such a collection contribute to Keita's undertaking? According to the latter, the first and most important step is to establish trust and transparency between the different stakeholders in Africa and Europe without pursuing hidden agendas. In this spirit, the first step in my research of the Frobenius collection was to inform the National Museum of Mali about the collection in Hamburg and meet Keita in order to provide him with an overview of my findings. Then, with the purpose of building trust and mutual understanding, we openly discussed how the collection came into Frobenius' possession and whether the objects were acquired by force. According to Keita, objects that were taken without consent should not stay where they are but should be returned.

To foster collaboration, it is important to create a space of transparency and trust. This includes questioning the hegemonic structures still in place today. Furthermore, Samuel Sidibé rightfully points out that in order to exploit the potential of repatriating ethnographic objects, specific requirements and regulations must be adhered to. This means that trust and confidence are also necessary on the European side. European museums must acknowledge the capability of African museums to take care of collections and, if they are loaned, trust them that their objects will return safely and undamaged. Furthermore, Sidibé stresses the importance of going beyond colonial ethnological discourses and focusing on current African perspectives.

In order to realize the full potential of the Frobenius collection, it is, therefore, necessary to open up new ways to see and interpret the collection. My research so far has been an important step in creating links between Hamburg and Bamako in order to expand the knowledge about the Frobenius collection and reveal its potential for community-focused and reciprocity-oriented projects. The collection offers a means of critically engaging Europe's colonial past, while simultaneously restoring a source of pride and identity for African diaspora groups in Europe.[7] Contemporary postcolonial consciousness of African identity coheres with Frobenius' collection, which, under critical consideration, engenders cross-cultural conversations that could unveil previously unknown perspectives and symbolic attributions.

Notes

1 Cf. Oberhofer, 2016.
2 Cf. Atkins, 1993.
3 All citations translated by the author.
4 Cf. Ivanoff, 2017.
5 Keita, 2019.
6 Appadurai, 1986, p. 34; see also Hoskins, 1998.
7 Cf. Basu, 2011.

References

Ackermann, Andreas; Röschenthaler, Ute; Steigerwald, Peter. *Im Schatten des Kongo. Leo Frobenius. Stereofotografien von 1904–1906.* Frankfurt/Main: Frobenius-Institut. 2005.
Álvarez, R.; Vidal, M.C. Translating: A Political Act. In R. Álvarez; M. C. Vidal (Eds.). *Translation, Power, Subversion*. Philadelphia, PA: Multilingual Matters. 1996. pp. 1–9.
Appadurai, Arjun. Disjuncture and Difference in the Global Cultural Economy. In: *Theory, Culture & Society*, vol. 7, no. 2, 1990. pp. 295–310.
Appadurai, Arjun. "Introduction: Commodities and the Politics of Value." In: Appadurai, Arjun (Ed.). *The Social Life of Things: Commodities in Cultural Perspectives*. Cambridge: Cambridge University Press, 1986. pp. 3–63.
Atkins, Keletso E. *The Moon Is Dead! Give Us Our Money! The Cultural Origins of an African Work Ethic, Natal, South Africa, 1843–1900* (Social History of Africa.) London: Portsmouth, NH: Heinemann or James Currey. 1993.
Basu, Paul. Object Diasporas, Resourcing Communities: Sierra Leonean Collections in the Global Museumscape. In: *Museum Anthropology*, vol. 34, no. 1, 2011. pp. 28–42.
Biro, Yaëlle. *Fabriquer le regard – Marchands, réseaux et objets d'art africains à l'aube du XXe siècle*. Les presses du Réel, 2018.
Clifford, James. *Routes. Travel and Translation in the Late Twentieth Century*. Cambridge, MA: Harvard University Press, 1997.
Fabian, Johannes. "Curios and Curiosity. Notes on Reading Torday and Frobenius." In: Schildkrout, Enid; Kaim, Curtis A. (Eds.). *The Scramble for Art in Central Africa*. Cambridge and New York: Cambridge University Press, 1998. pp. 79–100.
Förster, Larissa; Edenheiser, Iris; Fründt, Sarah; Hartmann, Heike (Eds.). *Provenienzforschung zu ethnografischen Sammlungen der Kolonialzeit. Positionen in der aktuellen Debatte*. 2018. Online: https://edoc.hu-berlin.de/handle/18452/19769 (accessed 9.7.2018).
Frobenius, Leo. *Auf dem Weg nach Atlantis. Bericht über den Verlauf der zweiten Reise-Periode der D. I. A. F. E. in den Jahren 1908 bis 1910. Mit 48 Tafeln, 27 Illustrationen, einem bunten Bild und 2 Karten*. Berlin-Charlottenburg: Vita Deutsches Verlagshaus, 1911.
Greenblatt, Stephen (Ed.). *Cultural Mobility: A Manifesto*. Cambridge and New York: Cambridge University Press, 2009.
Haberland, Eike (Ed.). *Leo Frobenius 1873–1973. Eine Anthologie*. Wiesbaden: Franz Steiner Verlag, 1973.

Hahn, Hans-Peter. "Leo Frobenius' Reise durch Nord-Togo in den Jahren 1908/09: Ethnologische Dokumentation und koloniale Sichtweise." In: Heine, Peter; Heyden van der, Ulrich (Eds.). *Studien zur Geschichte des deutschen Kolonialismus in Afrika. Festschrift zum 60. Geburtstag von Peter Sebald*. Pfaffenweiler: Centaurus, 1995. pp. 259–279.

Hahn, Hans Peter; Weiss, Hadas (Eds.). *Mobility, Meaning and Transformations of Things: Shifting Contexts of Material Culture Through Time and Space*. Oxford: Oxbow Books. 2013.

Heinrichs, Hans-Jürgen. *Die fremde Welt, das bin ich. Leo Frobenius: Ethnologe, Forschungsreisender, Abenteurer*. Wuppertal: Peter Hammer Verlag, 1998.

Hoskins, Janet. *Biographical Objects: How Things Tell the Stories of People's Lives*. Hove: Psychology Press. 1998.

Imperato, Pascal James. "Sogoni Koun." *African Arts*, vol. 14, no. 2, 1981. pp. 38–47, 72, 88.

Ivanoff, Hélène. "Les 'compagnons obscurs' des expéditions de Leo Frobenius." In: Kuba, Richard; Ivanoff, Hélène; Kassé, Maguèye (Eds.). *Art Rupestre Africain. De la contribution africaine à la découverte d'un patrimoine universel*. Frobenius-Institut: Frankfurt/Main, 2017.

Jahn, Karl-Heinz. *Leo Frobenius: The Demonic Child*. Austin, TX: African and Afro-American Studies and Research Center. 1974.

Kuba, Richard. "Portraits of Distant Worlds. Frobenius' Pictorial Archive and Its Legacy." In: Helff, Sissy; Michels, Stefanie (Eds.). *Global Photographies. Memory – History – Archives*. Bielefeld: Transcript, 2018. pp. 109–131. https://doi.org/10.25969/mediarep/1652.

Kuba, Richard. "Leo Frobenius et la politique colonial." In: Georget, Jean-Louis; Ivanoff, Hélène; Kuba, Richard (Eds.). *Construire l'Ethnologie en Afrique Coloniale. Politique, collections et médiations africaines*. Paris: Presses Sorbonne Nouvelle, 2020. pp. 67–99.

Küchler, S. "Why Knot? Towards a Theory of Art and Mathematics." In: Pinney, Christopher; Thomas, Nicolas (Eds.). *Beyond Aesthetics: Art and the Technologies of Enchantment*. Oxford and New York: Berg, 2001. pp. 57–77.

Laely, Thomas; Meyer, Marc; Schwere, Raphael. *Museum Cooperations between Africa and Europe. A new field for museum studies*. Bielefeld/Kampala: transcript/Fountain Publishers, 2018.

Lawrance, Benjamin N.; Osborn, Emily Lynn; Roberts, Richard L. (Eds.). *Intermediaries, Interpreters, and Clerks: African Employees in the Making of Colonial Africa*. Madison: University of Wisconsin Press. 2015.

Maquet, Jacques. "Art by Metamorphosis." In: *African Arts*, vol. 12, no. 4, 1979. pp. 32–91.

Oberhofer, Michaela. "Der Wert von Stroh, Eisen und Holz. Leo Frobenius als Händler und Sammler." In: Georget, Jean Louis; Ivanoff, Hélène; Kuba, Richard (Eds.). *Kulturkreise. Leo Frobenius und seine Zeit*. Berlin: Reimer Verlag, 2016. pp. 217–239.

Peers, Laura/Brown, Alison K. *Museums and Source Communities: A Routledge Reader*. London and New York: Routledge. 2003.

Peffer, John. "Africa's Diasporas of Images." In: *Third Text*, vol. 19, no. 4, 2005. pp. 339–355.

Price, Sally. *Paris Primitive: Jacques Chirac's Museum on the Quai Branly*. Chicago: Chicago University Press, 2007.

Sarr, Felwine and Savoy, Bénédicte. *Rapport sur la restitution du patrimoine culturel africain. Vers une nouvelle éthique relationnelle.* 2018. Online: https://restitutionreport2018.com/ (accessed 18.1.2019).

Streck, Bernhard. *Leo Frobenius: Forscher und Ethnologe (Gründer, Gönner und Gelehrte).* Frankfurt am Main: Societäts Verla, 2014.

Thomas, Nicholas. *Entangled Objects. Exchange, Material Culture, and Colonialism in the Pacific.* Cambridge, MA: Harvard University Press, 1991.

Zwernemann, Jürgen. "Leo Frobenius und das Hamburgische Museum für Völkerkunde. Eine Dokumentation nach der Korrespondenz." In: Zwernemann, Jürgen; Thode-Arora, Hilke (Eds.). *Mitteilungen aus dem Museum für Völkerkunde Hamburg* (17), 1987. pp. 111–127.

4 The Museum as a Colonial Archive
The Collection of Victor and Marie Solioz and Its Role in Forgetting the Colonial Past

Samuel B. Bachmann

Introduction

Dead Ends, Missing Links, and Widening Gaps in Ethnographic Museums

Ethnographic collecting was part of a euro-centric system of knowledge production that supported the exertion of colonial power, as it directly contributed to a body of knowledge about the 'nature of the colonized' that was in demand.[1] Ethnographic collecting entailed classifying those who would become the subjects of colonization. While ethnographic collecting in the field might have developed either way, its actual historical development cannot be reckoned outside European colonial expansion. As Glenn Penny described it for the development of German ethnographic museum collections, colonialism was the "conditio sine qua non" (2002, 13) of ethnographic collecting. This conclusion also holds for the Solioz collection and for the foundation of many other Swiss ethnographic museum collections.

Considering the description of colonial Switzerland as a method of "rethinking colonialism from the margins" (Purtschert and Fischer-Tiné 2015, 7), the Swiss colonial complicity refigures in actors, such as the Solioz couple, who were traditionally not part of a national historiography of colonialism or spatial conceptions such as 'metropole and colony' or 'center and periphery'.[2] While identifying themselves as colonial outsiders, Swiss private actors as much as public institutions acted within trans-national and trans-imperial networks in a multiplicity of ways and they might, "in a paradoxical manner, (…) lead us right into the heart of current imperial formations" (9). Thus, in analyzing forgotten players of European imperialism, the provenance of the Solioz collection and the involvement of the museum in its formation and perpetuation, also sheds light on Switzerland's means of actively forgetting its own colonial past.

Although once collected with scientific ambition and appreciated by a Swiss public and academia, the current fate of the German Southwest Africa collection is a decidedly more somber one: confined to a storage room in an industrial building somewhere in a suburban area. Like in many other

DOI: 10.4324/9781003282334-6

museum storages, massive amounts of trinkets, vessels, clothes, or weapons, to name only a few, are waiting to further fulfil their once ascribed purpose, which was to become an important medium of scientific evidence and cultural memory. Eventually, only very few objects were regularly selected for research or exhibition projects and allowed to publicly unfold their narrative potential. A considerable portion of the ethnographic objects in European museum collections encounters a dead end in their everyday museal use.[3]

Ethnographic museums as archives of material culture are not only dead ends in the physical meaning of the term. The knowledge that is ascribed and documented with regard to artifacts is often so scarce, fragmentary, or adulterated that research questions regarding an artifact's cultural or historical value are often met with a museal archive that is silent. The absence of identities, histories, and epistemologies of those initially intended to be represented and the euro-centric categorization and description of the materials of the 'others' calls attention to the incompleteness and deceptions of the ethnographic museum as an archive. In fact, the longer they remain hidden in a European storage space, the more the gaps widen between the museum and those for whom these materials could be meaningful. Today, many of these ethnographic objects remain largely disconnected from the distant cultural environments of their producers and sources (Schorch, McCarthy and Dürr 2018, 7).

Dead ends, missing links, and widening gaps in ethnographic museums, however, do not imply that these artifacts do not possess a narrative potential as instruments of knowledge transfer or material evidence of historicity. By following the microhistories of object biographies, their trajectories shed light on the different meanings people ascribed to them and how these meanings have transformed over time as they traverse different spaces and periods, human transactions, and exchanges. It is the 'the social life of things' as Arjun Appadurai sustainably argued, that illuminates their concrete, historical circulation:

> It is only through the analysis of these trajectories that we can interpret the human transactions and calculations that enliven things. Thus, even though from a *theoretical* point of view human actors encode things with significance, from a *methodological* point of view it is the things-in-motion that illuminate their human and social context.
>
> (1986, 5)

Many social biographies of ethnographic objects in European museum collections lead back to colonial contexts. In the metropoles of colonial powers, ethnographic museums served as target institutions for endless numbers of acquisitions and lootings as much as they served as recipients of material collections of scientific expeditions intended to investigate the 'nature of the colonized'. Public museums in the colonial metropole were directly entangled with the project of European colonial expansion and, consequently, have become mighty archives of colonialism.[4] It seems surprising, however, that ethnographic museums in formally non-colonial European states, such as in Switzerland, which was supposedly less directly interconnected with a given empire, managed to assemble ethnographic collections from former colonies that were often just as vast. Although Swiss ethnographic collections might have been more provincial and smaller in size than those in the metropoles, the museums still managed to assemble overwhelming amounts of ethnographic collections from a broad variety of different colonial contexts.[5]

Agents of Empires

The Swiss couple Marie and Victor Solioz set out to German Southwest Africa in summer 1903, where, on behalf of the German colonial administration, Victor was assigned the construction of the Otavi railroad, with the purpose of connecting the mines in Tsumeb, in the north-east of the colony, with Swakopmund on the coast.[6] As an experienced engineer, Victor had previously been involved in different railway construction projects abroad. Although very little is known about his career, his involvement has been linked to a railway construction project in Somalia. On behalf of the *Otavi Minen- und Eisenbahngesellschaft (OMEG)*, he was employed as the chief engineer of the contracting executive construction company Arthur Koppel AG.[7] Today, Solioz is remembered mainly for the vast collections of ethnographic objects acquired during the course of his assignment, which he sold to different museums after his returns.[8]

Several hundred ethnographic objects from his collections can be found in museums in Switzerland, while an unknown number is also assumed to be found in German collections.[9] The majority, however, seems to be preserved in the Historical Museum of Bern that counts 524 ethnographic objects handed over by Victor Solioz, originating from over a dozen countries. A purchase of 54 objects acquired by Victor Solioz are documented in Bern for the year 1902. From the correspondence with the museum at the beginning of 1903, it is assumed that the collector was eager to professionalize his 'hobby' considerably leading up to his departure to Namibia, where he knew he would be stationed approximately three years until the construction of the railroad was to be completed.[10]

After his return in 1906, he deposited his "complete collection" of "Herero, Bergdamara and Ovambo things"[11] in the museum of Bern. His motives for beginning to collect more extensively and systematically in German Southwest Africa than before are not entirely clear. Still, it is outlined in archival files that the couple envisioned eventually building a "pavillon" in Delémont, their hometown, where they would exhibit their collections on their own.[12] Ultimately, the private museum was never built. Further the couple's vehement refusal to consider transforming their deposits into a donation in 1913 – a request made by the museum's ethnographic curator at the time, Rudolf Zeller – shows that collecting was not only about achieving prestige, providing patriotic services, or contributing to ethnographic knowledge production, but was also an investment in tradable goods with expected revenue.[13] Especially given the precedent of 1902, when the museum of Bern was willing to pay for what he had to offer.

Although Victor Solioz was Swiss, in his role as the chief engineer of the Otavi Railroad, he was an incontestable agent of the German colonial empire.[14] The construction of the railroad played a significant role in the development of events in the colony in the first decade of the twentieth century. The project was one of the most visible manifestations of colonial occupation of the land and a central element of the projected exploitation of natural resources in the colony. The infrastructure of the railway, among others, became the target of local resistance, including violent attacks, which led to retaliatory actions by the Germans that resulted in what is generally agreed to be the first genocide of the twentieth century.[15]

Several sources in colonial literature suggest that the engineer and his wife were well integrated into the colonizer and settler community in Swakopmund, where at least Marie Solioz was based most of the time, while Victor was traveling along with the progress of the construction.[16] A quote from a letter addressed to the *Reichskolonialamt* suggests Victor Solioz's support for the German policy of oppression and eviction by assuring concerned members of his patronage that "it is clear for everyone in the colony, (…) that this uprising must be put down very energetically and that tabula rasa must be made with the guilty" (Drechsler 1996, 297).[17] This quote only provides a clue with regard to the degree of Solioz's ideological entanglement with the military exertion of power. Practically, however, the example of Solioz shows that in most cases – and regarding the logistics of assembling and shipping hundreds of ethnographic artifacts across the globe in particular – private Swiss actors had to establish numerous reliable contacts in colonial milieus to successfully pursue their different missions.

The story of Victor Solioz portrays a prototype of Swiss private actors' entanglements with European colonial expansion. Biographies of well-educated, high-skilled 'experts', such as engineers, physicians, natural scientists, anthropologists, merchants, and also missionaries, show that many of them were active in different empires, traversing across colonial frontiers and forming part of rather more international than national communities to be found in the different colonies.[18] The motives and incentives for Swiss private actors to pursue a career within European projects of colonial expansion, however, were manifold.

Around 1900, like in the case of Solioz, many of these private actors' endeavors also resulted in material collections, which differed in size and grade of systematization, but which often included a variety of types of artifacts, such as ethnographic, anthropological, zoological, botanical, or archaeological materials. Collecting was driven by scientific interests in the first place, and it was, especially for those collectors for whom this was a sideline activity, a chance for achieving a certain degree of scientific recognition. While many of them have never been really acknowledged as such, they were crucial actors in the circulation of knowledge within imperial networks (Habermas and Przyrembel 2013, 14). The biographical information about Victor Solioz, however, portrays him as a figure representing both the exertion of colonial dominance through his role on behalf of the *OMEG* and as an actor involved in the production and transfer of knowledge, mainly through the creation of his ethnographic collection.

After the demise of Victor Solioz in 1921, in a letter of condolence to Marie Solioz, curator Rudolf Zeller portrayed the collector in a heroic manner:

> With his collections (…) the deceased has set a monument for himself that will last forever and that will give knowledge to future generations about the energy and creative power of a man who found time, besides his exhausting profession, to study the culture of peoples and to collect their material culture.[19]

He further describes him as "sharp-witted", having a "remarkable eye for the unspoilt native". In particular, Solioz's identity as a direct witness in the field made him and his collection stand out so much for Zeller who publicly expressed a certain discontent with Switzerland's "lack of direct connections" to owning colonial possessions and thus a lack of "direct contacts for the procurement of ethnographic collections" (BHM 1906, 9).[20] He preferred collection additions that were not mediated through third parties, but found their way into the museum directly through the collector in the field for two reasons. First due to the fact that foregoing middlemen made prices for artifacts remain lower (BHM 1905, 2). Second, because these artifacts and the knowledge they were about to incorporate had been transferred directly by those witnessing the *Naturvölker* themselves.[21]

The "unequally greater value" of material culture collected "on the spot" (BHM 1900, 19; 1916, 3) was constructed upon the belief that they more directly documented a specific cultural encounter and were more promising regarding the transfer of knowledge about the people they ought to represent in the museum. The social practice of witnessing, however, also reveals that these private actors were always more than just engineers, merchants, or missionaries but also confidants of very specific colonial events (Przyrembel 2013, 211). In the case of Solioz, these events were particularly horrifying, as, between 1904 and 1908, tens of thousands of Herero and Nama people were killed by the German *Schutztruppe* or left to die in the Omaheke Desert.[22] It is as puzzling as it is frightening to ask the question of how he could have possibly managed to collect hundreds of artifacts amid the situation 'on the spot' in Namibia.

The analysis of ethnographic collections provides a promising access point to biographies of forgotten agents of empires because many of these

The Museum as a Colonial Archive 83

Figure 4.1 Victor Solioz (second from the right) at work on the Otavi Railroad in Central Namibia.
© National Archives of Namibia, Photographer unknown.

collections were not compiled by the Humboldts or Bastians, but by amateur collectors, acquiring material culture in terms of leisure activity.[23] Nonetheless, they were entangled with the colonizer in different respects. From the perspective of the colonized, the color of Solioz's passport was probably irrelevant when identifying him as a representative of the colonizer. It is however the more subtle and ideological aspects of his colonial entanglements that are of interest here because they highlight how formally non-colonial European actors acted as agents of empires. Swiss merchants, missionaries, or scientists did not always display the degree of commitment to a specific colonial power like Solioz. Some were also explicitly distancing themselves from any colonial interests, and yet in many ways, they acted in its service (Figure 4.1).

Emphasis and Omittance in Ethnographic Collecting

Victor Solioz provided two catalogues for his collections, which, together with scattered descriptions of specific objects in the correspondences between Zeller and Solioz, provide the primary source regarding the knowledge that was originally transferred from the field to the museum via the artifacts. The catalogues index and number all items separately. While the order of the overall catalogues is geographical, the costumes, accessories, jewelry, weapons, or household items within a geographical category are not listed in any particular order. But specific information for each item is systematically documented in seven columns: German name; local name; kind of use; tribe and people; materials it is made of; geographical origin, special peculiarities and comments.

Number 23, for instance, is thus documented as a "Haarfrisur", called "Ondyise" in *Otjiherero*. They were used by "old Herero women", made of human "hair" and a certain kind of unspecified "fiber". The piece was collected in "Damaraland" and as its special peculiarity, Solioz noted that they were "rare, as only worn by older women".[24] Interestingly, the information about this particular object offers some insightful information since it actually refers to a certain degree of historicity of the people by the notion of the changing trends in hairstyles.

In most cases, however, the information would rather sound like this documented for number 73: an "apron, made of leather, worn by men, Herero, Damaraland".[25] For the entirety of the Herero catalogue, the geographical reference is simply Damaraland, and no single name of a local protagonist is mentioned anywhere. Thus, the destiny of many of these ethnographic objects resembles the one befallen by this apron, for which the only non-visible information, transferred to the museum, is that it was worn by Herero men. Furthermore, no information regarding its intangible value in terms of its potential for ethnographic knowledge production has been added in over a hundred years of it being recorded in the museum collection. The story of the apron has, nevertheless, dramatically transformed.

In different respects, the accuracy of the term *material culture* is obviously questionable when referring to the Solioz collection. The definition of culture or cultural units upon which the Solioz collection was compiled and categorized was not only biased by euro-centrism, but also denied inclusion to anything that, in the eyes of the collector, represented a European influence; no matter the cultural significance of those materials, which the Europeans considered not to be original or authentic enough.[26] Although there might be some individual exceptions, the idea of systematic self-representation of the ethnographic subjects via their material culture was far from even being considered around 1900, and from today's perspective, there is no one left from what often gets referred to as the 'source community'.

As Silvester and Shiweda champion the preference of the term "descendant communities" in this regard by making "the simple argument that culture and cultural identities change over time" (2020, 31), the allegedly ethnographic value of the Solioz collection has transformed into a historical one. As historical evidence, the objects represent, on the one hand, the ways in which ethnographic collections contributed to the circulation of knowledge in colonial networks. On the other hand, they have the potential to be regarded as heritage relevant to the historicity and identity of a descendant community, much like the case of the *Haarfrisur*. As the term 'material culture' itself lacks a historical dimension, the term 'heritage' is more directly applicable to colonial collections, which ultimately is what the Solioz collection has become.

Ethnographic collecting, until well into the twentieth century, is to be understood as a method of natural science (Zimmerman 2013, 251). Similar to collecting specimens of fauna and flora, the material culture of the colonized was compiled, categorized, and preserved in museum collections, where they were intended to serve the production of knowledge about the nature of humankind. The explicit goal of collecting the materials of all *Naturvölker* was to achieve a total and complete picture of all humans, and the conviction was that the simplest way there was to collect the materials of the allegedly primitive (249). Ethnography, in particular in Germany, was a discipline concentrating heavily on collecting objects and the rhetoric of salvaging the material cultures of perishing cultures (endangered, ironically, by the contact with the 'civilized') through systematic and extensive collecting was particularly dominant (Penny 2002, 29ff.).

The scientific method of ethnographic collecting, of classifying material culture and ordering it within a system of difference and alterity, however, was a method of decidedly ahistoricizing the represented people through their material culture, because the artifacts of the colonized were neither conceived as "historical curiosities" nor as "artistic masterpieces", but as "natural science objects" (Zimmerman 2013, 251). Information ascribed to ethnographic collections was often detached from the idea of cultural historicity and denied the idea of the subjects' own pasts. They rather emphasized the specific differences by othering them and by actively defining an analytical framework of 'them' and 'us' (Thomas 1991, 3). Both the emphasis and the denial of specific information in this context contributed to a narrative of European cultural and scientific dominance.

Thus, around 1900, ethnographic collecting was an instrument of categorizing the colonized in order of various homogenous races and tribes, of highlighting their 'authentic' and 'original' inherent otherness, thereby denying them historicity. The then established scientific categories – along which collectors compiled their objects, or emphasis, and denials of information embodied by these objects – however, were not merely the result of collector's practices on the spot. Particularly regarding amateur collections such as Solioz's, scientific processing of all incoming materials fell within the expertise of the ethnographic museum. Although collections were crucial for the transfer of knowledge, they rather represent the preparatory material for future research. The production of knowledge was supposed to be undertaken after their arrival in the scientific target institutions (247). Categorization, emphasis, and denial of material culture and immaterial knowledge transferred by ethnographic collections were no random

86 *Samuel B. Bachmann*

Figure 4.2 "Hairdress No. 23" from Namibia in the Solioz collection. Inv. Nr. E/1906.342.0023.
© Bernisches Historisches Museum, Photo: Christine Moor.

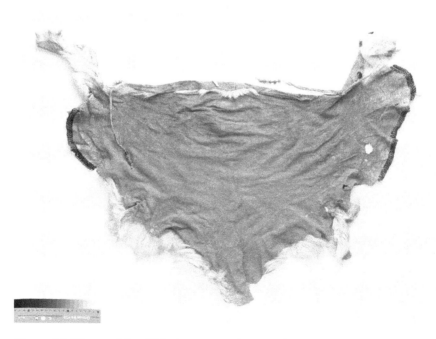

Figure 4.3 "Apron No. 73" from Namibia in the Solioz collection. Inv. Nr. E/1906.342.0073.
© Bernisches Historisches Museum, Photo: Christine Moor.

products, but depended considerably on administrative settings, collecting strategies, research domains, outreach goals, or available resources of museums (Figures 4.2 and 4.3).

The Museum as a Colonial Archive

When analyzing ethnographic collecting as a specific mode of colonial knowledge production, the focus of the analysis must go beyond the mere scrutiny of the collectors' practices. It, too, must take the role of the collecting institution into account. The Historical Museum of Bern opened its doors in 1894 and when Rudolf Zeller was officially elected by the supervisory board of the museum in 1904, he would become the first professional curator of the ethnographic collections of the museum.[27] In summer 1903, Zeller embarked on a study trip to German and Dutch museums in order to prepare for the ambitious task of systematically supplementing the basic stock and transforming it into a representative ethnographic collection.[28] The following years were marked by an enormous increase in the collection and can be described as the awakening of a scientific self-consciousness of the ethnographic department of the museum. During this process, Zeller enjoyed almost unlimited room for maneuver, and he pursued a clear vision of Bern's ethnographic collection's future and purpose.

After his return from the trip, Zeller was "full of courage and conviction" that "something can be made of the proficient basic stock in Bern". But he was also "desperate at what is to be seen elsewhere"[29] and knew that it could not be his goal in Bern to compete with the large colonial collections in Leiden or Berlin. Thus, he did not envision a large scientific institute but a collection that would perform a twofold service for science. First, via the "cultural property of the *Naturvölker*" it would be possible, by comparison, to "illuminate the life of the pile dwellers" of which the museum already held considerable archaeological collections, since many of the associated excavations took place in the canton of Bern and in alpine regions in general. Second, collections from "higher-ranked peoples from the Orient and East Asia" would allow for "valuable relations and comparisons to what has become historical for us". In this evolutionist manner, he further concluded for the future that the ethnographic collection ought to:

> Allow one to perceive one's own culture and its development all the more clearly in the mirror of foreign peoples and thus only apparently different in aim, subordinating itself to the whole, but serving the ideal purpose of a historical museum: the love of the fatherland and its history.
> (BHM 1903, 49)[30]

In the 36 years in office, Zeller managed to build up a vast network of collectors, museums, and dealers all over the world and, eventually, he became responsible for more than half of the total additions ever made to the ethnographic collections in Bern.[31] In order to compensate for missing direct links to colonial territories, he targeted private Swiss actors like Solioz, who would travel and collect on Zeller's behalf. He prepared a brochure named "instructions for the creation of ethnographic collections" that he handed out to his "employees"[32] before departure. In the name of the museum, Zeller would exert influence on what kind of items collectors ought to bring home and how they were supposed to document information regarding these materials. Some of these amateur collectors would eventually donate their collections to the museum and if they were hesitant, Zeller would appeal to their conscience and remind them of the important implications of such a service to the "fatherland". In other cases, when collectors were not as economically potent, the museum would also provide resources to them, with which they were supposed to acquire specific materials at its request.[33]

The way the collections were increased during these years denotes the significance and impact that museums had with regard to ethnographic collecting in colonial contexts. Most importantly, the collection strategy of the Historical Museum of Bern demonstrates how ethnographic collections were often preformulated before they were assembled. Thus, the selection of objects that were eventually to become the material representatives of the '*Naturvölker*' and 'higher-ranked peoples' in exhibition halls were not primarily made up of what actually was to be found 'on the spot'. It rather worked the other way around and collectors would check the boxes off Zeller's list of desiderata. The ethnographic collection of the museum, in those years, was therefore guided and developed mainly by one single person who impacted selection, acquisitional modalities, and ordering and classifying of materials. Ostensibly, the museum created the narratives of representation of, primarily, colonized people. Museums, including those in Switzerland, were agents of empires as they were instrumental to the practice of colonial collecting and representation and to the processes of emphasis and omittance of knowledge about 'them' and 'us'.

As colonial archives, ethnographic museums should be places of remembering the manifold ways in which the institution and collectors were entangled with European colonial expansion. Although around 1900, they were taking the lead in the circulation of knowledge in imperial networks, they were also preventers of this circulation. They furthermore contributed to the active construction of misleading narratives and memories. Andrew Zimmerman, referring to the analysis of the colonial collections of the *Königliches Museums für Völkerkunde* in Berlin, in this sense, identified the museum as a place of "threefold misremembering" (2013, 250).[34] First, it remembered the colonized as humans with no history. Second, it remembered the origin of mankind based on colonized people who, themselves, had been denied any past. Third, it remembered the colonial encounter to be an encounter between culture and nature. While this observation could probably be applied to many other ethnographic collections as well, the case of Solioz's collection demonstrates the manifold possible interpretations for the idea of 'misremembering'. It further spotlights the missing links and the absence of information in particular, to highlight the ways in which the museum as a colonial archive is to be read.

While the narrative of the Solioz collection, well beyond the period of the German colonial occupation of Namibia, was one dominated by notions such as 'completeness' and 'representativity', it could also be shown that the museum was instrumental for this specific way of storytelling. The role of the museum as the main actor behind a collection, as simple as this might sound, is one missing link and an aspect of misremembering its own impact. The lack of self-reflection regarding the institution's own role in the context of the transfer, the production, and the documentation of knowledge is so common that it is quickly overlooked. Moreover, museums are exposed to different administrative settings, political conditions, or public expectations which, up until today, considerably influence the museums' agency. Civil organizations and private as well as public bodies provide the financial resources and create a political environment, upon which collecting and archiving knowledge of non-European worlds becomes possible after all (Vogel 2013, 262).

During the analysis of archival materials of the Solioz collection, another element of narrative omission by the museum became obvious: the role of Marie Solioz. Although she is neither mentioned in the inventory books nor in any other documentation system of the museum, Marie Solioz was not only responsible for most of the correspondences with the museum. It has now become clear that she was the author of the original catalogues.[35] Moreover, she was particularly active with regard to one specific set of objects within the collection, a Herero costume for women. When the museum received the female Herero figurine, which was ordered by Solioz from *Umlauff's Welt-Museum und Naturalienhandel* in Hamburg and which was supposed to allow for a 'true-to-life' representation of the Herero costume in the museum, she was asked to assist in correctly dressing it up.[36] Not only did she obviously have, or at least pretend to have, the relevant knowledge, but the constant presence of her voice in the archival files indicates that her involvement in collecting and arranging the items was most likely far more significant than it was actively portrayed in the museum's public narrative of the Solioz collection. In any case, it can be assumed that the wives of those "heroic" male amateur collectors remembered for finding time besides their "exhausting profession", in general, were more often involved in compiling and administering their collections than commonly documented in the museums.

The most obvious absence of information in line with the Solioz collection, however, regards the collectors' encounters and exchanges in the local context with producers or traders and the identities of the many intermediaries that must have been involved in the transfer of knowledge as well as in the transfer of the materials itself. Intermediaries were the representatives of the different colonized communities who would work as interpreters or facilitators for encounters and exchanges on the spot. In these roles, they became crucial actors in the provision of information on the given community and its material culture. Ethnographic collectors, amateur ones in particular, who would often stay in a place for only a very short period of time, were heavily dependent on intermediaries who would have authority over the information that was provided, creatively added or deliberately omitted and would therefore impact the processes of knowledge transfer considerably (Habermas 2013, 39).[37] Intermediaries were also directly involved in scientific endeavors such as archaeological excavations, collecting expeditions, or the development of dictionaries, to name only a few. Or, as Felix Driver has put it: "(…) whisper it quietly, but Europeans were not all the masters of all they surveyed. Most of the surveying here, it turns out, was done by those others (…)" (14).

In many respects, colonialism in general and ethnographic collecting in particular was a collective enterprise that required a diverse labor force. In colonial archives, however, many of the voices of these local actors were muted or de-personalized in the context of documentation and institutionalization (Konishi, Nugent and Shellam 2015, 5). The Solioz collection provides an all-too representative example of an archive, in which evidence of the presence of any local individual is entirely missing. Indigenous agency does not appear, neither in the catalogues responsible for the transfer of knowledge, nor in further research or outreach projects from the museum. Either their identities were deliberately left out of the story because they were found to be irrelevant, or there were no direct encounters. While the latter seems unlikely given the size of the Solioz collection and his role on the railway construction sites, it is possible that Solioz bought his collection in one piece and did not collect piece by piece in different places. This would also explain why the geographical references remained as vague.

Correspondence between Solioz and Zeller omits any information regarding the actual methods of acquisition in the colony but provides reasons to assume that it was bought *en bloc*: Solioz wrote to Zeller that they "(…) have brought a numerous collection from South-West, and after I have chosen two complete collections (i.e. two pieces of each) for myself, the large rest goes to Germany".[38] From the sources of the museum archive, this is as close as it gets to answering questions as to how Solioz managed to assemble hundreds of objects during a colonial war. Most likely, however, he collected the artifacts in Namibia as he had collected them in all the other countries where his collections come from. For instance, as there are collection entries from Angola, Nigeria, Ghana, and Liberia, it is known that, at least in the words of Zeller, Solioz was able "in a few hours of a ship stop" to "gather such good things", whereas otherwise "one only gets globetrotter goods on such occasions".[39]

Finally, Solioz and the museum never really considered the historical events in German Southwest Africa to be of relevance for the ways in which they wanted to document and use the collection after its arrival in Bern. The only archival notion of the war in Namibia is to be found in the annual report of the museum from 1906, where it soberly states that "it was high time to collect the ergology of these peoples, because due to the war that has broken out in the meantime, the indigenous culture of these natives is practically wiped out".[40] The atrocities committed in this war have never been considered of relevance in terms of ethnographic knowledge production and outreach for the museum. Today, however, the Solioz collection has transformed into unambiguous colonial heritage, primarily providing evidence for the events that these artifacts 'witnessed' at the beginning of their journeys. The *Ondyise*, in this regard, on which strands of wear are still visible and which obviously had to be cut off to become a collectable object, provides a thought-provoking example when imagining the according way of appropriation with regard to the historical context at the time in Namibia.

Conclusion

Ethnographic collecting around 1900 was a method of colonial knowledge production and served the narrative of European cultural and scientific dominance by creating and serving concepts of otherness, alterity, and race.[41] The analysis of the Solioz collection shows the processes of assembling and institutionalizing an ethnographic collection from a specific colonial context, in which the collector and the museum have contributed to processes of accentuating otherness and difference as much as to processes of omitting information and of preventing the circulation of certain knowledge. Considering the museum as a colonial archive, however, does not only open new avenues for taking these artifacts out of their shadowy existence, but it also highlights the significance of identifying missing links and the absence of information when reading the colonial archive.

Ethnographic museum collections in Europe rarely represent the contemporary material culture of living people but, at best, rather fragmented parts of their heritage. Still, in contemporary ethnographic museum work, the diversity-celebrating world-culture approach has become very common. Yet, the diversity documented within these collections, very often, is deceptive. It is permeated with colonial ideology, one within which the 'primitive people' remain homogenous collectives without any form of historicity or transformative potential. It is a diversity that was often constructed by white men for other white men to assure themselves of their superiority. Since colonialism is the *sine qua non* of ethnographic collecting history, the ideological imprints of coloniality within these collections must be the necessary disclaimer for any form of celebration of diversity in the contemporary ethnographic museum.

This case study additionally exemplifies a Swiss context in which Swiss collectors in colonial contexts and recipient museums may have distanced themselves from colonial interests while continuing to act in their service

92 *Samuel B. Bachmann*

in manifold ways. Therefore, it is equally essential in Switzerland to start reversing the gaze when working with colonial heritage. Thus, when attempting to reconnect these artifacts with the people for whom they might be meaningful, it is not a question of how the museums can use the source communities to decolonize the institution, but of how the descendant communities can connect with the "source museums" (Silvester and Shiweda 2020, 31) to access and use these parts of their heritage in post-colonial and post-ethnographic times.

Notes

1. Cp. Habermas and Przyrembel 2013; Zimmerman 2013.
2. Cp. Rüther 2013.
3. Cp. Macdonald and Morgan 2019.
4. Cp. Förster 2018; Zimmerman 2013; Penny 2002.
5. Cp. Cladders 2015; Reubi 2011.
6. NAN, ref. no.: EVE 42 A.10.A.1 1; EVE 281 36 1; BBW 11 B6; BBW 11 B6A 1.
7. Cp. ibid. For more information on the *OMEG*, also see Drechsler 1996.
8. Collection entries by Victor Solioz are also documented in *Musée d'ethnographie de Genève* (1920; 1921; 1922; 279 inv. no.) and in *Museum der Kulturen Basel* (1902; 1907; 5 inv. no.).
9. BHM archive, ref. no.: A.001.036, see V. Solioz to R. Zeller, 11.11.1905.
10. BHM archive, ref. no.: A.001.036, see V. Solioz to R. Zeller, 02.06.1903.
11. BHM 1906. p. 11.
12. BHM archive, ref. no.: A.001.036, see M. Solioz to R. Zeller, 09.05.1905; V. Solioz to R. Zeller, 11.11.1905.
    M. Solioz to R. Zeller, 14.06.1913.
13. BHM archive, ref. no.: A.001.036, see M. Solioz to R. Zeller, 18.05.1913; M. Solioz to R. Zeller, 14.06.1913.
14. The understanding of private actors acting as 'agents of empire' pursued here is inspired by Vogel 2013, 279ff.
15. Cp. Kautondokwa and Silvester 2019. For more background information on the history of Namibia, see, that is, Zimmerer and Zeller 2003, Wallace 2011, Krüger 2016.
16. Marie and Victor Solioz are mentioned prominently in the memoires of the German *Schutztruppen Offizier* Viktor Franke (1866–1936), who spent more than 20 years in Namibia between 1896 and 1920 and who was a close friend of the Swiss couple. They are also mentioned in the published diaries of Hulda Rautenberg (1913–2002) about her life in *Südwestafrika* 1967.
17. RKolA No. 2112, 60-86 Solioz to Golinelli, 19.01.1904, original in German: "*Dass dieser Aufstand energisch niedergeschlagen werden muss und dass mit den Schuldigen tabula rasa (sic!) gemacht werden muss, steht hier bei jedermann in der Kolonie fest*".
18. Cp. Purtschert and Fischer-Tiné 2015, Schär 2015. On the different actors in line with the circulation of knowledge in imperial networks, see Habermas 2013.
19. BHM archive, ref. no.: A.001.036. Original in German: "*In seinen Sammlungen (…) hat der Verstorbene sich ein Denkmal gesetzt, welches ewig dauern wird und*

The Museum as a Colonial Archive 93

künftigen Generationen Kenntnis geben wird von der Energie und Schaffenskraft eines Mannes, der neben seinem anstrengenden Berufe Zeit gefunden hat, die Kultur der Völker zu studieren und ihren materiellen Kulturbesitz zu sammeln" and ibid.: *"Scharfsinn (...) mit einem merkwürdigen Blick für das urwüchsig Eingeborene".*

20 Original in German: *"Während bei Holland, England und Deutschland die Beziehungen durch den dortigen Kolonialbesitz gegeben sind, entbehrt die Schweiz jeder direkten Verbindung und dadurch auch direkter Anknüpfungspunkte für die Beschaffung ethnographischer Sammlungen".*
21 In the history of the German-speaking development of *Ethnologie* as a discipline, the term '*Naturvölker*' was prominently used and established, that is, by Adolf Bastian (1826–1905), the founder of *Museum für Völkerkunde* in Berlin. Rudolf Zeller also used the term frequently, see *"Bericht über eine Studienreise an die Ethnographischen Museen Deutschlands und Hollands"*, in: BHM 1903, 39ff.
22 Background information on the history of the genocide in Namibia, see, that is, Zimmerer and Zeller 2003, Krüger 2016.
23 This assumption is based on a survey in the Bernisches Historisches Museum undertaken by the author, April–June 2020. The survey analyzed collection entries between 1883 and 1918 from German colonial territories. Of the 40 different entries, consisting of 713 inventory items, none of the 'collectors' became known as an anthropologist or an ethnographer. The provenance information on the entries listed missionaries (11), antiques dealers (8), unknown (8), private collectors and philanthropies (6), merchants (6), engineer (1).
24 BHM archive, ref. no.: A.001.002.002. Full description of the "hairdress" in German: *"23; Haarfrisur; Ondyise; von alten Herero-Weibern; Hereros; Haar mit Faser geflochten; Damaraland; selten, da nur noch die älteren Frauen die tragen".*
25 Full description of the "apron" in German: *"73; Schamschurz; von Männern; Hereros; Leder; Damaraland".*
26 Cp. Beckmann 2012.
27 BHM 1903, p. 7.
28 See chapter: "Bericht über eine Studienreise an die Ethnographischen Museen Deutschlands und Hollands", in: BHM 1903, 39ff.
29 BHM 1903, p. 48.
30 Original in German: *"So kehrte der Berichterstatter zurück voll von Anregungen verschiedenster Art, entzückt von dem liebenswürdigen Empfang, den er überall gefunden, bescheiden und fast verzweifelt in Anbetracht dessen, was anderwärts zu sehen ist, und doch wieder voll Mut und voll fester Überzeugung, dass aus der Berner Sammlung mit ihrem tüchtigen alten Grundstock etwas zu machen sei, nicht ein grosses, wissenschaftliches Institut, aber eine Sammlung, die einerseits gestattet, das Leben des Pfahlbauers zu beleuchten an Hand des Kulturbesitzes der Naturvölker und anderseits in den höher stehenden Völkern des Orients und Ostasiens wertvolle Beziehungen und Vergleiche gestattet mit dem, was bei uns historisch geworden, kurz ein Glied des Museums, das im Spiegel fremder Völker die eigene Kultur und ihre Entwicklung um so deutlicher wahrnehmen lässt und so im Ziele nur scheinbar verschieden, dem Ganzen sich unterordnend, doch dem idealen Zwecke eines historischen Museums dient: der Liebe zum Vaterlande und seiner Geschichte".*

31 Excluding photographic material, the ethnographic collections of the BHM counts 48'743 inventory numbers, of which 25'419 were accessed between 1904 and 1940. Source: Database of the museum (status: 11.03.2021).
32 BHM 1915, p. 11.
33 BHM archive, ref. no.: A.001.036, A.001.037. That is, the museum financed the collection expedition of the young geologist and botanist Walter A. Volz (1875–1907) to Sierra Leone and Liberia 1906–1907, see BHM 1908, p. 7.
34 Original in German: "*Das Museum war folglich ein Ort des dreifachen Misserinnerns*".
35 BHM archive, ref. no.: A.001.036, see M. Solioz to R. Zeller, 13.05.1906.
36 BHM archive, ref. no.: A.001.036, see M. Solioz to R. Zeller, 03.05.1906.
37 Cp. Konishi, Nugent and Shellam 2015.
38 Original in German: "*Wir haben eine zahlreiche Sammlung von Süd-West mitgebracht, und nachdem ich zwei vollständige Sammlungen (d.h. zwei Stück von jedem) für mich ausgesucht habe, geht der grosse Rest nach Deutschland*".
39 BHM archive, ref. no.: A.001.036, see R. Zeller to M. Solioz, 09.11.1921.
40 BHM 1906, p.11. Original in German: "*Es war die höchste Zeit, die Ergologie dieser Völker zu sammeln, denn durch den inzwischen ausgebrochenen Krieg ist die autochthone Kultur der Eingebornen so gut wie vernichtet*".
41 Cp. Golding and Modest 2018; Schröder 2013; Zimmerman 2013; Thomas 1991.

References

Appadurai, Arjun. *The Social Life of Things. Commodities in Cultural Perspective*. Cambridge: University Press, 1986.

BHM, Bernisches Historisches Museum, *Jahresbericht(e)*: 1900, 1903, 1905, 1906, 1908 and 1916. Bern.

Drechsler, Horst. *Südwestafrika unter deutscher Kolonialherrschaft: Die grossen Land-und Minengesellschaften (1885–1914)*. Stuttgart: Franz Steiner Verlag, 1996.

Driver, Felix. "Intermediaries and the Archive of Exploration", in: Konishi, Shino, Nugent, Maria, Shellam, Tiffany, ed. *Indigenous Intermediaries: New Perspectives on Exploration Archives*. Canberra: ANU Press and Aboriginal History. 2015. pp. 11–30.

Habermas, Rebekka. "Intermediaries. Kaufleute, Missionare, Forscher und Diakonissen. Akteure und Akteurinnen im Wissenstranfer", in: Habermas, Rebekka and Przyremebel, Alexandra, ed. *Von Käfern, Märkten und Menschen. Kolonialismus und Wissen in der Moderne*. Göttingen: Vandehoeck & Ruprecht, 2013. pp. 27–48.

Habermas, Rebekka and Przyrembel, Alexandra. "Einleitung", in: Habermas, Rebekka and Przyremebel, Alexandra, ed. *Von Käfern, Märkten und Menschen. Kolonialismus und Wissen in der Moderne*. Göttingen: Vandehoeck & Ruprecht, 2013. pp. 9–26.

Konishi, Shino, Nugent, Maria and Shellam, Tiffany (Eds.). *Indigenous Intermediaries: New Perspectives on Exploration Archives*. Canberra: ANU Press and Aboriginal History, 2015.

Penny, Glenn. *Objects of Culture. Ethnology and Ethnographic Museums in Imperial Germany*. Chapel Hill and London: University of North Carolina Press, 2002.
Przyrembel, Alexandra. "Empire, Medien und die Globalisierung von Wissen im Jahrhundert. Einführung", in: Habermas, Rebekka and Przyrembel, Alexandra, eds. *Von Käfern, Märkten und Menschen. Kolonialismus und Wissen in der Moderne*. Göttingen: Vandehoeck & Ruprecht, 2013. pp. 197–220.
Purtschert, Patricia and Fischer-Tiné, Harald, ed. *Colonial Switzerland. Rethinking Colonialism from the Margins*. Imperial & Post-Colonial Studies. Cambridge: Palgrave Macmillan, 2015.
Schorch, Philipp, Mccarthy, Conal and Dürr, Eveline. "Introduction: Conceptualising Curatopia", in: Schorch, Philipp and McCarthy, Conal, eds. *CURATOPIA. Museums and the Future of Curatorship*. Manchester: University Press, 2018. pp. 1–18.
Silvester, Jeremy and Shiweda, Napandulwe. "The Return of the Sacred Stones of the Ovambo Kingdoms: Restitution and the Revision of the Past", in: Schorch, Philipp, ed. *Museum & Society*, vol. 18, no. 1. Leicester: University Press, 2020. pp. 31–39.
Thomas, Nicholas. *Entangled Objects. Exchange, Material Culture, and Colonialism in the Pacific*. Cambridge, MA; London: Harvard University Press, 1991.
Vogel, Jakob. "Public-Private Partnerships. Das koloniale Wissen und seine Ressourcen im langen 19. Jahrhundert. Einführung", in: Habermas, Rebekka and Przyrembel, Alexandra, eds. *Von Käfern, Märkten und Menschen. Kolonialismus und Wissen in der Moderne*. Göttingen: Vandehoeck & Ruprecht, 2013. pp. 261–284.
Zimmerman, Andrew. "*Bewegliche Objekte und globales Wissen. Die Kolonialsammlungen des Königlichen Museums für Völkerkunde in Berlin*", in: Habermas, Rebekka and Przyrembel, Alexandra, eds. *Von Käfern, Märkten und Menschen. Kolonialismus und Wissen in der Moderne*. Göttingen: Vandehoeck & Ruprecht, 2013. pp. 247–258.

Archival Files Cited

BHM, Bernisches Historisches Museum, archival ref. no.: A.001.036: *Sammlung V. Solioz. Korrespondenz; Transkription der Korrespondenz*, 1903–2018.
BHM, Bernisches Historisches Museum, archival ref. no.: A.001.037: *Sammlung W. A. Volz. Inventare; Korrespondenz; Manuskript "Die Industrien der Eingebornen. Die Herstellung des afrikanischen Gewebes"; Fotografien zu verschiedenen Themen (Webstuhl, Töpferei, Piassona, Kürbisse, Fischerei, Musikinstrumente, Stöcke, Flechtarbeiten, Körbe, Löffel, Kämme, Holzarbeiten)*, 1906–1909.
BHM, Bernisches Historisches Museum, archival ref. no.: A.001.002.001: *Originalkatalog der Sammlung Solioz: Ovambo etc*, 1906.
BHM, Bernisches Historisches Museum, archival ref. no.: A.001.002.002: *Originalkatalog der Sammlung Solioz: Herero*, 1906.
NAN, National Archives of Namibia, archival ref. no.: NAN EVE 42 A.10.A.1 1: *Verkehr mit der Firma Koppel*, 1902–1906.
NAN, National Archives of Namibia, archival ref. no.: NAN EVE 281 36 1: *Betriebsleitung Otavi, Koppel Akten*, 1904–1905.

NAN, National Archives of Namibia, archival ref. no.: NAN BBW 11 B6: *Otavi Minen- und Eisenbahngesellschaft*, 1905–1912.
NAN, National Archives of Namibia, archival ref. no.: NAN BBW 11 B6A 1: *OMEG Geschäftberichte*, 1905–1914.
RKolA, REICHSKOLONIALAMT, Archive, RKolA No. 2112, 60-86 Solioz to Golinelli, 19.01.1904.

Further References

Beckmann, Gitte, ed. *"Man muss eben Alles sammeln". Der Zürcher Botaniker und Forschungsreisende Hans Schinz und seine ethnographische Sammlung Südwestafrika*. Zürich: Verlag NZZ/Völkerkundemuseum der Universität Zürich, 2012.
Cladders, Lukas. *Das Basler Museum für Völkerkunde. Grundzüge einer Sammlungsgeschichte zwischen 1914–1945*. Basel: Museum der Kulturen Basel, 2015.
Förster, Larissa. "Der Umgang mit der Kolonialzeit. Provenienz und Rückgabe", in: Edenheiser, Iris and Förster, Larissa, ed. *Museumsethnologie. Eine Einführung. Theorien, Debatten, Praktiken*. Berlin: Dietrich Reimer Verlag 2018. pp. 78–103.
Golding, Viv and Modest, Wayne. "Thinking and Working through Difference: Remaking the Ethnographic Museum in the Global Contemporary", in: Schorch, Philipp and McCarthy, Conal, eds. *CURATOPIA. Museums and the Future of Curatorship*. Manchester: University Press, 2018. pp. 29–43.
Habermas, Rebekka and Przyrembel, Alexandra, ed. *Von Käfern, Märkten und Menschen. Kolonialismus und Wissen in der Moderne*. Göttingen: Vandehoeck & Ruprecht, 2013.
Kautondokwa, Nehoa Hilma and Silvester, Jeremy. *The Ovaherero and Nama Genocide. Learning from the Past. A Handbook for Teachers*. Windhoek: Museum Association of Namibia, Solitaire Press (Pty) Ltd, 2019.
Krüger, Gesine. "Das goldene Zeitalter der Viehzüchter. Namibia im 19. Jahrhundert", in: Zimmerer, Jürgen and Zeller, Joachim, ed. *Völkermord in Deutsch-Südwestafrika: Der Kolonialkrieg (1904–1908) in Namibia und seine Folgen*. Berlin: Chr. Links, 3rd edition, 2016. pp. 13–25.
Macdonald, Sharon and Morgan, Jennie. "What Not to Collect? Post-connoisseurial Dystopia and the Profusion of Things", in: Schorch, Philipp and McCarthy, Conal, eds. *CURATOPIA. Museums and the Future of Curatorship*. Manchester: University Press, 2019. pp. 29–43.
Reubi, Serge. *Gentlemen, prolétaire et primitifs: institutionnalisation, pratiques de collection et choix muséographiques dans l'ethnographie suisse, 1880–1950*. L'Atelier, Travaux d'Histoire de l'art et de Muséologie, vol. 4, Peter Lang, 2011.
Rüther, Kerstin. "Räume jenseits von Kolonie und Metropole. Einführung", in: Habermas, Rebekka and Przyremebel, Alexandra, ed. *Von Käfern, Märkten und Menschen. Kolonialismus und Wissen in der Moderne*. Göttingen: Vandehoeck & Ruprecht, 2013. pp. 97–114.
Schär, Bernhard, C. *Tropenliebe. Schweizer Naturforscher und niederländischer Imperialismus in Südostasien um 1900*. Frankfurt a. M.: Campus, 2015.
Schorch, Philipp and Mccarthy, Conal (Eds.). *CURATOPIA. Museums and the Future of Curatorship*. Manchester: University Press, 2018.

Schröder, Iris. *"Disziplinen. Zum Wandel der Wissensordnungen im 19. Jahrhundert. Einführung"*, in: Habermas, Rebekka and Przyremebel, Alexandra, eds. *Von Käfern, Märkten und Menschen. Kolonialismus und Wissen in der Moderne.* Göttingen: Vandehoeck & Ruprecht, 2013. pp. 147–161.

Wallace, Marion. *A History of Namibia. From the Beginning to 1990*. London: Hurst & Co. Publishers, 2011.

Zimmerer, Jürgen an Zeller, Joachim (Eds.). *Völkermord in Deutsch-Südwestafrika. Der Kolonialkrieg in Namibia (1904-1908) und die Folgen*. Berlin: Chr. Links, 3rd edition, 2003.

5 Museum Collections in Transit
Towards a History of the Artefacts of the *Endeavour* Voyage[1]

Nicholas Thomas

Artefacts

Artefacts have three qualities that are salient to the revival of material culture studies and to related fields such as the history of collections. First, they are portable; second, they are durable; and third, they are mutable. They are portable in the sense that they are susceptible to being taken, bought, trafficked or otherwise acquired, removed from places of creation or use, and transported over shorter or longer distances, indeed from hemisphere to hemisphere, across continents and oceans, to be relocated in private homes or in institutional settings of one sort or another. They may include large objects, such as actual canoes and houses, or more typically models of boats and houses; or substantial parts of buildings; but even these substantial forms nevertheless can, if typically at considerable cost, be dissembled or cut into pieces, packed and moved. Artefacts are durable or relatively so, meaning that they can be retained and preserved, even if in the case of textiles, paper or fibre assemblages, doing so entails careful attention to their care and the conditions under which they are preserved. Portability and durability are conducive to mutability. Not, or not necessarily in the sense that an object is susceptible to physical adaptation, though it may well be, and museum specimens have commonly been cleaned, painted, conserved or otherwise materially modified. In the sense, rather, that the meanings, values and narrative an artefact bears or is associated with may be more or less profoundly changed – in the direction of both impoverishment and enhancement. The relative physical stability that makes it possible for something to be a museum artefact thus makes it inevitable that its identity is not stable, that it outlives the character and significance that it starts with, or possesses at any given moment.

Provenance

Research into the provenance of artworks, artefacts and archival documents has long been undertaken, particularly in support of the art market. Over recent decades, methods focused on the documentation of ownership and

DOI: 10.4324/9781003282334-7

of transactions have assumed great legal and political significance in the context of the identification and restitution of works appropriated from their owners during the Nazi period, and in relation to antiquities illegally exported from their countries of origin, in some cases to be subsequently acquired by major art museums. Holdings of ethnographic artefacts in Western museums have been contested for decades, the histories of such collections have been intensively scrutinized in recent years, and restitution vigorously advocated. In this context, it has been recognized that 'provenance research' is as necessary to a museum as conservation science; in some countries significant levels of funding have been made available to cultural institutions and independent programmes to undertake it.[2]

Given the prominence of debate around contentious collections, it is not surprising that 'provenance research' has mostly been approached technically and in positivistic terms. Through often painstaking research in auction catalogues and archives, it attends to dates, names and incidents of appropriation, in order to provide 'yes' or 'no' answers to questions of whether artefacts and collections were legitimately or illegitimately acquired. In some instances, a 'traffic light' categorization (amber indicating ambiguity or uncertainty) is employed.

Provenance can also be thought in what, in another context, has been called 'an expanded field'. An 'expanded' conceptualization may be both necessary and productive, given the sheer heterogeneity of the holdings of museums, which may be at issue. Across Cambridge, and similar older universities in Europe, collections were developed through different knowledge frameworks over the early modern and modern periods. They reflect engagement with travel, trade, empire and markets in art, artefacts, specimens, books and documents over centuries, and they embrace natural specimens, scientific instruments, artworks, archaeological finds, ethnographic objects, manuscripts and books. These materials were at various times more or less randomly acquired (through bequests, for example), or actively gathered in support of particular scientific projects. Many disciplines and forms of knowledge were subsequently refocused, and the material infrastructure of the collection, at one time considered essential to advanced comparative inquiry, lost its utility, thus constituting what are referred to as 'orphan collections'. Such 'orphans' may, however, subsequently be rediscovered by their 'parent' discipline or adopted by different disciplines or novel cross-disciplinary fields, and recognized to constitute scholarly resources, albeit in terms entirely different to those envisaged by the makers of such collections, or those who shaped their former institutional contexts.

The instrumental rationale and orientation of provenance research is perforce inattentive to the issues thrown up by an artefact's mutability. The provenance researcher is, in principle, concerned to know how a certain object left one owner at a certain date and reached the hands of another at a later time. How are the intervening transactions to be characterized? Such investigation, in principle, may not consider questions of identity (things are not only what they were but what they are becoming), nor matters of narrative. That is, what stories do people concerned want to tell about the history of particular artefacts? How are those stories morally inflected? Among past and present owners, who is credited with agency? And what future does historical narrative point towards?

Thinking Provenance, Cross-Culturally

It is to state the obvious to say that provenance doesn't matter in the same terms to all of those concerned. In the case of an antiquity taken by agents of the Nazi regime from a Jewish family in Germany after 1933, the salient fact is that the piece was legally owned by them prior to its appropriation; how they acquired it, where it came from and how it was initially obtained from an archaeological site are irrelevant. Yet this may be so in less predictable respects. If a Pacific artefact was acquired by a European naval officer during an eighteenth- or nineteenth-century voyage of exploration, the issue from the perspective of provenance research, undertaken at the direction of museum management, is one of legitimacy. Was it seized or stolen? Or was it willingly and fairly exchanged? An Islander may well be interested in that question. But he or she may be more interested in the question of *from whom* it was acquired. It may, for example, be well documented that the object came from a certain island, or was acquired during a visit to a particular harbour. But that information may be insufficient, if the piece was taken from or sold by a person or people associated with any one of a number of different local groups. This may be – and actually is, as I discuss below – a critical question insofar as the descendants of people associated with those groups remain interested parties today. That is, if the question now arises of *who speaks for these artefacts?*

The Artefacts of the *Endeavour* Voyage

For over a century, the collections of art and artefacts made during the voyages of Captain James Cook to the Pacific have been studied by archaeologists, anthropologists, historians and museum curators. Research that might at one time have appeared antiquarian and arcane now has growing academic, cultural and political resonance. Most obviously, historic artefacts are of profound significance for Indigenous people, as embodiments of ancestral agency, culture and ways of life. The Gweagal (Sydney region) elder, Shayne Williams, has, for example, said of early artefacts collected during Cook's voyages that 'For us, they feel like our national treasure'. From the perspective of academic inquiry, ethnographic collections are at the crux of work on cross-cultural relationships, travel, exploration, cosmopolitan science and the histories of collecting, art markets and scientific institutions.

All historic artefacts potentially speak across such fields, and of course, also are the stuff at issue, in the restitution debate. But the collections made on Cook's three voyages are acutely significant, particularly in places such as Australia, Hawai'i and New Zealand, where encounters with Cook have long been associated with national narrative. Whether the meetings were 'first contacts' or not (both New Zealand and Australia had been visited by Dutch and other navigators well before Cook), they have long been construed as foundational and have accordingly been celebrated and lamented in varied terms over time. What might be called the convenient notoriety of the historical events was exemplified at the start of the pandemic, in a comment posted on social media on 29 April 2020 by Annelise van Diemen, the deputy chief health officer in the state of Victoria: 'Sudden arrival of an invader from another land, decimating populations, creating terror. Forces the population to make enormous sacrifices & completely change how they live in order to survive. COVID19 or Cook 1770?'[3] Whether considered a punchy way of drawing attention to risks to public health or a 'tortured, non-relevant, attempted analogy' (in the view of a conservative member of the Australian senate), the post highlights the contested monumentality of the historic events that constitute these artefacts' contexts.

In the more conventional terms of scholars, curators and connoisseurs, Cook voyage artefacts owed their importance to them being the first from Oceania to enter European collections, with the exception of a handful of pieces associated with the voyages of Dampier, Carteret and Wallis. They have thus long been seen as the most representative of 'traditional' techniques and of styles unaffected by European influence. Though such dubious notions of authenticity and acculturation have been displaced by the more dynamic perspectives of historical anthropology, the associations between Cook voyage artefacts and formative early encounters continue to render the objects the foci of intense interest, for scholars, Indigenous people and wider publics alike.

From the 1890s through to the 1960s museum curators and ethnographers published occasional papers and monographs on Cook voyage collections, notably those in Florence, Dublin and Stockholm. A decade of Cook bicentenaries from 1969 onward were marked by exhibitions and stimulated new work, inaugurating a body of scholarship that has steadily grown since. From the early 1970s, the US anthropologist Adrienne L. Kaeppler began publishing studies now recognized as seminal, which brought rigorous archival investigation to the identification of artefacts collected during the voyages, and began a career-long inquiry into the late eighteenth-century museum of Sir Ashton Lever.[4] The institution, known as the Holophusicon or Leverian, held over a thousand artefacts from Cook's voyages which were widely dispersed following the sale of the collection in 1806. Given the publication of numerous essays and catalogues since, it might reasonably be presumed that some 50 years of sustained inquiry has by now documented the voyage collections, more or less definitively. Yet Kaeppler's work on the artefacts once in the Leverian Museum made it clear just how challenging the history of collections could be. An assemblage of artefacts which was at one time in a single institution has suffered astonishing dispersal, in some instances passing through the hands of many private collectors and their descendants, and through museums that themselves were periodically divided, reconstituted, amalgamated and renamed, ending up in dozens of institutions in many countries. The evidence for objects' movements was often limited to marginalia in printed auction catalogues, documents that were themselves extremely scarce, in some cases known through a single extant copy.

Both the interviewer and interviewee in an Australian morning news programme discussing an initiative to return Aboriginal cultural heritage from northern hemisphere museums made the understandable assumption – given that Cook's voyages were official British naval expeditions – that the artefacts might primarily be in the British Museum. But Cook voyage objects are in fact distributed across institutions in at least 14 countries, and the British Museum's collection is not the largest. Poor records make it very difficult to establish how many Cook voyage pieces are in the British Museum – perhaps 200 to 250 from all three voyages – but there are about as many, or more in Vienna, Berlin, Göttingen, Dublin, Oxford and Cambridge as well as smaller collections in many other museums.

Inquiry into the artefacts collected during Cook's voyages thus still has a long way to go. Much of the recent wave of research has been undertaken by curator-scholars on the collections that they themselves are responsible for, which therefore has had an institution-specific focus. This chapter aims to evoke the complex trajectories of artefacts which at one time constituted a single collection. Its scope is thus not the holdings of any particular museum, but the collections made during a single expedition, in this case Cook's first voyage, undertaken in a single ship, the *Endeavour*, over 1768 to 1771 (Figure 5.1).

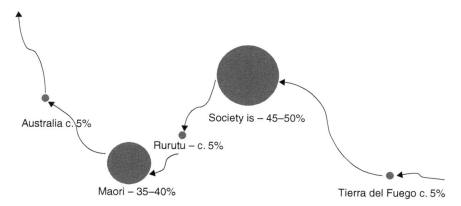

Figure 5.1 Collections made during the voyage of the *Endeavour*, 1768–1771, illustrating the likely proportions of artefacts collected during encounters in the places shown.

Fewer artefacts were collected by participants on this voyage than during the second or third expeditions, not least because the interest in material brought back on the *Endeavour* stimulated a market, and prompted everyone from ordinary seamen to officers and naturalists to assemble collections subsequently. The first voyage collection was made up of fewer artefacts from a more limited range of cultures than those of the second and third voyages. But it has a distinctive, foundational character. It appears to have been the very first collection made of Indigenous material culture by Europeans in the field, which was documented systematically and subsequently deposited in educational institutions. There were, of course, all sorts of precursors – individual artefacts from the New World and elsewhere had reached the Ashmolean and the Museum Wormianum in Copenhagen in the seventeenth century and the British Museum earlier in the eighteenth, but it seems that, before the *Endeavour*, despite a long history of European voyages to remote regions, some with quasi-scientific aims, there was little interest in acquiring artefacts, or, in any case, little interest in documenting or curating artefacts which may have been collected. In effect, it extrapolated the kind of collecting, undertaken for example by the 'apostles' of Linnaeus and other scientists of the period from plants, animals and mineralogical samples to what were at the time called 'artificial curiosities'. These pieces were moreover typically contemporary 'implements', 'utensils' or 'ornaments', they were things *in use*, rather than antiquities or relics of the kinds long gathered by travellers within Europe. If, needless to say, there were many continuities between the collections of the voyages and various precursors, those of the 1770s nevertheless inaugurated new modes of collecting, a new and sometimes prolific market in ethnographic material, and the novel representation of non-Western culture in private, civic, educational and national collections and institutions.

This chapter offers a sketch map for a fuller future inquiry. It addresses questions that appear simple: what artefacts were collected? Where from? How many? What became of them? Where are they now? These cannot be answered, other than very provisionally. Here the aim is to begin to explain some of the many empirical and conceptual complexities present around seemingly simple questions and indicate what is at stake in inquiries that perhaps look like a postcolonial antiquarianism.

The Voyage

The years following the war of 1758–1763 enabled scientific co-operation among European nations that were otherwise almost continually involved in conflict. One aspect of co-operation was a co-ordinated effort to observe the Transit of Venus of 1769 from many points around the world. It was hoped that precise observations would enable, for the first time, an accurate measurement of the distance between the earth and the sun. The ostensible purpose of the *Endeavour* voyage was to undertake the observations from

Tahiti, which from a European perspective had been discovered just a few years earlier by Captain Samuel Wallis. Following initially violent encounters with the local Polynesian people, peace had been made, and it was therefore anticipated that Cook and a party of astronomers and naturalists might be able to establish a secure shore base from which the Transit could be observed.

An undeclared purpose of the voyage was to engage in a search for the 'Great South Land' or southern continent, a longstanding object of geographical and commercial speculation, explicitly motivated by a colonial vision of opportunities for lucrative trade. Following the Tahitian sojourn, Cook was secretly instructed to venture south and investigate areas where previous sightings of land had fuelled rumours of the likely location of a continent.

While the voyage's larger story need not be addressed in detail here, the ship passed Tierra del Fuego and made its way to the Society Islands, the archipelago which incorporates Tahiti, where an unusually protracted stay was needed to establish facilities and relationships with locals in the lead-up to the astronomical observations. Afterwards, Cook called at Huahine, in the same archipelago, passed Rurutu in the Austral Islands, and then reached the North Island of New Zealand towards the end of 1769. In order to establish whether New Zealand (previously visited by the Dutch navigator

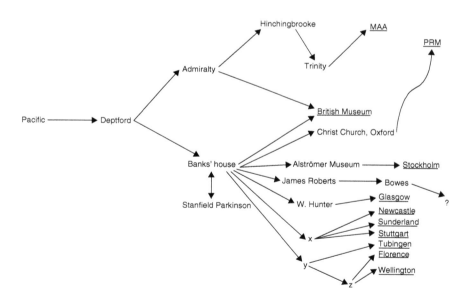

Figure 5.2 The movements and destinations of the artefacts brought back on the *Endeavour*: a selective illustration of the movements of objects between collections and institutions. Those museums underlined hold *Endeavour* voyage artefacts today.

Abel Tasman in the mid-seventeenth century) formed part of any continental mass, he circumnavigated and charted both the North and South Islands, before crossing the Tasman Sea to the eastern Australian coast, which was charted from Point Hicks (which marks the border between the present states of Victoria and New South Wales) and Cape York. There were limited contacts with Indigenous Australians in Botany Bay (later selected as the site for a British penal colony, which was relocated slightly north in Port Jackson and developed into the city of Sydney; hence the notoriety and foundational status of the contacts with the Gweagal people). The ship almost sank on the Great Barrier Reef, but was successfully beached in the Endeavour River in north Queensland for a period of repair, where there were more extended contacts with local people. Following a passage through Torres Strait, the Endeavour returned to England via Batavia and the Cape of Good Hope (Figure 5.2).

Where Did Artefacts Come from?

Contacts with Indigenous peoples and such traffic in artefacts as took place were very different at different stages of the voyage. Those in Tierra del Fuego were brief, involving barter for small ornaments such as shell necklaces and utilitarian things people had with them, such as a bow, quiver and arrows. In the Society Islands, Cook's crew included people who had travelled to the islands before and already had some familiarity with the language. While this must have been basic, some among the crew were linguistically gifted and acquired, over the three-month stay, the capacity to communicate, reflected in the extensive wordlists that were recorded. A significant proportion of crew and officers were based on shore through the period; notwithstanding moments of tension and violence, interaction was mostly cordial and indeed intimate. Polynesians of rank 'exchanged names' (a form of friendship contract) with Cook, Banks and other naturalists and officers, meals and sexual intimacies were extensively shared, and towards the end of the stay, Cook, Banks and others undertook a tour on foot around the greater part of the island's coast. On departing from Tahiti, Huahine and other parts of the archipelago were visited. Under these circumstances, it is not surprising that Europeans took away a very wide range of artefacts, including many significant higher-status objects, which appear to have been gifted in ceremonial contexts, but notably including many kinds of things, from fish hooks and fabrics to musical instruments. There was no deliberate effort to assemble a representative collection, but because collecting ended up being so extensive, the resulting assemblage – distributed among a number of different actors on the vessel – had something approaching a representative character.

Following the period in the Society Islands, just a few pieces changed hands off Rurutu in the Austral Islands, in the course of fleeting contact. This was, notably, offshore exchange, between canoe and ship, so the local partners offered items that they happened to have in their canoe. As Europeans did not land, they had no opportunity to seek objects they were not immediately offered.

Contacts over the extended cruise around the coastlines of Aotearoa were also varied. Over the initial period there was much violence, and more Indigenous people were killed during initial confrontations around Poverty Bay and subsequently than at any other point in Cook's three voyages, up until the aftermath of his own death in Hawai'i in 1779. However, other interactions were more cordial and at times as friendly as those in Tahiti. There was much barter between the ship and canoes at various locations; some artefacts of great *mana* (spiritual power) were presented, most likely to the Society Islands priest and navigator, Tupaia, who accompanied and guided Cook and Banks but died in Batavia on the voyage back to England. Others were presented or sold to officers, naturalists and crew members under varied circumstances. Again, though neither Cook nor Banks explicitly expressed an interest in assembling a representative collection, the range of material gathered was very wide, and included weapons, paddles, vessels, musical instruments, fish hooks, tattooing implements and garments, notably including large woven flax capes with decorated borders.

On the Australian coast, at both Kamay (Botany Bay) and Cooktown in the north, the experience was entirely different. Indigenous Australians resisted the intrusion, were cautious, and avoided or ignored those mariners who did land. There was slightly more interaction at Cooktown, enabling the transcription of a short vocabulary (when the word kangaroo was famously first recorded by a European visitor), but there is no record of any actual barter. The Australian artefacts obtained during the voyage were primarily spears, appropriated from a camp, very soon after first landing; a shield, also taken on the same occasion; and possibly other pieces picked up under similar circumstances.

How Many Were Collected?

In an important passage about the acquisition of artefacts in his second voyage journals, Cook made it clear that while large numbers of artefacts were eagerly sought and acquired, not all were retained: some mariners gave things from island away at another, or used them to traffic for unfamiliar things that aroused their curiosity; other artefacts, he wrote, were simply lost, disposed of, or broken. Hence the numbers eventually brought back to England represent only a proportion of what was at one time received or taken.

For example, it is recorded that following Gweagal resistance on 28 April 1770, the British took away some '40 to 50' spears, which they feared were poisoned; this was thus in the first instance an operation of disarmament, rather than ethnographic collecting. It was quickly realized that the spears were for fishing and were not poisoned, but there is no indication that any of the number were therefore returned. How many actually reached England is unclear; the three multi-pronged fishing spears and one lance at the Museum of Archaeology and Anthropology in Cambridge are the only examples that are extant and documented today, but there is evidence that others were in other collections in the eighteenth century.

No overall inventory of objects on the Endeavour appears ever to have been prepared, but data provides some basis for an estimate of the number of artefacts brought back on the ship. The picture can be summarised as follows. The voyage naturalist and scientific entrepreneur Joseph Banks was individually probably the most avid collector, and some or most artefacts acquired by his assistants were, together with natural specimens, treated as part of their employer's collection. Cook himself was certainly presented with objects, he may have actively sought them, and he may have gathered together objects acquired by other mariners, if he at some point formed the view that the collection was a semi-official part of the voyage's findings or record. That he did think in such terms is suggested by the fact that soon after the ship reached the dock, at Deptford in the Thames, he forwarded several boxes of artefacts with a letter and a partial list to Lord Sandwich, his patron at the Admiralty. It is not explicit in the letter that this presentation represented any kind of official deposit, rather than a personal gift. On the one hand the fact that the material was delivered to Sandwich at the Admiralty rather than his residence might suggest the former; the fact that Sandwich then had the artefacts or most of them taken to his country house not far from Cambridge in contrast implies the latter.

The two sources which hint at the range and size of the entire assemblage are first, the single largest collection with a documented association with the first voyage, which is at the Museum of Archaeology and Anthropology at the University of Cambridge, and second, a substantial series of drawings of artefacts in Banks' possession, meticulously executed for him by John Frederick Miller, a scientific artist of German descent who was then a member of his scientific staff (British Library Add. Ms. 15508).

It is known that Sandwich retained some of the artefacts that Cook gave him. The bulk, however, was divided between the British Museum and Trinity College, Cambridge. The gift to Trinity, Sandwich's alma mater, was fully listed at the time of transfer, within three months of the Endeavour's return, and the 102 artefacts, which include objects from Tierra del Fuego, the Society Islands, Ruruta, New Zealand and Australia, are all extant. They remain the property of the College but were placed 'on deposit' at MAA in two stages, in 1914 and 1924, and since then the Museum has managed care, conservation and curation, including loan to exhibitions elsewhere in Britain and in North America, Europe, Australia and New Zealand. Some of the artefacts bear parchment labels, and there are similar parchment labels associated with a number of artefacts at the British Museum, but the BM holds no listing of material presented by Sandwich, though a presentation certainly was made at about the same time as the gift to Trinity. There is no particular reason to assume that the collection was evenly divided between London and Cambridge, but if that assumption is made, and if it assumed that only a comparatively small number of artefacts was retained by Sandwich personally (which is suggested by the fact that his descendants in the early twentieth century gave the few pieces they had to MAA), that would imply that Cook sent over 200, but probably fewer than 250 artefacts to the Admiralty in 1771.

Miller's drawings, now among extensive Banks papers, including other Endeavour voyage visual records, at the British Library number 30, depicting a total of 108 artefacts. It is clear that those illustrated can only have been a representative sample. Although just a few can be matched with pieces in the British Museum, the University of Tübingen and in one case in a private collection, artefacts in Oxford collections known to have been collected during the first voyage and donated by Banks are in some cases of similar genres, but the examples are not the same. And while Miller's drawings are, we may assume, of a representative sample of three-dimensional objects, he made no attempt to depict textiles, such as woven Maori flax cloaks, or smaller or larger pieces of barkcloth from Tahiti or elsewhere; Banks certainly owned examples of both woven and beaten fabrics. If the drawings are of a selection of artefacts, it is hard to say whether that selection is likely to have represented a tenth of the collection, half the collection or some larger proportion. In the absence of any helpful pointer, it could be assumed that at the time the Endeavour returned, there was some equivalence between the collection held by Cook, which he sent on to Sandwich, and the collection of Banks, though it would not be surprising if Banks, charged with natural history, hence with collecting, was considered the appropriate holder of a larger group of artefacts than the expedition's commander. Banks cannot have brought back fewer than about 150 artefacts, excluding textiles, since those in the drawings and those he is otherwise known to have owned (now in Oxford or elsewhere) add up to near that figure. If it is assumed that he also possessed a dozen or so Maori woven capes and cloaks, and a similar number of larger sheets of Tahitian barkcloth (as well as, probably, a larger number of tapa samples) the minimum number of artefacts he owned must have been about 180; it is likely that his collection was larger, perhaps by a considerable margin.

By the second and third voyages, it is clear that many individual sailors, as well as other officers, made their own collections of artefacts. This was in part because the enthusiastic interest in material brought back on the first voyage generated a market in Pacific curiosities: objects were subsequently acquired in part specifically for financial gain. This was not the case during the first voyage itself, but it may be presumed that a number of participants brought back pieces as souvenirs; how many individuals did so, how many artefacts they might typically have owned, is more or less impossible to determine. The only documented collection owned by a more junior participant is that of Banks' artist, Sidney Parkinson. He had died at Cape Town on the return voyage, but his journal was published by his brother, and it included two engraved images, one depicting Society Islands, the other Maori artefacts, showing a total of 53 pieces. Again, we have no idea whether this was just a sample, the bulk or all of what Parkinson owned; again, the images included none of the flat textiles, which could not be intelligibly depicted in this kind of print. But if we believe that Cook sent Sandwich 220–250 artefacts, and that the commander also retained some personally, the collection of a young draughtsman is unlikely to have been nearly as extensive. It may be reasonable to assume that the 53, plus say a dozen fabrics, amounted to most of what Parkinson had owned, adding up to say 70–80 pieces in total.

While this reasoning is entirely but unavoidably speculative, a conservative conclusion is that at least 500 Pacific artefacts were brought back to England on the Endeavour. That number would have consisted of about 250 pieces from the Society Islands, some 220 from Aotearoa New Zealand and the remainder from Tierra del Fuego, Rurutu, eastern Australia and New Guinea. The figure of 500 may well be a significant underestimate, if Banks in fact returned with many more artefacts than Cook. Given the naturalist's enthusiasm and acquisitiveness, it is, on balance, likely that he did collect more than these cautious estimates suggest; Endeavour collections may hence have totalled 600 to 800 objects.

Where Are They Now?

The picture has been as unclear as the preceding discussion implies, in part because the trajectories and destinations of the collections have been far wider than might be assumed. A provisional diagram attempts to map only some paths that these artefacts in transit have followed.

As was stated earlier, a reasonable assumption might have been that voyage collections would primarily have been deposited at the British Museum, as some material indeed was. The relevant deposits include one from Sandwich and the Admiralty of 1771. It is unfortunate that records for the period refer to groups of acquisitions but not individual artefacts, so that while it may be assumed that the group was similar in numbers and range to what went to Trinity that is unclear, and there are only half a dozen BM objects linked with the parchment labels associated with the Sandwich transfer.

Joseph Banks was also a significant donor to the British Museum, but the provenances of what he gave are complicated by two considerations. The first is that he made no deposit in the immediate aftermath of the Endeavour voyage, but did give material in 1778 (following the return of Cook's second voyage), in 1780 (after the third) and possibly subsequently, as he also referred in correspondence in 1782 to having sent substantial loads of artefacts, possibly referring to the two listed deposits, or to some other transfer. In other words, the earliest of these gifts presumably combined first and second voyage material, and later gifts combined materials from all three voyages.

But the history of Banks's collections is complicated above all for a different reason. By 1784, he was said to be annoyed that the materials he had sent across to the Museum, or some of them, remained unpacked, unsorted and uncatalogued. He therefore gave his friend and scientific associate Johan Christian Fabricius, a Danish zoologist, and two of Fabricius's friends, the opportunity to go to the BM and take away as much of this material as they wished. Fabricius 'received no small quantity of different objects' and anticipated that he would 'certainly have some trouble in transporting everything of this precious freight' back to the continent. The names of Fabricius's friends, presumably also European scientific associates, are not known. While a number of museums in Britain, France, Germany and Denmark hold parts of Fabricius's zoological collections, none retain ethnographic artefacts that were at one time in his possession. What appears to have been a substantial part of Banks's collection of 'artificial curiosities', derived from his own participation in the first voyage, as well as from others on the second and third, thus evidently reached continental Europe in this way during the 1780s. But there appears to be no information as to how many artefacts travelled, and only oblique indications of what became of them.

This makes it easier to understand that first voyage objects appear in collections in many institutions, in cities including Florence, Stuttgart, Wellington, Tübingen, Stockholm, Glasgow, Newcastle, Sunderland and Brighton. The British Museum and the universities of Cambridge and Oxford were 'primary' destinations for voyage artefacts, in the sense that Sandwich and the Admiralty presented material directly to the BM and to Trinity, as Banks later did to Christ Church, an Oxford college (while, following the second voyage, Johann Reinbold Forster likewise presented material to Oxford). The university donations ended up being physically located in different institutions (the Pitt Rivers and MAA) to those they were originally presented to (though in the case of Cambridge, Trinity remains the owner of the collection), but these were nevertheless in effect direct transfers of a field collection to collecting and educational institutions. The other British, European and New Zealand institutions that now hold first voyage objects were, on the other hand, not 'primary' destinations in this sense. Artefacts appear in the first instance to have been given by Banks to scientific colleagues or associates who presented them in turn to scientific societies, or passed them down to descendants, who in some cases sold them.

There is a more general point to be made in this context about tracing provenance. In some instances the circumstances of field collection are established through documentation. A succession of labels, sale documents, lists, registers, catalogues or similar records enables a work to be firmly associated with a maker and an acquisition history. The four spears in Cambridge are known to be from Kamay, from Botany Bay, because they are listed in the 1771 register for the Cook-Sandwich collection, given to Trinity College in October of that year. There can be no doubt that they were brought back on the Endeavour at that time. They are not artefacts obtained at a later date, or from some other place. Yet conversely, it is possible for pieces for which no chain of documentation is extant to be provenanced in a similar, specific way, because the distinctive qualities of the artefacts themselves in effect document their origins. A salient example concerns a group of *hoe*, Maori canoe paddles. These were passed to members of the Endeavour's crew at a very early stage in interaction, off the shores of the great opening that Cook called Poverty Bay (as he was disappointed by the resources available), the location of the modern town of Gisborne, on the east coast of New Zealand's North Island. On 12 October 1769, mariners interacted with Maori in a canoe who were said to be eager, not to obtain European commodities, but pieces of beaten Tahitian barkcloth which they were offered in trade. As the men in the canoe had little with them other than their paddles, they exchanged the bulk of those with the seamen, having, it was observed, barely sufficient left among them to paddle back to the shore.

The *hoe* are remarkable artefacts in themselves, as they feature kowhaiwhai, a highly distinctive Maori painting style known much better from the painted rafters of meeting houses and certain other artefacts than from portable forms such as paddles. Yet this group constitute the earliest artefacts known to bear the complex curvilinear designs, represented through a series of distinctive variations – none of the paddles are the same. The artistic interest of the works was immediately recognized, in the sense that Banks's draughtsman, Sydney Parkinson, made a watercolour of three of the paddles. Importantly, however, what distinguishes the artefacts as a group is not only the painting, but a highly distinctive approach to the carving of what is referred to as the loom, the part of the object that connects the blade to the shaft. So far as is known, all the paddles collected on this occasion feature a bold combination of motifs distinguished by a denticulate, heavily incised structure.

These taonga are of enormous significance on a number of counts: as some of the very first Maori taonga obtained by any European, as the first exemplars of kowhaiwhai, as objects that can be associated with a particular Maori community, and so on. However, from the perspective of this essay, they are important also as *markers*. Their trajectories and destinations, in so far as they can be traced, suggest the potential trajectories of a wider range of Endeavour voyage artefacts, that cannot themselves be reconstructed or documented.

Given what has already been said about the initial primary division of the collections on the ship between Cook and Banks, the indication that other senior or junior participants also personally held artefact collections, and on the one hand the relatively coherent path of the material owned by Cook, from the ship to the Admiralty and then to the British Museum and

112 *Nicholas Thomas*

to Trinity, and on the other hand the notably more dispersed circulation of Banks-owned material, it might be assumed that a 'set' or artefacts of this kind might have been shared between Cook and Banks, and in turn by the various recipients of their collections. And indeed this is the case – two of the *hoe* are in Cambridge, and two are in the British Museum. Yet research undertaken over a number of years by Amiria Salmond, Billie Lythberg and Steve Gibbs, a Ngai Tamanuhiri artist from the area, that involved workshops in Gisborne as well as study visits to various European collections revealed in due course that examples in the Hancock Museum (now part of the Great North Museum, Newcastle) and in London matched pieces depicted by Parkinson and Miller, while another at Te Papa in Wellington appeared to match one depicted in a well-known portrait of Joseph Banks by Benjamin West. Further examples identified by various curators have been found in Oxford, Naples, Glasgow, Stuttgart and Stockholm. Not all the feature kowhaiwhai painting, but close affinities in the carving of the grips go beyond similarities of style, pointing to the work of the same carver, and a strong likelihood that most if not all of the paddles formed part of a set made for those who crewed a particular waka or canoe, probably made by the canoe-sculptors, and were stylistically and aesthetically consistent

Figure 5.3 The *hoe* collected in October 1769 in the collection of the Museum of Archaeology and Anthropology, Cambridge; on display in the 'Oceania' exhibition, Royal Academy of Arts, London, September–December 2018.

with the vessel itself, and all acquired by those on board the Endeavour on the same occasion (Figure 5.3).

The set may include as many as 18–20 paddles. In some instances, the passages of these artefacts from voyage participants to the museums that currently hold them can be straightforwardly reconstructed. As was noted earlier, the third voyage actor after Cook and Banks who held something over 50 pieces was Sydney Parkinson. He died during the voyage and his effects including his collection passed to his brother Stanfield Parkinson, who was subsequently involved in something of a feud with Banks, prior to financial settlement that enabled Banks to assume control of works, records and artefacts of Parkinson's. Some artefacts were however sold to the naturalist Fothergill (who had attempted to mediate the conflict) and those were subsequently sold or bequeathed to the eminent surgeon and collector William Hunter. His London museum was bequeathed to the University of Glasgow and re-established there. Though no documentation links the *hoe* in the Hunterian collections today with Parkinson, he was almost certainly the source, and Fothergill almost certainly the intermediary, which resulted in these and probably other Endeavour pieces reaching Hunter in the 1770s or early 1780s.

Similarly, a major donation by Banks of voyage artefacts to two Swedish naturalists, the Alstromers, was at first in their private museum, subsequently in those of the royal scientific academy and of state museums, and now in the Etnografiska Museet, Stockholm. The Banks gift was documented though a detailed 1961 publication, which however confuses pieces likely to have been acquired by Banks himself during the first voyage with others he received from second or third voyage participants such as Johann Reinhold Forster. (In other words, a single 'collection' is in fact composed of several field collections, made by different people at different times.) The 1961 volume was moreover incomplete: two *hoe* which clearly belong to the 'set' collected on 12 October 1769 were only recently discovered by Aoife O'Brien. Though the artefacts' identification was a surprise, it is not unexpected given the presence in the museum of a significant yet incompletely documented group of artefacts from Banks.

In other institutions, such as the Linden Museum in Stuttgart, the *hoe* which have been identified have no obvious connection with any participant in the eighteenth-century voyage. It may be most likely that they were among the pieces taken away from the BM in 1784, by Fabricius or one of his associates, that were subsequently passed on to others in Germany.

Does It Matter?

Investigations of this kind may be endless. If, returning to one of the initial conclusions, more than 500 artefacts were brought back on the Endeavour, it is not at all easy to locate and document more than approximately 150 of those now. Further research may well establish links between the voyage of

1768–1771 and artefacts that are at present seen merely as unprovenanced Tahitian or Maori pieces; it may prove possible to trace further some artefacts, such as a shield taken away from Kamay, from Botany Bay, at the same time as the spears, which is known to have been auctioned in Lincolnshire following the death of a servant of Banks who was a voyage participant. Is the detective work, of tracing objects of this kind simply a form of antiquarianism, that has nothing to contribute to social, cultural and historical analysis in the epoch of the digital humanities and of contemporary theory?

The questions of where an eighteenth-century fish hook has ended up, or of when and where a painted paddle that survives in a museum today was collected, may indeed seem arcane and inconsequential. But there is a broader case, that such inquiry is not 'still' important, but has new importance, precisely because disciplines such as history, art history and anthropology are reconfigured as decentred global disciplines, focusing in particular on north-south transactions, histories of encounter, travel, knowledge, science and colonization. In this context, the formative passages of these histories have proved compellingly interesting, not only to scholars trained and based in northern hemisphere universities and museums. Early voyages and expeditions, their encounters and confrontations with Indigenous peoples, and the collections they made, have increasingly fertile for Indigenous artists, writers, researchers and curators, in many countries including Aotearoa, Australia and various Pacific nations (Figure 5.4).

The artefacts collected during these voyages were at one time 'ethnological specimens', notionally representative of technologies and cultures at particular stages of their development. They then attracted interest as 'primitive art', again unevenly. But over recent decades their importance has been increasingly recognized in historical terms. Not exemplifications of an ahistorically conceived ethnicity or culture, they are seen as expressions of Indigenous art traditions at specific moments, and – as collections – as products of moments of encounter, exchange and appropriation. And of course they represent exceptionally important bodies of cultural heritage. Over recent years they have been 'in transit' in new ways, not only studied in European museums by Indigenous people, but taken back to 'Country' (to use the Australian term) or to local tribal terrain and to sites such as marae (tribal ritual precincts) in New Zealand. These travels have moreover involved not just standard exhibition loans, that involve the transfer of material, supervised by conservators, into display cases. Recently, a significant group of artefacts which travelled to the Tairawhiti Museum, Gisborne, for an extended exhibition which marked the 250th anniversary of the Endeavour's arrival went first to a local marae. There, some were removed from the art shipper's crates, and incorporated into the performance of a ceremonial welcome. Subsequently, the taonga were accessible for hands-on

Figure 5.4 Hoe from Cambridge, the British Museum and other UK institutions in Gisborne, Aotearoa, New Zealand. In late September 2019, community collections-study events took place prior to the installation of artefacts for the 'Tū te Whaihanga' exhibition (September 2019–May 2022).

access and study on the part of community members over a number of days, before the installation of the exhibition proceeded. Similarly, artefacts including three of the four Gweagal spears, back on ancestral land for the first time in 250 years, have been not only exhibited but made accessible for direct, private, small-group community access. As William Faulkner famously observed of the past, these artefacts are not dead, 'not even past'. They are animate, spiritually alive, and in transit, in new ways and with renewed energy.

Notes

1 This chapter outlines a larger project. It draws upon earlier studies of the collections of the Museum of Archaeology and Anthropology (Thomas 2016, 2018) as well as a related literature (Coote 2015); and on conceptual argument regarding the lives of artefacts and the constitution of collections (e.g. Thomas 2016).
2 See, for example, writings by Larissa Forster and her colleagues.
3 'Victorian defends deputy chief medical officer after she compared James Cook with Covid-19', *Guardian* 30 April 2020.
4 Kaeppler 1978, 2011.

References

Coote, Jeremy, ed. *Cook-Voyage Collections of 'Artificial Curiosities' in Britain and Ireland, 1771–2015*. Oxford: Museum Ethnographers' Group, 2015.

Kaeppler, Adrienne. *"Artificial Curiosities": Being an Exposition of Native Manufactures Collected on the Three Pacific Voyages of Captain James Cook, R.N.* Honolulu: Bishop Museum Press, 1978.

———. *Holophusicon: The Leverian Museum*. Altenstadt: ZKF, 2011

Thomas, Nicholas. *The Return of Curiosity: What Museums Are Good for in the Twenty-first Century*. London: Reaktion, 2016.

———. "A case of identity: The Artefacts of 1770 Kamay (Botany Bay) encounter." *Australian Historical Studies* 49: 2018. pp. 4–27.

Part II
Heuristic Materiality Meanings and Transformations

6 "To Give Away My Collection for Free Would Be Nonsense"

Decorations and the Emergence of Ethnology in Imperial Germany

Carl Deussen

Introduction

The research leading to this paper was sparked by a curious letter sent by German ethnographer and publicist Wilhelm Joest to the director of the *Koniglijke Museum voor Volkenkunde* in Leiden, Lindor Serrurier, at some date during the mid-1880s.[1] Joest and Serrurier already knew each other at this point and Joest had in 1882 donated a small collection of Ainu artefacts to the museum. Back then, Joest was trying hard to establish himself in the young ethnographic community and thus had divided the valuable collection he had brought from Hokkaido and given it to four major European museums for free. Now, however, he was writing as an already established scientist and this time, he wanted something in return. After some initial reflections on his work in Berlin, Joest cuts to the chase:

> In this regard, I have gotten older and wiser and I want to be open with you about my principles. I never sell parts of my collection, but I will happily present you objects as a donation, provided that you could show me your gratitude in form of a decoration. To give away my collection for free would be nonsense, would it not? In that case I would rather keep it for myself. Now, you will of course completely understand and say: "Sure, if you present us with a nice donation, I will arrange for you to receive a decoration." At least I assume that you share this conviction, which is the only sensible one for a museum director.[2]

Joest then goes on to explain that there was no need to behave like "haggling jews" [Schacherjuden] and to bargain for every single object, but that he was willing to be generous and even buy some additional objects if Serrurier so desired, all that, however, only if he would get his decoration. The letter is remarkable for two reasons. First, it shows the elaborate negotiations that could go on behind the scenes when 19th-century collectors gave their collections to ethnographic museums. Second, it shows how Joest was trying to frame this whole process not as a negotiation, but as a donation with

DOI: 10.4324/9781003282334-9

no bargaining involved. The letter not only raises questions concerning the role of decorations in the acquisition of ethnographic collections, but also how these decorations were conceptualised by the parties involved. In this essay, I will use the life and career of Wilhelm Joest as an initial case study to approach these questions. While the scope of one collector biography is not sufficient to answer them comprehensively, I hope to show that decorations could be an influential factor in ethnographic collecting in 19th-century Imperial Germany and beyond. Approaching decorations as decidedly material representations of collecting and donating in the young field of ethnography, I will argue that they played an important role in the development of ethnographic museums and simultaneously offer a valuable perspective for reflections on the history of these institutions today (Figure 6.1).

Although there has been no exhaustive discussion of decorations and ethnographic collecting so far, various authors have addressed the topic. Both Glenn Penny and Angela Zimmermann, in their monographs on

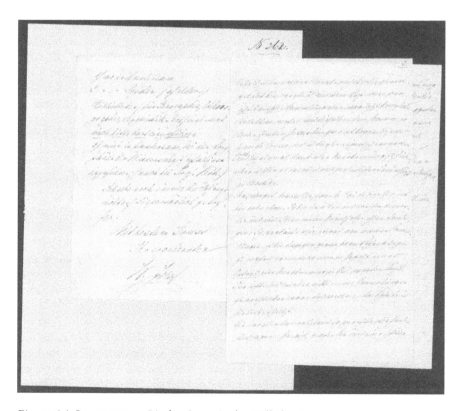

Figure 6.1 Letter sent to Lindor Serrurier by Wilhelm Joest.
© Collection Nationaal Museum van Wereldculturen. Coll.no. NL-LdnRMV_A01_010_00417.

ethnographic collecting in Imperial Germany, briefly indicate the importance of decorations. In *Objects of Culture*, Penny writes extensively about how the creation of networks of possible contributors and collectors was a necessity for ethnographic museums in Imperial Germany. He also mentions decorations, although only in passing.[3] In her monograph *Anthropology and Anti-Humanism*, Zimmermann discusses decorations with a focus on the colonies. She writes that

> [b]ecause the museum of ethnology was a royal museum, retaining traces of its origin as the king's cabinet of curiosities, donations of artifacts could be interpreted as service to the Prussian monarch. Royal orders conferred prestige on their members and gave them the privilege of wearing ribbons and medals with formal attire. Outward signs of social status such as royal orders were particularly important to European colonials.[4]

This interpretation explains why decorations were so useful to ethnographic museums. They were particularly popular with those potential colonial collectors who were closest to the objects desired and equipped with the necessary knowledge and authority to claim them. But a sole focus on the colonies does not explain the high interest a collector like Joest, living in Berlin, showed in decorations. And Joest was not the only collector living in the metropole and craving decorations: Claudia Kalka's short study on the collectors Hermann and Robert Schlagintweit presents a similar case.[5] The brothers Schlagintweit travelled and collected in Tibet and Central Asia and, once they returned, were repeatedly decorated for their donations of collections.

Finally, Rainer Buschmann has written extensively on the topic. In *Anthropology's Global History. The Ethnographic Frontier in German New Guinea, 1870–1935*, he focuses on the strategies of Count Karl von Linden in Stuttgart to attract donors by freely giving out decorations in exchange for donations.[6] Linden had identified what he called the "buttonhole aliment" [Knopflochschmerzen] of potential collectors living in the colonies, referring to a missing medal in their buttonholes. As a count, he was able to bestow decorations and hence he was ready to cure this alignment by generously bestowing decorations on potential donors to the Stuttgart Museum. Buschmann presents a well-interpreted case study, but he limits himself just to Stuttgart and, again, only to collectors residing in the colonies.[7]

There are several reasons for choosing Wilhelm Joest as a case study. First, most studies so far have focused on decorations given to stationary collectors in colonies who possessed only limited expertise in the field of ethnography, if any. Michael O'Hanlon has called these "secondary collections", as opposed to those assembled by actors with a theoretical background.[8] While Joest was not a theoretician such as Adolf Bastian, he was certainly a member of the ethnographic establishment and engaging with his collecting offers the chance of exploring the relationship between decorations and primary collections. Second, most studies have emphasised the perspectives of museums, showing how they gave out decorations to build their network. To look at a collector who received decorations for various institutions shifts this perspective, allowing a better understanding of how collectors moved within the decoration system. Finally, the rich archive documenting the life and career of Wilhelm Joest allows a deeper analysis of the motivations behind his craving for decorations and, as such, also indicates why decorations fell out of style eventually. In this paper, I follow his life closely through the decorations he received, a biographic approach defined not only by the materiality of the collections he amassed, but equally so by the material expressions of his success as a collector that he was wearing on his chest for the world to see.

Decorations and the Emergence of Ethnology in Imperial Germany

On September 3, 1881, after having crossed Siberia by land and while still staying in Moscow, Wilhelm Joest wrote a letter to Adolf Bastian. At this point, Joest had already published some travelogues covering his years-long voyage through Asia, but none of them had been received by the scientific community in Germany. Bastian, on the other hand, held the position of director of the *Königliches Museum für Völkerkunde* in Berlin and was one of the central figures in German ethnology. Hence Joest knew it was Bastian to whom he had to address his plan to become an ethnologist and "to act completely according to scientific standards and to leave behind the 'Globetrotter' fully."[9] After his return to Germany, Joest moved to Berlin and went ahead with his plans. He held two lectures at the *Gesellschaft für Anthropologie, Ethnologie und Urgeschichte* (BGEAU), donated his Ainu collection to four strategically important museums and completed his doctoral thesis on Gorontalo language in 1883. However, these steps did not seem to satisfy his desire for scientific prestige. He could have tried to gain an official position at the museum, the BGEAU or another scientific association. But these were available in a very limited number and near impossible to acquire for a newcomer to the field like Joest. In addition to this general difficulty, it is questionable whether Joest would have wanted such an ordinary position at a museum. His family's sugar trading fortune made Joest financially independent, and he preferred travelling and collecting to a steady job inside a museum. Hence Joest sought a way to demonstrate his legitimacy both within Berlin's academic circles and towards his family and bourgeois social sphere.[10]

This is where decorations came to play a crucial part in Joest's life. After the unification of Germany under Prussian leadership, the conditions for receiving a decoration were propitious. The newly established federal states had all kept the right to bestow honours and except for the Hanseatic city-states, they all did so to some extent.[11] Some smaller states with little political influence in the new *Reich* were especially prone to giving out decorations. Hence it is little surprising that Joest received his first "ethnographic" decoration from the duchy of Saxe-Coburg and Gotha, which was known for its liberal bestowal of titles.[12] There, he received the recently created *Medallie für Kunst und Wissenschaft* [Medal for the Arts and Sciences] for his travel report written on his traversing of Siberia. As this was a medal dedicated to honouring scientific achievement, Joest could claim it without giving objects in return. However, once he had set his eyes on higher decorations, new negotiation tactics seemed to have been required.

Joest had already tried to receive some kind of decoration for the aforementioned donations of Ainu objects. However, he might have underestimated how extensive a collection needed to be and how much lobbying was required to get more than a letter of gratitude. In a letter to Adolf Bernhard Meyer, director of the ethnographic museum in Dresden, he writes that

> in spite of the innumerable crates of objects that I have donated before I got into contact with the Ethnographic Museum [in Dresden], I have had enough negative experiences, I was promised decorations that have never materialized etc. etc. Thus, now my opinion is that we should be frank with each other so that there will not be any difference in the end.[13]

The letter shows that Joest's goal was clear: he wanted to receive a decoration in exchange for his services to the museum. And as the museum was under the King of Saxony's royal patronage, donations could indeed be rewarded with a royal decoration. Shortly before writing this letter, Joest had already been named an official representative of the museum. In the letter itself, he promised Meyer a share of the objects that he would collect during his planned journey to Africa and the Pacific. Such a promise by a wealthy and knowledgeable collector was worth a lot, but not enough to merit a decoration. Accordingly, Joest had to find something he could donate just then.

The promise of future donations explains why Joest was successful shortly thereafter, and for a relatively cheap exchange value. In June 1883, Joest had visited the colonial exhibition in Amsterdam, where he acquired an antique Celadon bowl from Seram. Joest had talked about these bowls during his lecture on Seram at the BGEAU and knew that Meyer was also interested in them. He proceeded to offer the bowl to Meyer on July 5, but the letter does not survive. Thus, it is unclear whether Joest informed Meyer that the bowl he was donating had been bought in Amsterdam.[14] In any case, Meyer was content to receive the rare piece and recommended Joest for a decoration. Already on July 20, Joest received a letter from the General Directorate of the Royal Collections for the Arts and Sciences stating that "His Majesty, the king, has most graciously deigned to award

Figure 6.2 Order of Albrecht, Knight's Cross First Class.
© Münzkabinett Dresden/SKD.

you, in recognition of your services to the science of ethnography and especially to the Royal Ethnographic Museum, the Knight's Cross First Class of the Order of Albrecht".[15] Joest had received his first major decoration in exchange for the celadon bowl and had given his striving for scientific and social recognition a material expression that he could present to the scientific community and, importantly, to persons outside of it.

There followed a row of other decorations received in exchange for collections, from Baden, Braunschweig, again from Saxe-Coburg and Gotha and, finally, from Prussia. Hence, when looking at the energy and other resources Joest invested in being named a Knight of these orders, a question arises regarding the actual role and importance of this exchange of material culture for material insignia: Were they a frivolous side effect of the imperial hunt for ethnografica or can they be seen as closer to the centre, as constitutive? The single case study of Joest does not provide sufficient material to answer these questions comprehensively, but it is occasion enough to formulate a hypothesis. I would argue that the case of Wilhelm Joest shows that in the early phase of ethnology as an organised science, decorations were crucial in determining scientific expertise and provided a pathway for those who wanted to professionalise in a profession not yet existing.

When Joest started his career in the early 1880s, there were no standard forms of ethnological scientific authority available to him – neither could he pursue a doctorate in this profession, nor had there been professorships created that would have distributed authority in the field. There were, of course, the newly created ethnographic museums and the collections that they housed. These collections were increasingly understood as ethnographic and scientific[16] and, in their sprawling materiality, were very effective arguments for why studying "primitive cultures" should be considered a science. This arrangement was working well for the few practitioners working in those museums, but access to these positions was highly competitive.[17] A second form of gaining legitimacy was becoming a collector, but there was a problem. Under the paradigm of salvage ethnography, museums accepted almost everything presented to them, and by everyone. This created an unclear hierarchy among collectors, raising the question who of them were legitimate travelling scientists – *Foschungsreisende* – and not merely colonial officials collecting on the side or, even worse, illegitimate "globetrotters" pretending to be ethnographers. Joest's diaries and published writings are riddled with anxiety concerning his own status and with fierce attacks on potential imposters:

> As of late, just about everyone can travel; there are no distances left uncovered. Countries that seemed hermetically closed only thirty years ago are today already swamped with those travelling for pleasure [Vergnügungsreisende]. In revenge, they are sending us their worst products, which we can no longer regard as novel or exotic.[18]

The quote shows Joest's sense of a world in which his role as an ethnographer was increasingly threatened by amateurs spoiling his pristine destinations, a sentiment that would continue to be relevant to ethnology's self-understanding for the next century. But in Joest's case, this anxiety is explicitly linked to the perceived quality of ethnographic objects and to his own sense of authority in judging them. The question was how he could materialise this authority and differentiate his own collections from those he so dreaded.

In this situation, in which neither universities nor museums could give sufficient credit to those collecting with scientific ambitions, decorations might have played precisely that role. They were imbued with stately authority and could thus provide the necessary legitimacy. Within the realm of the German Empire, their meaning was widely recognised, and they could be worn in various contexts, be they military, stately or academic. Their effectiveness was not only based on their wide currency but also on their excessive materiality. Worn on the chest, these medals made from silver, gold and gemstones looked spectacular, an authority based on splendour. On more than one occasion, Joest notes proudly in his diary that he went to a meeting of the BGEAU in full regalia. And indeed, he must have been a sight to behold (see Figure 6.3). Decorations, more than other titles or positions, had become the major point of reference for Joest's understanding of himself as a scientist. And this understanding was mirrored, if not by all, at least by a part of the ethnological community. When Joest died on his expedition to the island of Santa Cruz, Richard Andree wrote an obituary in the journal *Globus* and noted approvingly that "[Joest], by donating his ethnographic

Figure 6.3 Wilhelm Joest in June of 1896, wearing his uniform as a *Rittmeister* and all his medals.
© Berliner Gesellschaft für Anthropologie, Ethnologie und Urgeschichte, Inventarnummer FS-212.

collection brought from his travels, had earned a dozen of foreign and German decorations".¹⁹ This suggests that decorations did play a role in conferring legitimacy and value onto collectors and their collections in early Imperial German ethnology.

Decorations and the Determination of Value

As the negotiations in the letter to Serrurier cited at the beginning show, how this value was to be determined was far from clear. Various authors have commented on the many ambiguities that defined the determination of ethnographic value. Penny has named an array of categories that played into this process: aesthetics, scientific relevance, material composition, age, the completeness of a set or collection, rarity, how strange it seemed to a European eye and the available information regarding the function and origin of an object.²⁰ Additionally, he stresses that even though the relative importance of these criteria changed through the course of the 19th century, all of them remained important indicators of value.²¹ Thus how to integrate decorations into this already complex hierarchy? First, it is important to note that there was a clear difference in value between different kinds of decorations. While Joest got his first scientific decoration just for having published his travelogue, a Prussian decoration required years of lobbying and various donations to the Berlin museum. Already in 1885, he wrote to Bastian:

> I should have already received a Prussian decoration by now, but I know very well how things stand. However, you should keep in mind that, once I get an heir, my expenses will be naturally limited + that the matter will then become more difficult.²²

Joest used not only the donations he had already dedicated to the museum to lobby for a decoration, but also his future ability to do so. In the end, he did not get an heir to spend his money on, but Bastian's inability or unwillingness to procure the desired decoration led to a change in Joest's donation policy, with more objects going to museums outside Prussia, for example in Karlsruhe and Munich. The letter to Serrurier probably also falls into this period. Under the threat of losing an important collector to other museums, Bastian finally used his position to recommend Joest, and as Joest already sported a variety of other decorations at this point, he bypassed the lower-ranked Order of the Crown and was immediately awarded the Order of the Red Eagle, 4th class. This shows one of the advantages the Berlin museum had over other institutions in Germany: while figures like Karl von Linden were able to procure decorations more easily, those given out by the Prussian state were regarded as much more valuable and hence a promise of such a decoration alone could bind a collector to the museum for some time.

Decorations had their own hierarchy of value. How, however, did these relate to the value of objects? Or, to put it bluntly, how many objects did a certain decoration "cost"? Different from selling ethnographica for money on a piece-by-piece basis, decorations were rewarded only once a collection passed a certain threshold. Collectors were incentivised to create collections that fulfilled this criterion, while ideally not surpassing the required value so that additional objects could be used to negotiate with other museums. How this worked in practice can be gathered from the second part of the letter to Serrurier:

> There are still a number of objects left from my original collection, but nothing ordered: All kinds of ethnographica from all over the world; but an opportunity to supplement these will certainly arise and especially since, as museum director, you will certainly often be presented with objects that you would like to bring into your possession without making use of your museum's budget. That is, after all, what these crooks are for [...]. If you agree in principle, I will send you a list from Berlin containing everything I would be willing to give away; or, you may write me whenever something is offered to you. This should not be too expensive; however, I can tell you that, in this way, I already came to a satisfactory agreement with Dresden, Karlsruhe, Weimar etc.[23]

The quote highlights a central criterion: completeness. At the time of writing the letter, Joest had already donated many of the objects he had collected in Asia and Africa to the museum in Berlin or to other institutions. Others had become part of his private collection he displayed on the walls of his elaborate Berlin flat. While a variety of objects remained, Joest himself seems to have been sceptic whether they would merit a decoration. Thus, he came up with another suggestion: supplementation. He offered Serrurier to buy objects from other collectors who themselves were (supposedly) only interested in money and thus, to Joest, mere "crooks" and not real scholars. These objects would then supplement his own to form a complete collection worthy of a decoration.

Completeness hence manifests itself as one of the important conditions for exchanging objects for decorations. However, as the negotiations leading up to the awarding of the Order of Albrecht showed, sometimes a single rare object such as the celadon bowl could also be sufficient. And, as became clear both in the case of Dresden and Berlin, decorations could equally be awarded in hope of future donations and to bind a collector to a museum.[24] There emerges a picture that is similar to that described by Penny:[25] towards the end of the 19th century, the trend for value in ethnographic objects shifted towards collections deemed complete, but that did not mean that earlier criteria like rarity or strangeness lost all their importance. This could certainly be interpreted as a relation not only of similarity but of causality. While decorations probably were only one factor driving this change in valuation, their importance to some collectors cannot have been without consequences. Thus, when investigating the shift towards complete collections deemed sufficiently scientific, the structural incentive of collecting an assortment of material culture worthy of a decoration cannot be disregarded.

A further question would be how far collecting in the field was influenced by collectors' interest in decorations. Did they already calculate what kind of objects would get them the decorations they wanted?[26] While the case of Joest does not provide a clear answer to this question, there are some indications in that direction. First, in letters both to Dresden and Berlin, Joest inquires what kind of objects these museums would like to have him collect and later donate to them. This is not linked to decorations explicitly, but the subject of decorations comes up at other points in the same letters. Additionally, at one point in his diary, during a stay in East London, Joest notes that he "received a lot of things, half of them for Kassel, half of them for Berlin".[27] Thus while it remains unclear whether Joest already had decorations in mind while collecting, he spent some thought on how he might donate the objects he had just received. This topic merits more investigation, especially as decorations could also be conceptualised as a driving force for the most devastating effects of the colonial European collecting frenzy. As decorations required especially rare objects of complete collections, collectors might have been incentivised to try and overcome indigenous resistance to their desired acquisitions. At various points in his career, Joest used force or deceit to acquire specific objects or human remains. Thus, in how far was appropriation by force guided by a desire for remuneration in the form of decorations? While this question exceeds the frame of this essay, this question would be crucial in integrating the discussion on decorations into the broader engagement with the colonial legacy of ethnographic collecting.

Scientists and Decoration Hunters

I have shown that decorations could be used to determine both the value of objects and the scientific reputation of a collector. But while they could be effective in these regards, the tense negotiations required to receive them also made them ambiguous determinants of expertise. Because, after all, if one had to negotiate for this token of scientific expertise, in how far did it just reflect an ability to negotiate and exert pressure? This scepticism towards men sporting too many decorations is discussed lucidly by Kalka's study on the collectors Hermann and Robert Schlagintweit, who were skilled negotiators, exchanging their Tibetan collection for decorations from around Germany and the Netherlands.[28] Kalka presents the example of the Schlagintweit brothers trying to acquire a Hanoverian decoration and cites a document detailing the customary assessment of trustworthiness that was part of the decoration process. The letter lists the decoration they already possessed and their waning popularity at the Prussian court. It also includes the warning that "it is the prevailing belief among [Prussian] circles that the gentlemen Schlagintweit may be seen somewhat as decoration hunters [Ordensjäger]".[29] They hence provide an example for how a too pronounced interest in decorations to define one's role as a collector could backfire and diminish one's social and scientific reputation.

Hence Joest often accompanied his letters with remarks that he, in fact, was not hunting for decorations but merely asking for just compensation. Take, for example, the title of this essay taken from the letter to Serrurier – "to give away my collection for free would be nonsense". Here, Joest is creating a rationale for asking something in return for his donations without seeming greedy or overly ambitious. There are several other instances in which Joest tries to normalise the transaction: first, he builds up pressure by telling Serrurier that giving out decorations would be "the only sensible [conviction] for a museum director" and later calms him down by referring to the other big museums he has successfully interacted with in "Dresden, Karlsruhe, Weimar etc.". Interesting in this regard is Joest's invocation of the racialised figure of the "haggling Jew" [Schacherjude]. Joest's behaviour can clearly be described as haggling over the price of a decoration. However, by naming this anxiety explicitly and at the same time rejecting it via an anti-Semitic stereotype, Joest can pre-empt this accusation and convince both Serrurier and himself of the legitimacy of their interaction. Still, in the end, he closes by stating that "in any case, I naturally ask for and promise discretion".[30]

As eager as Joest was to receive decorations, he was very careful not to appear too interested. He tried to avoid giving the impression that he was only collecting to receive decorations, something that would have flipped his reputation from being a scientist that could prove it by displaying decorations to a mere decoration hunter abusing ethnographic collecting to gain social prestige. This point is further underlined in a letter to Ernst Wagner, director of the *Großherzogliche Sammlung für Altertums- und Völkerkunde* in Karlsruhe (which later became the *Badisches Landesmuseum*):

> As a Prussian, I would be expected to present my collection to Berlin, and I have indeed given very valuable things to that city, but – I take the liberty of sharing this with you in the hope of being able to be sure of your discretion from the outset – I have not earned any thanks for it. That my things are now rotting in some cellar – I have no satisfaction in that. Since I'm not selling <u>anything</u>, but I am willing to give away further objects from my collection, if I can get some recognition in the form of a decoration. In such a case, I would remain a friend and sponsor of the museum in question, as I am currently in Dresden, for example. This is not decoration hunting [Ordensjägerei] on my part, but I want at least <u>something</u> to gain from it, otherwise, I can keep these things for myself or rather, I would not collect them at all.[31] (Emphasis added)

The letter shows many of the points raised so far and, in its rhetoric strategies, resembles the letter sent to Serrurier. Yet it emphasises the fine line between scientific collecting and decoration hunting. In the last line, it seems as if Joest would almost slip. While pre-emptively rejecting the accusation of decoration hunting, he implicitly admits that he would not be collecting at all if there was not some form of remuneration, a statement that technically contradicts his scientific self-fashioning. Other scholars noticed the tension around this fine line. For example, even though Andree comments positively on Joest's decorations in his obituary, he also has to ward off the potentially damning conclusion of decoration hunting by adding that Joest "certainly pursued the acquisition of decorations rather 'as sport', as he once told me, and to show how one might get them".[32]

A possible reaction to the sources I have presented would be to reject Joest's claim to scientific authenticity and to argue that he, indeed, was solely a decoration hunter. However, such an interpretation would miss the crucial questions his career raises. Because despite his interest in decorations and social standing, Joest was a successful member of the Berlin academic community. His books went through several editions and in the end, he might have contributed more to the public image of ethnology than someone like Bastian, whose writing was considered cryptic even by fellow ethnologists.[33] Thus, a more likely conclusion is that in late 19th-century German ethnology, covert decoration hunting was simply part of scientific practice for a number of participants. To rise to a position of scientific prominence that was also accepted by figures outside of the closest academic circles, decorations presented a viable and sometimes inevitable way. Rather than rejecting the scientific character of decorations, it might be worthwhile to try and conceptualise the structures of ethnology with practices such as seeking decoration at its centre. A question could be how the materiality of decorations, together with other forms of materialisation of scientific practice, such as museum buildings and displays, allowed ethnology to gain legitimacy as a science in a relatively short period. How does a new discipline materialise, in addition to its emergence on a theoretical level? These questions lay beyond the source material and scope of this essay but are certainly worth asking in the future.

The End of Decorations as Signs of Scientific Authority

What I have discussed in this essay so far stands in contrast with the arguments brought forward by Alistair Thompson, whose article on the role of decorations in Imperial Germany is one of the most thorough discussions of the topic. Thompson discusses the widespread use of decorations and titles in Germany, but concludes that they were, in the end, not all that important.[34] Thompson points out that decorations were regarded as overly traditional by many and that they appealed only to a small group of nationalist conservatives. He describes an increasing process of commodification of certain decorations and the subsequent loss of value they experienced.³⁵ Thompson finally concludes that these decorations were no more relevant than they were in other European monarchies at the time.³⁶ While not addressing decorations in the realm of science specifically, Thompson does portray the rejection of decorations by the liberal establishment by giving an example from an excerpt of a speech held in honour of anthropologist Rudolf Virchow in 1901. In it, liberal politician Eugen Richter stated that

> [a]ll titles, orders and decorations cannot raise the importance of a man like Virchow a hair's breadth above what he commands by himself (loud, prolonged applause) and which the world recognizes ... I consider it proper that we should at least spare men of learning from all orders and titles (loud applause), from all the jewels and baubles that are more suited ... to chamberlains and court lackeys than to such men (loud applause).³⁷

How can this be understood in relation to Joest's academic trajectory? After all, Joest and Virchow were not political or academic enemies but belonged to the same Berlin community of ethnologists and anthropologists. For one, it seems clear from the explicitness of the quote that not all academics were interested in the reception of decorations and that for some, at least, not being decorated was more prestigious than wearing a colourful array of medals. Joest himself becomes the target of such a sentiment in the memoirs of art historian and museum director Wilhelm von Bode, who in 1930 relates an anecdote about the encounter between Joest and Prussian Crown Prince Friedrich III at the opening of the new ethnographic museum in Berlin:

> The new Museum of Ethnology was ceremonially opened in the fall of 1886, with the Crown Prince standing in for the Kaiser. He did not seem to have any real joy in building and therefore was more amused by the society. To a well-known traveller from Cologne, whose imposing figure was covered with ribbons and stars of exotic orders, he said, while examining these decorations close by: "Golly, if only I had had such merits!"³⁸

While von Bode does not criticise Joest directly, his tone suggests that he found the Crown Prince's and Joest's interest in decorations decidedly unscientific. Importantly, he calls Joest a mere "traveller" [Reisender] rather than scientific traveller [Forschungsreisender] or ethnographer. One reason for the different relationship to decorations certainly lies in the high positions both Virchow and von Bode held. They were leaders in their respective fields and did not need any decorations to prove it. However, for academics of less importance like Joest, this kind of honour without honours was not as easy a possibility. Even within the small academic community, decorations meant different things to different participants, a detail that gets lost in Thompson's overarching narrative.

Second, a crucial component that is missing from Thompson's analysis is time. He covers the importance of all decorations for the whole existence of the German Empire in the length of an article and hence has to generalise to a certain extent the role of decorations at specific moments. But as the case study shows, with regard to their role for ethnology, it makes a difference whether one considers decorations in 1882, when the field was still forming, or in 1901, when there were already more forms of purely academic recognition, or retroactively in 1930, when stately decorations in science were already a thing of the past. After being decorated in 1887 with his much-desired Prussian decoration, Joest also managed to be named titular professor for ethnology in 1890. After that point, he did no longer try to exchange objects for decorations and only received new decorations from foreign leaders in Bulgaria, Rumania and Venezuela for general academic merit. However, he still wore his decorations proudly, so they certainly remained an important point of reference for him. As we have seen above, when Joest died in 1897, his decorations were still worth a mention in his obituary, but other achievements clearly stood in the foreground. From this emerges a slightly more nuanced version than that proposed by Thompson: while the rejection of decorations seems to have been part of academic self-identification in 1901, it had not always been like that and, as I have shown earlier, the lack of other forms of authority had indeed favoured the use of decorations in ethnology. And, as with all paradigm changes, this one was gradual, with decorations falling out of style at different speeds depending on the position one had within the academic hierarchy.

Conclusion

Joest died before decorations went out of fashion for good. It is thus unclear how he would have reacted to this process and whether he would have stopped wearing them or whether he would have doubled down to become a somewhat anachronistic figure, still sporting the dress from another period. Decorations were highly important to Joest, and they also mattered to the development of Imperial German ethnology as a whole. Before the emerging discipline became formalised at the university, they fulfilled an important role in providing legitimacy to collectors who wanted to distinguish themselves by appealing to this new science. As such, they represented an alternative system of academic merit that was based on the donation of significant collections of ethnographic objects. The chance of exchanging objects for medals also influenced the conceptions of value that was attached to ethnographica. As only bigger collections deemed complete or extraordinary single objects could be exchanged for decorations, the desire to receive a medal might have contributed to the general trend towards collecting and valuing coherent collections.

Decorations offer a chance to better understand the relationship between museums, collectors and the state during ethnology's founding period. They highlight the fragile and contested character of concepts such as expertise and value. Joest's letters to museum directors reveal how thin and ill-defined the line between a decorated ethnologist and a decoration hunter abusing ethnographic collecting really was. Joest was trying to materialise the prestige he thought he deserved in exchange for his donations, but this process was accompanied by a constant danger of acquiring a reputation for being interested only in the decorations themselves. Hence with the creation of more formal academic titles within ethnology, the use of decorations quickly declined. Still, in the process that led to ethnology reaching this stage, decorations played an important role. And when ethnologists began to reject them, they might have also wanted to reject what they represented: the often-messy processes that lay behind the acquisition of those ethnographic collections that now, placed in the meticulous glass cases in the museum, seemed as if they had never been tainted by behind-the-scene negotiations.

Today, much interest is placed in exactly those background histories that have been made invisible for a long time. In this sense, this essay can also be read as a source of inspiration for how to make these complicated backgrounds visible in an exhibition context. Just like the objects that they were exchanged for, decorations endure and thus provide an opportunity to materialise the acquisition histories behind contemporary museum collections. They may allow visitors to make sense of how objects ended up in a museum – that they did not simply appear one day, but that long and complicated, and sometimes violent, processes led to their current place of existence. Visually, the inclusion of medals into displays promises stark contrasts that open new perspectives onto collections, as well as onto the collectors behind them and their motivations for engaging in this field.

I want to close this essay by completing the story of Joest's attempt to gain a Dutch decoration from Leiden. The response letter from Serrurier does not survive but the lack of an additional Joest collection in Leiden shows that, in the end, the deal did not happen. It seems that despite his efforts, Joest was not always successful. The reason why he could have failed in the Netherlands may present itself in the yearly report of the museum in Leiden. In it, Serrurier dedicates two whole pages to the refusal of the Dutch state to grant decorations to collectors and concludes that

> [i]n neighbouring empires one is more generous. The German Empire, France and Italy have on many occasions bestowed decorations for important donations. [...] At present, we are not practicing thrift in rewarding donations to the State Museums; in fact, we practice almost complete austerity. If we continue along this path, the Order of the Dutch Lion may seem to stand higher to some, because it has a few dozen knights less; but we will have to supplement our collections with

a great deal of money, and in spite of this they will remain poor and lag behind those of neighbouring empires.[39]

This quote seems to explain why Joest did not have any success with receiving a Dutch decoration: similar to the processes Thompson describes, the Order of the Dutch Lion was losing value and the Dutch government was attempting to prevent that by restricting its bestowal. That this fact led to such an alarmist response by Serrurier only emphasises the importance of decorations for the development of ethnographic museums. The excerpt also poses more questions: what were those decorating practices in France and Italy to which Serrurier refers? Were they as extensive as those in Germany? It is clear that there will be more research required to answer these questions.

By focussing in-depth on the career of one collector, I have argued for the importance decorations could have for some participants in early German ethnology and for the emergence of the discipline as a whole. I have shown the close connection between the materiality of ethnographic objects collected under imperialism and the materiality of prestige that incentivised this process. Bringing together these two different kinds of objects shows how their interactions transformed their meaning, creating new hierarchies of value. My analysis shows the contradictions inherent to the process of converting non-European artefacts into ethnographic objects and calls into question any straightforward understanding of the process of scientific collecting. Decorations, both conceptually as titles and materially as medals, created the social pull that mobilised collectors to appropriate artefacts on a global scale, fuelling the collecting frenzy that at the root of the contemporary debate about salvage ethnography and restitution. Addressing the history of decorations thus offers a chance to broaden the scope of this debate, shedding light on the multifaceted past of imperial ethnographic collecting and pointing out possible ways to display it in the museum of the future.

Notes

1 The letter is lacking a date; I have tentatively dated it in relation to Joest's overall writing.
2 Wilhelm Joest to Lindor Serrurier, Date Unknown, Archive Museum voor Volkenkunde Leiden. "Nonsense" is English in the original. All translations are mine.
3 Glenn Penny, *Objects of Culture: Ethnology and Ethnographic Museums in Imperial Germany* (Chapel Hill: University of North Carolina Press, 2002), 65–66.
4 A. Zimmerman, *Anthropology and Antihumanism in Imperial Germany* (Chicago: University of Chicago Press, 2001), 168–169.
5 Claudia Kalka, "Ordensjäger' – Miscellanea Zur Sammlung Schlagintweit Im Niedersächsischen Landesmuseum Hannover," in *Mit Begeisterung Und Langem Atem. Ethnologie Am Niedersächsichen Landesmuseum Hannover*, ed. Anna Schmid (Hannover: Niedersächsisches Landesmuseum Hannover, 2006), 89–95.

6 Rainer F. Buschmann, *Anthropology's Global Histories. The Ethnographic Frontier in German New Guinea, 1870–1935, Asia Pacific Journal of Anthropology*, vol. 10 (Honolulu: University of Hawai'i Press, 2009), 54–56.
7 For a more detailed study on the use of decorations in ethnographic collecting, see Buschmann's forthcoming publication *Hoarding New Guinea. Writing Colonial Ethnographic Collection Histories for Postcolonial Futures.*
8 Michael O'Hanlon and Robert L. Welsch, eds., *Hunting the Gatherers: Ethnographic Collectors, Agents, and Agency in Melanesia, 1870s–1930s* (New York: Berghahn Books, 2000), 12–15.
9 Wilhelm Joest to Adolf Bastian, 03/09/1881, Ethnologisches Museum der staatlichen Museen zu Berlin.
10 For a similar discussion on the importance of prestige in early ethnographic collecting, see Claire Wintle, *Colonial Collecting and Display – Encounters with Material Culture from the Andaman and Nicobar Islands* (New York/Oxford: Berghahn Books, 2013), 81.
11 Alastair Thompson, "Honours Uneven: Decorations, the State and Bourgeois Society in Imperial Germany," *The Past and Present Society* 144 (1994): 171.
12 Thompson, 173–174, 188.
13 Wilhelm Joest to Adolf Bernhard Meyer, 25/06/1883, Museum für Völkerkunde Dresden.
14 In his 1884 publication *Alterthümer aus dem Ostindischen Archipel*, pp. 10–11, Meyer gives the origin of the bowl as "donation by Dr. W. Joest, excavated on Seram," leaving it unclear whether he thought that Joest had excavated it himself or merely procured it for the museum.
15 Bär to Wilhelm Joest, 20/07/1883, Joest private archive.
16 A process portayed well by Nicolas Thomas, *Entangled Objects – Exchange, Material Culture, and Colonialism in the Pacific* (Cambridge/London: Harward University Press, 1991), 126–170.
17 Penny, *Objects of Culture: Ethnology and Ethnographic Museums in Imperial Germany*, 89.
18 Wilhelm Joest, *Aus Japan Nach Deutschland Durch Sibirien* (Köln: M. Dumont-Schauberg, 1882).
19 Richard Andree, "Wilhelm Joest," *Globus Zeitschrift Für Länder- Und Völkerkunde* 73 (1898): 46–48.
20 Penny, *Objects of Culture: Ethnology and Ethnographic Museums in Imperial Germany*, 80.
21 Penny, 80–85.
22 Wilhelm Joest to Adolf Bastian, 02/11/1885, Ethnologisches Museum der staatlichen Museen zu Berlin.
23 Wilhelm Joest to Lindor Serrurier, date unknown, Museum Volkenkunde Leiden.
24 A process described well by Buschmann in regard to Stuttgart. Buschmann, *Anthropology's Global Histories. The Ethnographic Frontier in German New Guinea, 1870–1935.*
25 Penny, *Objects of Culture: Ethnology and Ethnographic Museums in Imperial Germany*, 85.
26 For a similar discussion, see Gosden and Knowles' analysis of the collecting behavoiur of anthropologist Felix Speiser in Chris Gosden and Chantal Knowles,

Collecting Colonialism: Material Culture and Colonial Change (Oxford: Berg Publishers, 2001), 124.
27　Wilhelm Joest, Diary XIV, p. 126, Rautenstrauch-Joest-Museum, Sammlung Rautenstrauch.
28　Kalka, "Ordensjäger" – Miscellanea Zur Sammlung Schlagintweit Im Niedersächsischen Landesmuseum Hannover."
29　Kalka, 93.
30　Joest to Serrurier, date unknown, Museum Volkenkunde Leiden.
31　Wilhelm Joest to Ernst Wagner, 07/11/1884. Sammlung Darmstaedter, Berliner Staatsbibliothek.
32　Andree, "Wilhelm Joest," 48.
33　Manuela Fischer, Peter Bolz, and Susan Kamel, eds., *Adolf Bastian and His Universal Archive of Humanity: The Origins of German Anthropology* (Hildesheim: Georg Olms Verlag, 2007).
34　Thompson, "Honours Uneven: Decorations, the State and Bourgeois Society in Imperial Germany."
35　Thompson, 184.
36　Thompson, 201–202.
37　Thompson, 196.
38　Wilhelm von Bode, *Mein Leben. Zweiter Band* (Berlin: H. Reckendorf, 1930), 64.
39　Lindor Serrurier, "Verslag Omtrent Het Rijks Ethnographisch Museum Te Leiden" (Leiden, 1884), 68.

References

Andree, Richard. "Wilhelm Joest." *Globus Zeitschrift Für Länder- Und Völkerkunde* vol. 73, 1898. pp. 46–48.
Bode, Wilhelm von. *Mein Leben. Zweiter Band*. Berlin: H. Reckendorf, 1930.
Buschmann, Rainer F. *Anthropology's Global Histories. The Ethnographic Frontier in German New Guinea, 1870–1935*. Honolulu: University of Hawai'i Press, 2009.
Buschmann, Rainer F. *Hoarding New Guinea. Writing Colonial Ethnographic Collection Histories for Postcolonial Futures*. Lincoln: University of Nebraska Press, 2023 [forthcoming].
Fischer, Manuela, Peter Bolz, and Susan Kamel, eds. *Adolf Bastian and His Universal Archive of Humanity: The Origins of German Anthropology*. Hildesheim: Georg Olms Verlag, 2007.
Gosden, Chris, and Chantal Knowles. *Collecting Colonialism: Material Culture and Colonial Change*. Oxford: Berg Publishers, 2001.
Joest, Wilhelm. *Aus Japan Nach Deutschland Durch Sibirien*. Köln: M. Dumont-Schauberg, 1882.
Kalka, Claudia. "'Ordensjäger' – Miscellanea Zur Sammlung Schlagintweit Im Niedersächsischen Landesmuseum Hannover." In *Mit Begeisterung Und Langem Atem. Ethnologie Am Niedersächsischen Landesmuseum Hannover*, Anna Schmid (Ed.). Hannover: Niedersächsisches Landesmuseum Hannover, 2006. pp. 89–95.
O'Hanlon, Michael, and Robert L. Welsch, eds. *Hunting the Gatherers: Ethnographic Collectors, Agents, and Agency in Melanesia, 1870s–1930s*. New York: Berghahn Books, 2000.

Penny, Glenn. *Objects of Culture: Ethnology and Ethnographic Museums in Imperial Germany*. Chapel Hill: University of North Carolina Press, 2002.

Serrurier, Lindor. "Verslag Omtrent Het Rijks Ethnographisch Museum Te Leiden." Leiden, 1884.

Thomas, Nicolas. *Entangled Objects – Exchange, Material Culture, and Colonialism in the Pacific*. Cambridge/London: Harward University Press, 1991.

Thompson, Alastair. "Honours Uneven: Decorations, the State and Bourgeois Society in Imperial Germany." *The Past and Present Society* vol. 144, 1994. pp. 171–204.

Wintle, Claire. *Colonial Collecting and Display – Encounters with Material Culture from the Andaman and Nicobar Islands*. New York/Oxford: Berghahn Books, 2013.

Zimmerman, A. *Anthropology and Antihumanism in Imperial Germany*. Chicago: University of Chicago Press, 2001.

7 Discourse on Objectification and Personification

Modern Forms of Material Cultural Identity in the Touareg Society

Djouroukoro Diallo

Introduction

Nomadic life in Sub-Saharan Africa has changed considerably since the droughts of the 1970s and 1980s. In the Touareg society, this disruption happened at both economic and societal levels. This process triggered the exile of young Touareg men called *Ishumar*. Derived from the French word *chômeur* (Eng. unemployed), this phenomenon marked a twofold paradigm shift in society: the redefinition of the traditional nomadic way of life in the Sahara through a new ideology, a freedom movement called *teshumara*, and a new culture of warfare with the aim of securing a certain monopoly over expressions of violence.

After integrating into the Libyan army and gathering considerable experience in warfare on different battlefields throughout the Sahel region, the *Ishumar* imposed themselves as a new social class in Touareg society. This shift was influenced by the transfer into a society of new exogenous objects such as the Kalashnikov assault rifle and a four-wheel drive Toyota replacing traditional cultural objects fulfilling similar functions: for example, the sword and the dromedary (Bourgeot & Guillaume 1990). Even at the cultural level, the guitar (*al guitara*) played a significant role in the emergence of a new music style called *desert blues*, symbolizing the way of life corresponding to the *teshumara* ideology. In 2002, the German car manufacturer Volkswagen launched a new all-terrain SUV model with the name Touareg.[1] Within these examples, a twofold transfer of societal and material transfer of culture and social identity happens. First, the adoption of Western objects as expressions of Touareg cultural values and second, the projection of the ethnonym Touareg with its accompanying societal values onto a vehicle (Diallo 2018). Defining discourse as a *petitio principii* (Sökefeld 2007), it is argued in the foregoing that the Touareg identity, or more precisely its modern form, developed alongside the *teshumara* ideology as the result of the third space of enunciation happening in a postcolonial space of hybridity (Bhabha 1994). Furthermore, the overall discourse of mass media takes the Touareg identity for granted. This discourse does not consider the

DOI: 10.4324/9781003282334-10

relationship between traditional Touareg culture and its modern forms. This perception, or perhaps misperception, serves as the basis for constructing the stereotype of the blue people.

This essay investigates the emergence of the new social class, *Ishumar*, in the Touareg community, and questions the process of objectification and personification during the transfer of discursive notions such as *chômeur* describing a social phenomenon, *al guitara* symbolizing a modern cultural trend, and objects like the Kalashnikov and the four-wheel drive Toyota expressing cultural identity in modern Touareg society. For this purpose, the discussion will concentrate on the contributions of Bourgeot & Guillaume (1990) and Claudot-Hawad (1987, 1990b), as well as Klute (2013). The description of the two discursive strategies upon the ethnonym Touareg will refer to the understandings of Diallo (2018) as well. Furthermore, this essay demonstrates the relationship between discourse as a *petitio principii* and the emergence of a social phenomenon like the *teshumara* ideology associated with the musical and cultural trend of *desert blues* known as the music of resistance, in which *al guitara* represents a key instrument. Finally, the process of personification and objectification in expressing the Touareg cultural identity will be analysed by using samples of mass media data from COSMAS II of the German corpus of reference *Dereko* (Deutsches Refenzkorpus) (Diallo 2018).

The Touareg Society

As a famous nomadic community living mainly in the Sahara across parts of Algeria, Mali, Niger, Burkina Faso and Libya, the Touareg are considered marginalized groups in these countries, where they correspond respectively to specific denominations such as *Imuhar, Imuschar* or *Imascheren*. These various groups are also called *kel ajjer, kel ahaggar, kel adrar* or *kel aïr*, according to toponyms existing inside the borders of these countries (Diallo 2018; Fischer 2012). Politically structured in five confederations, the Touareg cultural area can be compared analogically to the five fingers of a hand distributed in the Sahara and the nomadic Sahel, from East to West, like the five fingers of a left hand spread out flat, with the forearm to the north (Mariko 1984: 124). The regional distribution corresponds to the postcolonial cultural space of the Touareg society divided into the countries bordering the Sahara and Sahel region. This situation represents a critical factor in the emergence of the *teshumara* ideology and the process of material culture transfer of a modern Touareg identity. These country-specific entities are recognized as part of the same ethnolinguistic community called by the endonym *kel tamashek*, even though the nomination Touareg itself constitutes an exonym.[2] This notion might derive from *terek* (Arabic), meaning abandoned by God. It could also refer to a region located in present-day Libya called *Targa*, which is a Berber word meaning gutter or channel. In a broader context, it could also mean garden.[3] Alongside this uncertain etymology, one can discover in the academic literature various orthographies, for example, *Tuareg, Touareg, Tuaregs* or *Touaregs*, even if they all represent plural forms of *targi* (fem. sing.) and *targia* (masc. sing.) (Fischer 2012). Traditionally, the socio-cultural and political system of this community presents characteristics of a strong class civilization composed of *amajagh* (nobles), *imghad* (vassals), *ighwallen* (freedmen), *inaden* (craftsmen) and *iklan* (enslaved people).[4]

But in this rigorously organized hierarchy, all the societal values refer to the status of the warrior aristocracy the noble class (Klute 2003, 2013; Lecocq 2010; Boilley 1999; Bourgeot & Guillaume 1990; Claudot-Hawad 1987, 1990b; Mariko 1984). The term *amajagh* (plural form *imajighen*) refers to the category of nobles, the highest social hierarchy in Touareg society. This term has regional variants such as *amashagh/imushagh* or *amahagh/imuhagh* and « se réfère au code culturel dans sa globalité et au système de comportements qu'il implique » (Claudot-Hawad 1990b: 49). This designation points to numerous characteristics of Touareg culture like honour and a robust warrior tradition. In a broader sense, the term *amajagh* refers to all members of this culture who are involved in its everyday public life and political decision-making (Bourgeot 1978, Bourgeot & Guillaume 1990; Claudot-Hawad 1987). However, the droughts of the 1970s and 1980s provoked a general poverty, famine, lack of work or prospects and, in some cases, discrimination which led most Touareg to go into some form of exile. In this context of cyclical and quasi-permanent crises formed a *lumpen-nomad* of wanderers, vagabonds and unemployed people in search of food and a home. Some moved to the cities, grouping together by ethnicity and forming communities of nomads who have become sedentary through impoverishment. Others ended up in refugee camps in Algeria, or in Libya in camps directly under the control of the Libyan authorities. Among this latter group, some integrated into the Islamic legions and learned the techniques of modern warfare by fighting in Chad, Lebanon, Palestine and Iraq (Bourgeot & Guillaume 140). As a result of the Touareg exile mainly in Algeria and Libya subculture emerged. The young male followers of this new way of life became known as *Ishumar*.

Expressions of Cultural Identity in Touareg Society: Between Tradition and Modernity

Generally, the Touareg community is portrayed as a traditionally authentic nomadic culture. Developed since colonial times, the blue people stereotype incorporates a whole range of implicit characteristics attributing to this society values such as bravery and chivalrous warrior traditions. The Touareg are perceived as Berbers of white race, strange and mysterious people wearing veils in the desert. The positive representation of women as important key players in this society constitutes a significant aspect, too. Moreover, these nomads living in the Sahara practiced a very superficial belief of Islam (Pandolfi 2004). Criticizing this interpretation of Touareg societal values, Bourgeot (1990) asserts that this *pars pro toto* perception does not correspond to the realities of their everyday life.

Indeed, the Touareg civilization is not excluded from modernity. It undergoes the same process of hybridity (Bhabha 1994) as other colonized cultures engaged in since colonial time. Referring to Bhabha (ibid.), Mambrol (2016)[5] argues that the concept of hybridity is considered one of the most widely employed and most disputed terms in postcolonial theory. This term refers to the creation of new transnational forms within the contact zone produced by colonization. Commenting on Bhabha (1994), Mambrol (2016) asserts that all cultural statements and systems are constructed in a third space of enunciation in postcolonial contexts. In the foregoing, normative as well as modern expressions of Touareg cultural identity are discussed. The modern expressions are produced in this third space as they result from colonial and postcolonial circumstances.

Despite its singularity, the Touareg identity itself is considered to be the result of a hybrid process: "We are a perfectly noble metal, but we could not stand without any alloy" (Claudot-Hawad 1996: 8).[6] Analysing the evolutions inside the Touareg culture over a period of 40 years, Bourgeot & Guillaume (1990) distinguishes three diverse representations of identity in this society. Hence, the normative expression of identity is based upon a traditional endogenous development process. The second type results from the various political and economic upheavals that Touareg society experienced. The last expression of identity in this culture refers to the *Ishumar* phenomenon claiming the ideology of *teshumara*.

The normative expression of Touareg identity manifests itself under five traits: the language, the head veil, the sword, the dromedary and the nomadic pastoral life. Language forms the central pillar of Touareg culture and is far more than just an instrument of communication. It constitutes the first feature of identity formation in such an ethnolinguistic community and enables self-nomination and self-recognition in the process of inclusion to a group. Understood as the main instrument of communication for constructing cultural and political discourse, it creates thanks to this epistemological process corresponding spaces for these spheres. It serves to include or exclude individuals as well as social groups by connecting politics and culture (Bourgeot & Guillaume 1990:133).

Despite this key function, the *kel tamasheq* or Tamashek language alone cannot cover all dimensions of Touareg identity. The head veil called *tagelmust* is used to complement this process of identity construction. It consists mainly of a blue veil covering the entire head area up to the face. This is more than a simple protective mechanism against the warm, dry winds of the desert. In the various Touareg cultural spaces, the veil also symbolizes the initiation or acceptance of young people into adult life. For young females, it signifies the transition to puberty, which is the completion of a process of individualization and socialization. Metaphorically, the head veil is compared to trousers. Like the intimate genitals, the face must also remain covered from the outside. For males, a face without a veil is synonymous with an affront. The head scarf directly concerns the relationship to the father and, by extension, to ones male ancestors both patriarchal and matrilineal. Moreover, it embodies a genealogical identity that is very affectively and emotionally charged (Bourgeot & Guillaume 1990: 135). Like the veil, the sword establishes a link to the family and represents traditionally the intrinsic symbols of society. This additional expression of the normative identity of Touareg culture symbolizes military prowess, punishment and positions of power: « Transmis de père en fils, il peut également entrer dans la circulation des biens indivis ... par voie utérine, ce qui en souligne la valeur sociale et affective » (138). This instrument accompanies the Touareg fighter in every place and in all situations. It guarantees his safety as well as his honour.

For various reasons, I refrain from going into the other symbols of Touareg identity such as the dromedary and the nomadic life, as they are quite simply inherent to all representations of this group. Moreover, they constitute the very basis of the stereotype of the blue people. And, research on the hybrid specificity of nomadic life and identity would go far beyond the scope of this article. For the same reason, I refrain from defining the concept of identity in this essay. Considering the socio-cultural and political situation since Postcolony, the *teshumara* ideology results directly or indirectly from the consequences of political and economic turmoil that occurred in the postcolonial nations of Mali and Niger after the regular droughts in the 1970s and 1980s. This natural disaster and the lack of political will to mount an effective response to it provoked chronic unemployment and a lack of prospects for young Touareg men. This specific situation produced the given conditions for the emergence of a revolutionary fundamentalist mentality viewing war as the only solution: the *teshumara* ideology (Klute 2013; Lecocq 2010; Boilley 1999; Bourgeot & Guillaume1990; Claudot-Hawad 1987, 1990b).

Towards the end of the 1970s and the beginning of the 1980s, many *Ishumar* were recruited into the Islamic Legion of Libya as mercenaries. They fought for Libya in various conflicts around the world. Many participated in the war between Libya and Chad, while others were involved in Lebanon and Iraq. The experience of modern warfare constitutes another stage in the establishment of the *Ishumar* movement. This stage introduces a modern external instrument, namely the Kalashnikov assault rifle, as the *Ishumar* mastered this weapon thanks to combat operations abroad. This newly acquired knowledge provides the basis for an armed struggle against the postcolonial states and their representatives. Moreover, the *Ishumar* are perceived in the Touareg society as returnees who will free the homeland from its shackles. They give hope that this culture can be restructured. In warfare, modern objects are available; the *Ishumar* now prefer the Kalashnikov to the sword. Instead of riding dromedaries, they drive most efficiently with a four-wheel drive 4 × 4 Toyota pick-up. This technique, learned in Chad, represents the new and efficient leadership style of war in the desert (see Diallo 2018; Klute 2013; Magassa 2012; Lecocq 2010; Bourgeot & Guillaume 1990; Claudot-Hawad 1987, 1990b). Analogous to camels, the four-wheel drive vehicle represents a status symbol and implies power that determines social hierarchies. Similarly, the Kalashnikov now plays a central role in the establishment of the social categories due to its efficiency over the sword. Using these modern, external, linguistic and cultural indicators, the *Ishumar*, under exogenous influence, introduced new means of reference into Touareg culture, marking a break with the traditional way of life.[7] This modern and cheeky class of experienced young men gives new impetus to Touareg society and invites the other members of society to revolution, as it has brought with it the necessary external gaze. According to Lecocq (2010), the *Ishumar* perceive themselves as "the new illelan: the strong protectors of society who should defend the tilaqqiwin, the weak".

The social category of the *Ishumar* emerged from the loss of traditional values and learning the techniques of modern warfare while in exile. Claudot-Hawad (1990b) claims that this social phenomenon of the exiled Touareg laid the foundations of renewal in Touareg society. Moreover, it has torn down the traditional social barriers to create the basis of an egalitarian society. Claudot-Hawad highlights the process of development of the two designations *Ishumar* and *teshumara*. She defines this doctrine as follows: « La teshumara désigne un état d'esprit, un mode de vie, un courant idéologique, une vision politique, qui se sont développés en marge de la société touarègue ».[8] As such, *teshumara* is interpreted as the embodiment of the constant Touareg resistance against foreign occupying powers. In their jargon, the followers refer to themselves as *Ishumar*, while the doctrine is called *teshumara*. These two terms have evolved from the French word *chômeur* (Eng. unemployed), which have been *targised* to *Ishumar* and *teshumara* as new notions in Tamashek.[9] In this process of *targisation*, the feminine forms of *Ishumar tashamurt* (plural: *tishumar*) were formed. While *tishamuren* refers to the musical and poetic genre of *teshumara*, *eshumer* symbolizes the action of *teshumara*. The instrument *al guitara* the targised name of the guitar constitutes the core element of the new musical genre and the emergence of *desert blues* known in world music and represented worldwide by the Touareg band *Tinariwen*. This musical movement contains many elements of the Malian repertoire. The members of *Tinariwen* admit to having been influenced by well-known Malian musicians such as Ali Farka Touré and Boubacar Traoré *Karkar* (Diallo 2018; Lecocq 2010).

Furthermore, Claudot-Hawad (1990b) uncovered different stages of development of this freedom movement. She links the first stage to the making of bracelets, which the first *Ishumar* made in the 1960s from barbed wire fences of the housing estates of oil company employees in southern Algeria. They sold these bracelets in the markets of Tamanrasset, In Salah, Djanet and even Gao in order to send the proceeds to their relatives. Initially, they had sent their families the handmade bracelets directly. Since then, this exogenous barbed wire art has symbolized the young Touareg in exile, the *Ishumar*. In this context, the *Ishumar* renounce national borders and adopt the whole Sahara as their homeland. They contradict the state orders and are important actors in all smuggling activities in the region. Thus, they form a parallel market system to secure their autonomy vis-à-vis the state. This phase denotes the process of self-marginalization whereby most of the Touareg in exile exclude themselves from the national systems of the countries bordering the Sahara.

After the *étape du bracero*,[10] the consequences of the droughts in the 1970s led to another phase of development of the Teshumara doctrine. The central features of the *Ishumar* movement such as self-marginalization and the parallel economic system through smuggling operations could only take place in an illegal framework. The *Ishumar* reinforced this illegality with the constant movement in the Sahara region to escape the control mechanism of the states. This behaviour is what Claudot-Hawad calls *le don de l'ubiquité*, the ability of a person to be present in a wide variety of places without giving any clues about their destination. This represents a modern form of nomadic life that differs from the traditional way of life. Traditionally, nomads follow known routes also associated with certain cultural referents such as dromedaries, other animals as well as seasons. There is a clear ethnographic identification with the territory, ranging from the most familiar to the most distant spaces and areas.

Unlike tradition, the *Ishumar* do not want to leave any traces. They see themselves as nomads, but they cannot and must not be controlled. Their destinations and routes remain secret. They can be anywhere and nowhere because they possess the gift of ubiquity. In the course of this constant movement, they always carry a *sac marin* (shoulder bag). In turn, the French term *sac marin* also has been *targised* as *shakmara*.[11] The use of the *shakmara* instead of the customary goatskin bag marks another break with tradition. In addition, the *Ishumar* carry motor oil canisters. These two accessories established themselves as additional emblems of the *teshumara*. Through this integration, the aforementioned borrowings from French form metaphors for the same social group that introduced new means of reference into Touareg culture. The presence of these new symbols of identification manifests itself from various points of view. While *chômeur* represents an exclusively Western perception of man's occupation, *sac marin* signifies the journey into exile. These characteristics indicate clearly that the *Ishumar* movement is under external and exogenous cultural influences. It reveals features of a hybrid postcolonial third space in the sense of Bhabha (1994).

Objectification and Personification as Transcultural Forms of Touareg Identity

Concepts and notions function like a *petitio principii*; they describe what they presuppose. So, they represent a central component of discourse, which is a main means of representing social reality (Sökefeld 2007).

This representation can happen through various strategies of discursive constructions such as personification or objectification. Both expressions are widely used in the social sciences. In the foregoing, they are understood as figures of speech serving as metaphors for discursive strategies describing human groups, particularly the Touareg. Clearly defining the terms will help support our analysis. The *Oxford English Dictionary* defines objectification as "the action of objectifying, or condition of being objectified; an instance of this, an external thing in which an idea, principle etc., is expressed concretely".[12] In contrast, personification is "the action of personifying or something in which such action is embodied. Concretely, it means ... the attribution of personal form, nature, or characteristics; the representation of a thing or abstraction as a person".[13]

In representing Touareg in German-speaking media discourse, these discursive processes are also common. Diallo (2018) analysed this phenomenon widely in collected data from COSMAS II of the German reference corpus (dereko).[14] The analysis of word forms and KWICs (key word in context) in this corpus reveals various forms of word compositions as well as typologies expressing contexts of objectification and personification of the ethnonym Touareg. In these word forms, the term Touareg is diversely personified according to the following patterns: A: *Persons + Objects* (Tuareg-Rallyes), B: *Persons + Objects + Persons* (Tuareg-Rallye-Experten), C: *Persons + Objects + Objects + Persons* (Tuareg-Rallye-Organisationsmitglieder)[15]. In pattern A, the object Tuareg rallies is personified by implicitly associating the rally with certain characteristics of the Touareg (people). Pattern B corresponds to the composition Tuareg rally expert, which denotes a person who is recognized as an expert for such events. Finally, the designation Tuareg Rally Organizer in pattern C addresses a social organization that could act politically and economically.

Furthermore, the co-occurrence data demonstrated the existence of Touareg and Tuareg. Both variants denote vehicles with all-wheel drive systems, which were brought to market by the car manufacturer Volkswagen in 2002. The difference between the two spellings is presumably due to the attempt to name the vehicle with an Anglicism such as Touareg instead of the German Tuareg. By choosing the Touareg name, the car manufacturer is tapping into prevailing stereotypes about this cultural group. Metaphorically, stereotyped implicit and explicit characteristics of the Touareg people, such as the psychological and physical disposition to deal with difficult living conditions in the Sahara, cultural imprinting for a suitable life under the naturally demanding challenges of the desert, a warrior culture as well as the austere nomadic life etc. are valourized by designing a vehicle to embody these traits. On the one hand, this naming choice corresponds to the rhetorical stylistic device of personification by attributing to the vehicle properties of a person or group of people. On the other hand, the nomination Touareg becomes the symbol of a thing or an object by replacing the collective designation Touareg with an object an all-terrain SUV. This fact triggers a procedure of objectification of these people resulting from the connection with the image of the off-roader. This last procedure seems to be more widespread because the four-wheel drive vehicle is probably better known worldwide than the eponymous ethnic group itself. In reference to Bhabha (1994), one can assume that this phenomenon of personification and objectivation is also related to aspects of postcolonial hybridity in a transcultural context, where the word Touareg receives a universal characteristic. Finally, it is remarkable that the stereotype of the blue people serves as a label for marketing communication.

Summary

Building a cultural bridge between North and Sub-Saharan Africa, the Touareg cultural space is intrinsically devoted to hybridity as Hainzl (2013) claims: "Social structures are never constant but are subject to constant change and reconstruction. Traditions are invented, developed and discarded. They serve ... to inculcate values and norms of behavior through repetition".[16] The colonial and postcolonial contexts, triggering both cultural and political upheavals, interrupted some aspects of the traditional Touareg way of life, while in other ways contributed to some continuity as well. Extension of Touareg culture occurred through new expressions of identity carried by the exiled Touareg young men known as *Ishumar* within the framework of a specific ideology—*teshumara*. The present paper broadly discussed this ideology and demonstrated key terms such as *tashamurt* (plural: *tishumar*), *tishamuren* (musical and poetic genre of *teshumura*) and *eshumer*, symbolizing the action of *teshumura*. The term *al guitara*, to name the main instrument used in *desert blues*, also belongs to the basic semantic field that has evolved from the birth of this ideology. All of these terms resulted from a cultural phenomenon whose proponents linguistically made use of *targisation* by domesticating and declining French words according to the rules of the Tamashek language. This represents a typical postcolonial hybridity and confirms the importance of language as a basic feature of Touareg identity and a unifying factor of all Tamashek speakers.

The analysis of the advent of the *Ishumar* social group and the corresponding cultural material transit proved that this phenomenon reveals characteristics of a third space of enunciation (Bhabha 1994), as illustrated in the discussion on societal features, structures and hierarchy of the Touareg society. The paper emphasized specificities of normative and modern forms of material and immaterial expressions of Touareg identity. Finally, this paper analysed examples of personification and objectification in German-speaking mass media discourse. Using data from COSMAS, the analysis showed a link between the stereotype of the blue people and discursive strategies taking place in a postcolonial hybrid and transcultural context to describe objects like vehicles. The topic of cultural hybridity using the case of the *teshumara* ideology and the evolution of its linguistic features provides a fertile soil for further research.

Notes

1. Source: www.volkswagen-newsroom.com/en/touareg-3627, accessed on 15 November 2021.
2. For more details, see Diallo, 2018. pp.70–73.
3. See Chaker, Gast & Claudot-Hawad, 1984. p.31.
4. I prefer to keep the names of these social classes in Tamashek.
5. See Nasrullah Mambrol published on 8 April 2016: https://literariness.org/2016/04/08/homi-bhabhas-concept-of-hybridity/, accessed on 15 April 2021.
6. Translated from French, Claudot-Hawad quoting a Touareg interviewee.
7. The concrete manifestation of the integration of the Kalashnikov and the four-wheel drive pick-up (4 × 4) into the tradition of warfare in Tuareg culture is the subject of Klute (2013).
8. Ibid., p.123.
9. Ibid., p.126.
10. Claudot-Hawad, 1990b.
11. Ibid.
12. *OED*, 1989, p.642.
13. Ibid., p.604.
14. For more detail see Diallo (2018: 273–370).
15. These features correspond to word forms in German language. And "Tuareg rallye" is a private institution organizing rallies in the desert in Algeria or Morocco, https://tuareg-rallye.webnode.com/en/, accessed on 23 April 2021.
16. p.111. Translated from German into English.

References

Bhabha, Homi. *The Location of Culture*. New York: Routledge, 1994.

Bourgeot, André & Guillaume, Henri. «Identité touarègue: de l'aristocratie à la révolution.» *Études rurales n 120* 1990. pp. 129–162. Online: DOI: https://doi.org/10.3406/rural.1990.3293

Bourgeot, André. *Les échanges transsahariens. la Senusiya et les révoltes twareg de 1916–17*. Cahiers d'Etudes Africaines, vol. 18, Cahier 69/70, 1978. pp. 159–185.

Chaker, Salem, Gast, Marceau & Claudot-Hawad, Hélène. *Textes touareg en prose de Charles de Foucauld et A. de Calassanti-Motylinski*. Edition Critique avec Traduction, Introduction et Annotation. Aix-en-Provence: Edisud, 1984.

Claudot-Hawad, Hélène. «Des États-Nations contre un peuple: le cas des Touaregs.» *Revue du monde musulman et de la Méditerranée*, no. 44, 1987. pp. 48–63.

Claudot-Hawad, Hélène. «Honneur et politique: les choix stratégiques des Touaregs pendant la colonisation française.» *Revue du monde musulman et de la Méditerranée*, no. 57, 1990a. pp. 11–48.

Claudot-Hawad, Hélène. *Tourages et autres Sahareins entre plusieurs mondes. Définitions et rédefinitions de soi et des autres*. Aixen-provence: CNRS, 1996. Print.

Claudot-Hawad, Hélène. «La teshumara, antidote de l'État.» *Revue du monde musulman et de la Méditerranée*, no. 57, 1990b. pp. 123–140.

Diallo, Djouroukoro. *Darstellung der Tuareg-Rebellionen in Mali in deutschsprachigen Massenmedien: Eine text- und diskurslinguistische Medienanalyse anhand ausgewählter Zeitungsartikel*. Bern: Peter Lang, 2018.

Fischer, Anja. *Sprechkunst der Tuareg. Interaktion und Sozialibilität bei Saharanomaden*. Berlin: Reimer, 2012.

Hainzl, Gerald. «Die ethnische Dimension des Konflikts in Mali.» *Wegweiser zur Geschichte Mali*. Hrsg. Hofbauer & Münch. Paderborn, München, Wien, Zürich: Schöningh, 2013.

Klute, Georg. «Der Tuaregkonflikt in Mali und Niger.» *Jahrbuch Dritte Welt 1996. Daten, Übersichten, Analysen*. Hrsg. Joachim Betz/Stefan Brüne. Deutsches Übersee-Institut, 1996.

Klute, Georg. «L'islamisation du Sahara (re)mise en scène. Les idéologies légitimatrices dans la guerre fratricide des Touareg maliens.» *Les relations transsahariennes à l'èpoque contemporaine. Un espace en constante mutation*. Hrsg. Laurence Marfaing/Steffen Wippel (Eds.). Paris: Kartala, 2003. pp. 361–378.

Klute, Georg. *Tuareg-Aufstand in der Wüste. Ein Beitrag zur Anthropolgie der Gewalt und des Krieges*. Köln: Köppe Verlag, 2013.

Lecocq, Baz. *Disputed desert. Decolonisation, competing nationalism and Tuareg rebellions in northern Mali*. Afrika-Studiecentrum series no. 19, Leiden: Brill, 2010.

Magassa, Hamidou et al. *L'occupation du Nord du Mali*. Bamako/Paris: La Sahélienne/L'Harmattan, 2012.

Mambrol, Nasrullah. «https://literariness.org.» *Homi Bhabha's Concept of Hybridity*. (accessed 15.04.2021).

Mariko, Kélétigui. *Les Touaregs Ouelleminden*. Paris: ACCT/Karthala, 1984.

Pandolfi, Paul. «La construction du mythe touareg: quelques remarques et hypothèses.» *Figures Sahariennes*, Ethnologies comparées no.7, printemps 2004. www.academia.edu. (accessed 25.04.2021).

Sökefeld, Martin. «Problematische Begriffe: "Ethnizität", "Rasse", "Kultur", "Minderheit".» Berlin: Reimer Verlag, 2007. pp. 31–49.

8 The Material Culture of Vodun
Case Studies from Ghana, Togo, Germany and In-Between

Niklas Wolf

Introduction

The material culture of West African Vodun can be understood as a supra-temporal, inter-national, and inter-medial[1] system of material and iconographic references, connecting past, present, and future with different localities and media. The term "Vodun" signifies the spirits themselves, as well as the spiritual and practical knowledge system and its material manifestations, with which spirits temporarily coincide categorically and ontologically by making use of those connections and ergo becoming present in a temporal, local, and material sense at the same time.[2] Besides the term "Juju", which seems to have partly pejorative connotations in Ghana and Togo, Vodun is one of the local terms. It considers the origins of the spiritual practice in West Africa and distinguishes itself from other regionally specific terminology like the generically spread term Voodoo. With the use of and reference to the material culture of Vodun, contemporary image authors situate themselves in specific discourses around history, identity, and alterity. In doing so, they often either create or trace visual networks of Vodun globally. While Vodun has long enjoyed a public audience in Benin, the same was not common for other West African countries such as Ghana and Togo. Especially in recent times, a more public perception and staging of Vodun can be observed, which is characterized by a comparatively high degree of pictorial openness as well as medial updating of the visual vocabulary and technique. As will be shown, new (and social) media and their approaches create new images of Vodun in inter-medial and inter-national interspaces that span between Africa and the diasporas. Image practices are thereby often associated with intercultural discourses of identity;[3] questions of authorship and meaning consequently demand thorough imagological analyses.

The practice of Vodun is generally open to *foreign* influences, be they images or their contents – as long as they are powerful.[4] Tangible formations of Vodun are thus characterized by iconographic, content-related, and material influences that are synthesized within them and, through the accumulation of material and content, legitimize and increase their power. By adopting

DOI: 10.4324/9781003282334-11

images and elements of material cultures that Vodun has encountered in the past and present in inner-African and global *contact zones*,[5] they gain mnemonic power by storing and remembering the past, which is accessible within them for the present and future. Elements of historicity can be transmitted through certain visually encoded forms, colours, materials, or performative elements from language, music, and bodily practices. Therefore, a claim to interpret the present and shape the future is derived from the ideas of history manifested in Vodun. Through techniques of display and order in archival spaces – shrines and museums, for example, can be such architectures of memory – Vodun participate in the material and immaterial cultural heritage of a society and thus in its culture of memory.

In Winneba, a flâneur will nowadays encounter images of the *Spiritual King of the River* in everyday public spaces. Large billboards in English and French promise solutions to marriage problems, child problems, or business improvement. The *Spiritual King of the River* takes the form of a visual representation enthroned on a pile of money, which makes use of both its local and foreign imagery to convey its power. Iconographically, the depiction resembles images of the Hindu Lord Shiva. The spirit holds the Trishula, a trident symbolizing the three main deities of Hinduism. On his forehead, the third eye of Shiva can be seen, around his neck, a snake (Naga) is coiled. It seems as if this intercultural synthesis, especially through its iconological foreignness, which does not correspond to local habits of seeing, is made available for supercharging the Vodun and, at the same time, to ennoble him.[6] Through visual connections to established pictorial knowledge, this specific imagery can be linked to tradition-based pictorial narratives of Ghanian Vodun, such as those regarding the power of snakes, whose form and body the Vodun of Ghana, Togo, and Benin often take.[7]

It is beginning to become apparent that spaces and contents of contemporary Vodun can hardly be thought of as being hermetically closed or being geographically or medially definite, but rather must be read in the form of intercultural hermeneutics (which rethinks the stereotypical genesis of images dealing with the *foreign* from the experiences of one's own). While their approaches to the classification, appropriation, or techniques of the visually rewriting of history in shrines, contemporary artistic practices, or museum displays serve superordinate discourses of ownership and provenance, as well as the ones about the construction of identity and alterity, the locations of things in their material or immaterial networks are not meant to be understood as static. Hans Peter Hahn writes, "by appearing in different places, material objects link the spaces of their presence through their materiality".[8] Spaces and networks of West African Vodun seem to be fluid and mutually permeating. Consequently, *The Shrine as an Archive*, *Material and medial interspaces*, and *The Musealization of Vodun* will be analyzed as sites and practices of Vodun based on specific case studies.

The Shrine as an Archive

Like museum displays, altars and shrines systematize the order of things, forming carefully curated archives of the respective material culture by using specific aesthetic approaches to address certain philosophical questions.[9] They are places of knowledge and performative texts, at the same time, displaying inventories of global and local networks and actors. Certain religiously connoted actions are the basis of a constant updating of Vodun and thus confirm their status again and again. Processes of updating the Vodun include formal-aesthetic practices in the sense of attachment and accumulation of material and thus the restructuring of the surface and corpus of the Voduns sculptures for example.[10] They also situate them specifically in the present through a kind of visual and semiotic flexibility that allows spiritual practices and the objects associated with them to respond to new social contexts and societal challenges. This kind of visual, material, and spatial flexibility is the basis of Voduns possibility for *presentification*,[11] an actual realization of what is otherwise intangible. In the sense of a definition of concepts of material culture (which would conceive objects as artefacts whose authors and modes of use are closely linked in an anthropocentric approach),[12] such a container-like *thing* (in this case) mutually reinforces and confirms the properties of materiality, aesthetics, and spirituality that are inscribed into it.[13] The connection of things with *practised ways of acting or the ambiguity of these and the changeability of object-related meanings and ways of using*[14] – their *cognitive stickiness*[15] as Alfred Gell would perhaps put it – makes them interesting for (equally anthropocentric) questions concerning material culture and the archive at the same time – although it is precisely at this point that methodological and analytical limits of such approaches start to reveal themselves.

Close to the mouth of the Volta River in the Volta region of Ghana, the shrine of the Mami Wata priestess Mamishie Rasta is located. The African water spirit Mami Wata is pictorially and sculpturally usually depicted as a light-skinned woman, often with open, flowing hair, bare torso, and a scaled fin tail. These depictions are inspired by the figureheads of European ships and by images of Indian serpent deities, with iconographic connections to 19th-century lithographs from Germany.[16] Characteristic of the equally feared and admired, punishing, and rewarding deity is her *internationalness*.[17]

The entrance to the shrine is guarded by the Vodun Amegavi. In human form, the sculpture of a saluting soldier, he meets the visitors in a green military uniform; a rifle is leaning against his lower body. The form and content of the image-like vessel coincide with the function of the Vodun: he supports security careers such as military and police, functions as a bodyguard and security coordinator of the whole house, and thus, like other Vodun, addresses a specific clientele with specific requests. His image seems to be able to function as a permanently materialized representative of the spirit.

On the inner walls of the shrine images based on Hindu gods and deities can be found. They are combined with local aesthetics, pictorial practices, and material cultures. Indian lithographs and images of the Bhagavad Gita served as iconographic models for the creation of new Vodun spirits. Even a pictorial interpretation and Vodun-appropriation of the Mesopotamian deity Ištar is found on one wall. In Middle Assyrian inscriptions, Ištar is described as a powerful goddess of love and war, who can determine the fate of people (and especially royal families) and was understood as a threat to the (at the time construct of) masculinity of non-obedient (male) rulers; she is thought of as a "(…) feminine figure who performs a masculine role in military contexts".[18] Being associated with the planet Venus, Mesopotamian images show Ištar as a beautiful, sometimes winged and mostly naked woman.

In Mamishie Rasta's shrine, however, Ištar is not so much recognizable by the repetition of established pictorial formulas – she is identified by corresponding annotations alone. The "*Queen of heaven and Thunder God*" has long, light hair, her uncovered arms and legs show light skin. She wears a kind of warlike garment, the lower end of which seems to be made of pteruges, which are parts of soldiers' armour from Roman antiquity (Figure 8.1). On her upper body she carries several flintlock pistols, over her shoulder she carries a quiver with arrows. Finally, Ištar's face is reminiscent of lizard-like creatures. The face's colour and its features clearly state that the Vodun Ištar is part of a different reality, foreign to the one of the viewers,

Figure 8.1 Ištar, Mamishie Rasta shrine, Volta (Ghana).
Photo: Niklas Wolf, 2019.

her dress, attributes, and the dedicated inscriptions next to her signify her as a martial and powerful Vodun.

The integration of visual and textual elements from Hinduism, Christianity, and even Mesopotamian deities and their compilation with local and tradition-based pictorial knowledge is evidence of the openness and iconic or mimetic flexibility of contemporary Vodun. Mamishie Rasta describes the depictions of Amegavi and Ištar as part of a *"solution"*, as part of "a *healing* process".[19] The images, she says, came to her in a dream. "Certain forms of the gods are common, other gods often want their form to be revealed. If they want to, they exactly describe how they would like to be represented".[20] The Ghanaian Ištar is imagined as controlling the entire universe, having a judging function in the legal sense and healing power – as the inscriptions clearly shows.

The depiction of the *Thunder God* is not the only one in Mamishies shrine who is identified by written annotations on the wall. This kind of inscriptions are especially remarkable: They identify spirits and their attributes and mostly refer to a specific function of the Vodun. The structure of the shrine is thus no longer purely architectural but takes on an educational character. The performative – and temporary – activation of the material culture in the ritual is thus expanded by a dimension of producing permanent knowledge, so the shrine itself can be read as an archive and history book for a society at the same time – an architecture of memory. The multiplicity of images in this shrine, in conjunction with local historiography and its iconic knowledge, attains unequivocal significance, creating a kind of comparative compendium of the Vodun Mamishie works with. In addition to the ephemeral pictorial qualities that characterize many Vodun, they attain educational permanence on the walls of the shrine. Loosely based on W.J.T Mitchell's idea of the intrinsic will of images[21] and foreshadowing some thoughts of Graham Harman, it could be argued that – besides the tangible characteristics of Vodun imagery – it very much matters what they *want*. On the walls of Mamishie Rasta's shrine, they demand performative encounters with their viewers to educate them via strategic modes of display, bringing the educative intentions of a museum's presentation to mind. Mimetic imitation of the foreign and its material culture is thus not only unproblematic for West African Vodun, a foreign provenance of the spirits sometimes was so important that it was attributed to Vodun purely fictitiously and retrospectively, as Dana Rush has stated,[22] but always related to effectiveness and ergo spiritual power: "The wonder of mimesis lies in the copy drawing on the character and power of the original, to the point whereby the representation may even assume that character and that power".[23] Mamishie Rasta understands possession by a Vodun as a kind of reincarnation, as a reference to the origin of the soul of the person being possessed. Similar to Tchamba Vodun, locating spirits in a specific or unspecific foreign and highlighting the imagological dimension of alterity on the walls of the shrine at the same time consequently serves a kind of ordering of the present.

An outstanding example of the combination of ephemeral and permanent object properties, characterized by questions about the provenance of effective artefacts and their possibilities to shape the ideas of identity and alterity of a specific social group, are spiritually and historically charged pictorial objects of the Tchamba Vodun in Ghana and Togo. They are "*projective transfigurations*"[24] of foreignness, based on the pre-colonial, inner-African slave trade.[25] If in the present certain symptoms do occur in the course of a lifetime, the cause of these may be that the origin of the affected person from a foreign society and the following integration into a new society generations ago has to be processed. In possession rituals, the bodies of dancers are performed by foreign spirits of the North,[26] who are identified as not belonging to the persons' culture through clothing and jewellery, as well as distinct ways of moving and behaving.[27] Such performances have a purifying effect and confirm the status of those concerned in the present, and are thus part of the self-reassurance and regulation of society. Parts of the material and immaterial culture of Vodun can consequently function as markers of identity and as triggers for trance, whose dance could be described as "danced ways of knowing",[28] a form of acquiring and performatively exhibiting knowledge. Highly specific objects not only create a connection between the material (things) and the immaterial (dance) cultural heritage but are consequently also knowledge-storing and communicating images, as are the images of the Vodun on the walls of the Mamishie Rasta shrine. Questions about the interstices of human and non-human actors begin to intersect in these visual practices, as do concepts of mimesis, symbolism, and metaphor.

In the Togolese village of Hahotoe, there are several shrines dedicated to Tchamba-Vodun. Since their form in tangible manifestations there, according to initial research, often seems to be unspecific, everyday objects associated with them and their materiality both gain wide-ranging significance. Using the example of a stool, which formally follows the typology of tradition-based Akan stools, it is possible to analyse mutually legitimizing connections between people and things, the networks and display of such connections, using a specific tangible manifestation. Akan stools have a straight base, elaborated and meaningfully carved centre parts, and a curved seat; the Adinkra symbol *Ohene Adwa*, like the shape of the stool, stands metaphorically for the king's authority. As utilitarian objects, this type of furniture is widespread in Ghana and Togo and part of the everyday culture; for example, the architecture of Jubilee House, the presidential palace in Accra, corresponds formally to such a stool, which can be read as an architectural equivalent and marker of political power.

In Hahotoe, different families tell slightly different stories about the provenance of a significant stool that legitimates social power in the present through incorporating history. In this object, the concepts of the mythological power of twins overlap with those of the aforementioned political significance. Ideas of the special significance of twins are common, and part

156 *Niklas Wolf*

of popular culture, in West Africa and its diasporas.[29] In the cosmology of the Yorùbá, for example, twins are thought of as an inseparable entity taking shape in physical duality. They are located between this world and the otherworld and endowed with the power of the Òrìṣà themselves and the concept of *àṣẹ*, a powerful life-force incorporated "in all objects of consciousness".[30] Consequently, after the death of a twin, s/he has to be (re)presented figuratively. This happens mostly by a so-called Ibeji, small wooden figures, which embody the absent human being in the literal sense and to which the same care and affection are given to in everyday life just as to its human counterpart.[31]

The stool in Haohotoe, however, was brought into the world together with its human twin by the same mother (Figure 8.2). Various families claim that the *original* stool today is located in their shrine, that they ergo have a share in the political power in the village. Questions can be raised about the identity and legitimation of the actors involved, as well as about originality and authenticity, (re)presentation and origin, and the history and identity-remembering functions of one specific object in the ritual.

After the death of the human twin, a carved representation of him was placed in shrines, taking the form of a stool, showing a pictorial technique of representation and objectification that seems to be similar to the Yorùbás

Figure 8.2 Mural, Hahotoe (Togo).
Photo: Niklas Wolf, 2019.

Ibeji practice. Both, the shrine of the Mami Wata priestess Mamishie Rasta and the shrinescape of Hahotoe, can be read as power centres of Vodun, as argumentative, visually and educationally powerful archives and places of display, whose material culture deposited therein evokes ideas of belonging and history as well as ideas of social and political regulation and power. By Vodun taking the shape and materiality of an everyday object, notions of what an object actually is or can be to Vodun are further diversified, as are the limitations of the museums understanding and framing of an object in a Western sense.

Material and Medial Interspaces

Parts of the African diasporas are currently revisiting pictorial practices of Vodun, using them to construct distinct diasporic identities with their own visual vocabulary, closely linked to the African continent and its visual and material practices. Vodun – and other religiously connoted bodily and object phenomena – are sometimes arranged into somewhat unspecific, summarizing or even eclectic pictorial configurations that seem to stand, as it were, for the material culture of Africa conceived as one. Particularly in African American contexts, discourses on cultural (re)appropriation and/or cultural appreciation and ergo the possibilities of images and media in the sense of a forthcoming syncretistic #*Wakandafication*[32] of Africa have recently developed in this context.

In the form of updated references, image authors from West Africa also address diasporas worldwide, as well as local audiences. In terms of cultural heritage, the medial and technical possibilities of Vodun are reimagined and subsequently open up new transatlantic spaces of inter-national networks. Christopher Voncujovi is the founder and spiritual director of the *Afrikan Magick Temple* in Accra. The hallmark of his philosophy is the internationality of the priest, which can be traced in his biography as well as in the spiritual orientation of his shrine. Trained by various teachers in Europe, Africa and Asia, in the ritual, he draws on elements of Kabbala (the mystical tradition of Judaism), the Sufi tradition (a mystical interpretation of Islam), Vodun and the yogic Ananda Marga teachings, which has its origins in Hinduism. The prerequisite for the use of images in the ritual is their "power to activate"[33] and – in contrast to tangible manifestations of Tchamba-Vodun – not their specific provenance. While in Hahotoe and Mamishie Rastas shrine, Vodun can only be experienced locally, images of the Afrikan Magick Temple address the whole world. In a specific aesthetic reminiscent of images in international fashion magazines and established strategies of the advertising and image medium Instagram, carefully and consciously staged and technically enhanced updates of a tradition-based image vocabulary is made available worldwide on various social media platforms. Photographs of performative actions that take on an encyclopaedic character are integrated into the visually based informational politics of the shrine. They show certain spirits ritual actions, plants, or animals associated with them, and thus link material and immaterial cultural heritage. What seems interesting in this context is not only the relocation of Vodun into a very public, virtual space but also the precise analysis and translation of Vodun into new, virtual and decidedly educational images. It could be argued that the camera becomes a mimetic machine,[34] as Michael Taussig notes, through which objects and images, which are by definition ephemeral and constantly in a state of unfinishedness and transformation,[35] are made permanent and fixed in time.

What are the special properties of the "prosaics of digital media"[36] and their technical "virtuosity"[37] in the reformulation and dissemination of Vodun in new intangible materiality – do records and the making available of ephemeral ritual practices create so-called ritual genealogies,[38] as Martin Zillinger postulated for images and media of North African Sufism, or can the virtualization of performative acts correspond precisely to the constant modes and techniques of actualization that Dana Rush argues are so typical for West African Vodun?[39]

Voncujovi uses the catchphrase *ReVodution* to frame his pictorial strategies. The practice of *ReVodution* seems to mark a kind of imagological and appreciative revaluation of Vodun and their material culture. Partly in contrast to some forms of displaying Vodun in European museum spaces, Voncujovi seems to be very much interested in a kind of globally receivable educative de-mystification of Vodun and its spiritual practice and knowledge.

For many contemporary visual artists, it might be precisely these open, not sharply delineated digital spaces that can function as a basis for the negotiation of contemporary Vodun. They make use of *liminal spaces*,[40] as Akwaeke Emezi, the author of *Freshwater*,[41] might put it. Music videos, in particular, to which a close and inter-medial interweaving of textual and visual representations is immanent, can attest to the global and local networks of Vodun.

Accra-born Samuel Bazawule, better known as Blitz the Ambassador, sees himself as a travelling ambassador mainly between Ghana and the United States, producing images of a mythical-spiritual and successful *Africanité*[42] of diasporic contemporaneity in films, music albums, and most recently, books.

The video work *Diasporadical Trilogìa* (2016)[43] tells a story between the realms of dreams and reality: a woman lives different lives, simultaneously, on different continents, connected through visual metaphors and the material and immaterial networks of Vodun. Episodically, closely interwoven encounters between times, spaces, and worlds are traced. The first chapter – *Trilogìa Chapter one (Yemaya and the singer)* – takes place in Accra City, 1957. In the year of the so-called independence of Ghana ("...*what the white man calls Independence*"),[44] a highlife band plays in a club, young people are dancing, showing off the current fashion and translating the images of Malick Sidibe into formulas of contemporary cinema. It is the title *JuJu Girl* that provides the acoustic framework. The song's lyrics talk about an obsession of a different kind, about the enchantment, the *Black Magic* by a young woman (Yemayá)⁴⁵ to which the male protagonist (Blitz) seems to succumb. Yemayá is wearing a white dress, dancing by the sea reminding of adepts of Mami Wata, *cowry shells* and *chicken bones* she uses for her magic. With the end of the song, the film begins to run backwards, the past seems to want to catch up with the present in the metaphor of images. *Act II* leads into the year 1997 and the *Trilogìa Chapter Two (Egun and the princess)*, situated in Brooklyn, New York. The previously adult Yemayá seems to have become a girl, 40 years later, on another continent. Arrived in the troubles of the African American diaspora, about which the title *Shine* reflects. She still wears the white dress. In the subway, an African mask appears next to her, which in the course dances with her, protecting her. It is a form of *Egun*, as the title of the chapter reveals, an Òrìsà of the Yorùbá connected to the ancestors. As if all powers were leaving her, the girl finally collapses. *Egun* creates the material, visual, and contextual connection to the final part of the trilogy, *Trilogìa Chapter Three (Ibeji and the wedding guest)*.

The question: "*What else can you remember?*" is used to transition to Salvador Bahia, the city of *Candomblé*, the Brazilian adaptation of West African Vodun, in 2017. The music of *Running*, the album's epilogue, kicks in as a young couple dances on the Brazilian coast. The seemingly lifeless body of a boy washes up in a boat, his mother seems to embody Yemayá now. In front of two Ibeji figures – which originate from the above-mentioned twin mythology of the Yorùbá – set up in a house, which is threatened with demolition, the boy awakens to new life just in time to make fearful construction workers run away. *You're running but you can't hide*. This line pointedly concludes the audiovisual *Gesamtkunstwerk*. *Diasporadical Trilogìa* shows a decidedly diasporic Ghanaian view of the networks of Vodun. Similar as to Awaeke Emezi's *Freshwater*, contemporary notions of corporeality, possession, protection, and belonging of diasporic identities are combined with an audiovisual metaphoric of West Africa in *magically realistic*⁴⁶ images, based on the imagery and materiality of Vodun.

The Ghanaian artist Azizaa Mystic describes herself as a *witch*, an enchantress of the Vodun, *aziza* is an Ewe term for small spirits of the forests.⁴⁷ In her image production, Azizaa Mystic makes use of the material culture of Vodun and transfers it through pictorial practices of social media photography and music videos into popular, explicit images of contemporary feminist hip-hop.⁴⁸ Her costumes show a multitude of material and aesthetic references to Vodun: she combines body paint, jewellery, and textiles to a partly somewhat eclectic aesthetic of contemporary spirits. In staged photographs, she expands established body practices and their materials by the dimension of fashion photography conditioned by social media. The result is a kind of updated fashion of Vodun with obvious material references to West African tradition-based spirituality.

The music video for the track *Black Magic Woman* (*Vodua*, 2018), which, with its quick cuts and fast-moving tracking shots, echoes West African cinema aesthetics in a kind of Nollywood way (which is often telling stories between real and surreal occurrences too),[49] is a multicoloured expression of this approach. The protagonists are wrapped in white cloths, partly marked with kaolin, they are wearing cowrie shells and the golden jewellery of the Akan; their movements are similar to the Agbadza dance of the Ewe. In this video, specific forms of body practices are combined with parts of the material culture of Vodun, generating a very contemporary and globally accessible media. Azizaa positions herself visually in the tradition of female priestesses (of Mami Wata, for example) and against the appropriation of tradition-based spirituality by Christianity. She curates an archive of visual metaphors and tradition-based systems of reference of material culture, deeply related to pressing issues of the present.

The video *Adze Kolo (Voodoo Pussy)* (*Vodua*, 2018) shows Azizaa as a kind of reincarnation of Mami Wata. Surrounded by waving white flags, the artist appears as a sea-dominating goddess, adorned all over with chains, carrying a bowl of cowries, which are in close spiritual and real connection with intra-African and transatlantic human trafficking and are repeatedly staged as the material of Vodun. A kind of linguist staff (an important symbol of power and part of the Akans (and other ethnic groups of Southern Ghana) material culture) marks the dancing artist as a mediator between worlds. The staff ends in a hand carrying a key, an Akan symbol of chieftaincy and the political and religious power associated with it. The proverb linked to this image in the sense of Herbert Cole's visual-verbal nexus[50] translates to being in authority can be likened to a key in one's hand which if not held properly can lead to lost position.[51]

West African Vodun, its human and non-human actors, not only seems to show a great deal of flexibility in terms of aesthetics and content, which is reflected upon and constantly updated in their spaces, materials, media, and networks. They also react extremely sensitive to current events, issues, and the changing possibilities of media, as a last example from Togo will show.

The Vodun Sakpata is the Vodun of the earth; the surface of its material manifestations, which grow organically out of the ground, often show pock-like spots. Sakpata is capable of punishing people with (epidemic) disease but is also associated, especially in recent times, with protective functions in the sense of vaccination.[52] The Vodun is an embodiment of the formal, material, performative, and conceptual nexus of the duality and dichotomy between punishment and protection that characterizes many Vodun. In the context of the global spread of COVID-19, Sakpata gained new attention in 2020, also in social media.[53]

The Togolese musician Elom 20ce describes himself as an archivist and activist at the same time (*une Arctivist*). The lyrics of his songs reflect in image-rich metaphors contemporary and historical experiences of violence, hegemony, and (neo)colonialism without veiling them in a magic-realistic way. Historical references in texts and images embed Eloms imagery in the past, present, and future of Togo, questioning the powers of the authors of historiography, their narratives, and, therefore, the orders of the archives themselves. The powerful potential of Sakpata, his media, actors, and techniques are updated and visually reflected upon in the track *Vodoo Sakpata* (2015). The corresponding video does not show an actual materialization of the spirit, it is rather an expressive visual metaphor for the interpretation and fixation of history and its materiality. The video begins with the playing of a music cassette on a radio, a medium of recording, playback, and audio-performative access to archived documents of sound at once. Elom prefaces a visual narrative with a reflection on archival media between image and sound and their approaches to material culture. The stage for doing so is a space reminiscent of sales booths of touristic sites in West Africa and thus the selling off of cultural heritage of African countries. The camera moves over various books, reflecting on the media and material of historiography, the processes of archiving, and the meaning of authorship. The image and sound document thus forces uncertainties between time and space in a visual metaphor, showing a palimpsest of collage-like interconnections. The Vodun Sakpata seems to be the driving force behind a modification of actualized history through body and object practices.

The experience of history is not fixed in the aforementioned artistic positions, it happens in close connection with the visual and material culture of Vodun and seems to be the basis of negotiations of the present and the future. The artist Larry Achimpong writes about his idea of a contemporary Pan-African flag to materially mark the transnationality resulting from such inter-national networks and the related reflection on history, future, technology, and media:

> Taking place across various landscapes and locations, the project builds upon a postcolonial perspective informed by technology, agency, and the body, and narratives of migration. (...) The work does not frame Pan African Futurism as a utopian vision of the African continent, but one that considers aspects of responsibility in relation to the hidden tremors of history. [54]

The hidden tremors of history clearly emerge through Val Jeanty's music and the way sound formulates a completely immaterial archive of the Voduns materiality. Through analytical de- or reconstruction, Jeanty transfers musical essences of West Africa into sonic interspace. Driven by electronic beats, rhythmically beaten drums or bright sounding gankogui push their way into the foreground of a quasi-meditative sound canvas. The Haitian musician's sonic archive establishes a much stronger and more specific connection to Vodun, dematerializing them by dissecting and rearranging their electronic traces in a global and contemporary frame of reference. The artist defines herself as a *Vodou Child*,[55] thinking of the spiritual practice and its actors in terms of an overall performative experience and as manifestations of inter- and transnational connections between Haiti and

West Africa. In a scientific subtext, various Lwa (spirits of Haitian Vodou) are being presented in a performance by Jeanty, wherein the Lwa's sonic essences are mixed and distorted. Legba, the spirit of the crossroads and thus the spirit of the in-between, is introduced as the connecting link between visible and invisible spaces, as the *"axis of the universe"*.[56] In Jeanty's music, the hardly tangible spirits, which are only temporarily bound to material culture, appear in a sounding garment in digital spheres. Accompanying lyrics, presented as a reminiscence of spoken word performances, acquire a far-reaching educational and historical significance in the likes of previously mentioned imagery and its strategies. In Val Jeanty's performances, sound is the timeless and intangible material of electronic Vodun, the form of the display reveals a hybrid sonic and archival exhibition of Vodun between tradition-based sounds of West Africa and the equally associative sounds of decidedly contemporary inter-national electronic music.

The Musealization of Vodun

Non-European objects in Western museums often function as signifiers of the curators' intention.[57] Through the inscription of curatorial truths, they are often misappropriated as cursory evidence of alienating narratives. The arrangement of efficacious things on the altars of museums no longer functions as a spatial marker of a religious ritual.[58] The form of the mensa is understood as installational, encompassing all objects involved in it, demanding a material and formal iconography of the museum display. The Mami Wata Altar of the Museum *Soul of Africa* in Essen functions quite differently. Commissioned by the director of the museum, filmmaker, photographer, curator, and collector Henning Christoph, parts of the installation were brought to Germany in a performative journey. Since the erection of the altar, which is equipped with figures, bowls, fabrics, and utilitarian objects, visitors have had the opportunity to constantly update and re-legitimize the form and material of the altar through veneration. The space of the conserving museum begins to overlap with the constantly changing space of the shrine.

Access to the small museum located in a private apartment in Essen is only possible via taking a guided tour. Henning Christoph is the narrator of tense and well-rehearsed stories, accompanying the visitors' way around the Vodun and their material, which are gradually brought out of the semi-darkness of the exhibition rooms by switching on hidden light sources by Christoph. The collector could be understood as an European archivist of Vodun, he could be read as a scenographer, expanding the experience of the museum's space by theatrical modes of reception without losing an educational claim. The museum, which seems to ignore most of the museum's techniques and terminologies, could be understood as a space for the performative and shrine-like staging of Vodun. Some Vodun shown in the exhibition have been deactivated before integrating them into the collection.

But especially the ones still being active – like the ones associated with the Mami Wata altar – seem to contribute to an immersive experiential space, that in theory and practice is closer to artistic modes of understanding (and performing) things than to the ones of a cerebral clean and contemporary museums space.

From October 19, 2019, to September 27, 2020, the Roemer- und Pelizaeus-Museum in Hildesheim hosted an exhibition simply titled *Voodoo*.

> A term whose spelling refers particularly to African American forms of practice and also to a colloquial understanding of Vodun and is often "fraught with racist categories about black religious practice [...]".

The poster for the show depicts the *Apotheosis Altar* (2004) by Edouard Duval-Carrié. Typical for the works of the Port-au-Prince-born artist are visual and material references to religiously powerful objects such as altars and reliquaries, as well as content-related and aesthetic connections to the Lwa of Haiti and their tradition-based iconographies.[59] On the Hildesheim exhibition poster, the altar formation seems to float in front of a deep black background above a nebulously billowing sea of clouds; in the centre, a mask-like face gazes out of the void, imponderable in its depth. The letters of the title seem to be made of cold-grey flames, creating an eerie, ethereal, otherworldly mood in the quite literal sense. The cloudy waves of the underground allow associations to the transatlantic space, but above all to an otherness that cannot possibly be part of the reality of contemporary viewers. The alienating design cites common stereotypes of *Voodoo*, in the sense of American and eventually West African horror movies, and thus perpetuates Western and African imaginaries of *Voodoo* as a threatening, dark, and possibly exclusively punishing power of the Other, manifested in maliciously powerful objects that stand above the laws of nature.

In Hildesheim, mainly objects from the Henning Christoph Collection (and a few pieces from other lenders) from African countries, the United States, Haiti, Brazil, and the Caribbean were displayed; the visual prelude to the exhibition and the iconic setting of the objects were photographs by the collector. The entrance area was dominated by a floor-to-ceiling brown-and-yellow world map, illuminated from behind. In an antiquing manner, its graphic design was reminiscent of 16th- and 17th-century atlases, thus citing the idea of European world discovery and measurement and invoking memories of Europe's colonial expansion. The Mami Wata Altar from the Essen Museum was also brought to Hildesheim in its entirety and displayed behind glass, unlike in the Soul of Africa Museum. As if it were a work of art by the artist Henning Christoph, all ephemeral and permanent components of the installation were transferred and built up in detail according to Christoph's instructions – they were re-staged in the literal sense of the word. The display seemed to immobilize Vodun and its material culture in a museum-like way, the altar seemed to be at least

164 *Niklas Wolf*

Figure 8.3 Mami Wata Altar, installation view, *Voodoo*, Roemer- und Pelizaeus Museum Hildesheim (Germany).
Photo: Niklas Wolf, 2020.

temporarily deactivated, whereby special attention was given to material traces of its former activity (Figure 8.3).

The Vodun of West Africa were shown in the same room as the altar, being framed by a naturalistic mode of display whose walls cited adobe architecture of African countries in terms of colour and texture. The exhibition remained largely in darkness (probably partly for conservation reasons), the display cases showed accumulations of efficacious objects; the display culminated, literally, in the raffia-like rooftops of the architectures. Similarly, as suggested by the exhibition's poster, Vodun were framed as museumized evidence of alterity, an impression sonically amplified by the soundscape of a ritual filmed by Christoph, shown in the adjacent room.

Unlike Christoph's museum Soul of Africa, this exhibition seemed only to want to be performative in a museum's context. It must ergo be read in the history of the exhibition of alterity in Western spaces – without these connections being explicitly and ideally critically addressed or marked in Hildesheim. The display left the Other – whatever that was in the curators' view – obscured in its state of the greatest possible foreignness and far from the *own* habits of seeing, partly conditioned by museums. When asked what the relocation of Vodun to museum spaces means, Mamishie Rasta replied, "*taking gods to museums would bring a curse on those who do*". But it is not the physical displacement of sacred sculptures, but the lack of attention meeting them there; the priestess says Vodun must be continuously activated, "*so in exhibitions give them what they demand*".[60] While in Essen, certain objects can act performatively in collaboration with human actors, in Hildesheim, a kind of immobilized naturalism curating Vodun could have been observed.

From the examples discussed, it becomes obvious that contemporary Vodun of West Africa can hardly be defined by media, material, or national borders. If one takes the *will* of images – again, following W.J.T. Mitchell here – seriously, Vodun have an active part in the formulation of contemporary identities of transcultural spaces and the (re)production of archival knowledge at the places of their appearance. All the examples discussed have the intent to create knowledge, being educational in some sense. Consequently, they cannot be disentangled from the authorship, they mark, in Donna Haraway's sense, not neutral but places of "*situated knowledge*".[61] However, it is obvious that methods and tools of material culture and its focus on artefacts, therefore, soon reach their limits when considering the close connections of human with non-human actors. By definition, objects of material culture would generally be artefacts,[62] that is, produced by humans, just as the modes of action and rules associated with them are. An actor-network-theory in the spirit of Alfred Gell, on the other hand, can be used to precisely analyze inter-national and inter-medial connections across spatial, content-related, and temporal boundaries. To the material culture – to use the somewhat simplifying term in this context again – of West African Vodun, however, there is more. Both, tools and terms of material culture, as well as those of Actory Network Theory (ANT), are somewhat limited when it comes to Vodun since both methodological approaches are based on the tangible interactions and networks between human and non-human actors and are therefore anthropocentric. Although the connections between human and non-human actors in all interstices and their networking communication, which seems to be part of the effective power stored in Vodun, deserve special attention. But both theoretical approaches could be – based on the understanding of intercultural hermeneutics – broadened up by reflecting upon the ideas of an object-oriented ontology (OOO).[63] Such an approach seems – especially following Graham Harman's ideas here "(…) if everything were defined by its relations, then nothing could ever change"[64] – to be inherent to Vodun and can be thought of as an uncompromising extension of ANT. The ontological dimension of Vodun thus might be freed from the partly exclusionary influence of human actors. The methodology and terminology of OOO would focus on the autonomy of Vodun, that is, an objective autonomy that lies beyond the boundaries of categorical (human) knowledge and science. They would, therefore, be thought of as independent actors in networks of posthuman relationism, rejecting materialism as a category only found in tangible objects but would argue that materialism could also be part of immaterial, object-independent constructions, forming holistic networks of performative identities based on social objects.[65] The Vodun of West Africa could then reveal themselves for what they are. Namely, more than history-storing and triggering residues of material culture, more than repositories of authorship and display, but active and performative intentional objects of global contemporaneity.

Notes

1. Some hyphenations are used in this article to materialize the *inbetweenness of things* (Basu 2017) in the medium of text.
2. They therefore produce significance *naturally* by the fact that the pictorial object (*Signifikant*) naturally evokes the concept of Vodun (*Signifikat*) Barthes 2010, p. 278.
   In the case of Vodun, the signifier ergo loses its pictorial qualities becoming one with the spirit. The kind of dichotomic distinction between material culture (a tangible thing) and spirits (an intangible idea) therefore becomes blurred, esp. for the period of coincidence of material and immaterial aspects of Vodun.
3. It's a given that concepts of identity are "constructed, fluid, and multiple" and therefore tend to reveal the term to either "mean too much (when understood in a strong sense), too little (when understood in a weak sense), or nothing at all (because of its sheer ambiguity)". Brubaker and Cooper 2000, p. 1.
4. On the pictures "power to activate", see p. 9.
5. "(...) social spaces where cultures meet, clash, and grapple with each other, often in contexts of highly asymmetrical relations of power, such as colonialism, slavery, or their aftermaths as they are lived out in many parts of the world today". Pratt 1991, p. 34.
6. Rush 1999.
7. Aronson 2007.
8. Hahn and Neumann 2018, p. 18.
   All translations were done by the author.
9. And would therefore also be open to methods of autoethnographic and practice-based artistic research. In these contexts, especially research that has previously been done by some Western researchers on the understanding of the aesthetics of Vodun has been heavily criticized for being Eurocentric, veiled, biased, and poorly worded.
   Adjei 2019, p. 133.
10. The structuring of surfaces is of great importance for many religiously or politically significant objects in West African contexts, as is the adherence of material (and ergo efficacy) to them.
    MacGaffey 2001.
11. Vernant and Zeitlin 1991, p. 151.
12. Samida et al. 2014, p. 169.
13. A term of European intellectual history that would be close to these phenomena could be Heidegger's Zeugganzes.
14. Hahn and Neumann 2018, p. 11.

15 Gell 1998, p. 86.
16 Drewal 1988.
17 Frank 1995.
18 Pacifying kings in this context would mean to take away their weapons, their power, and (therefore) in the end their masculinity.
Zsolnay 2010, p. 401.
19 Mamishie Rasta. Interview. By Niklas Wolf. September 2019.
20 Mamishie Rasta. Interview. By Niklas Wolf. September 2019.
21 Mitchell 2006.
22 Rush 2010, p. 62.
23 Taussig 1993, p. xiii.
24 Rush 2011, p. 44.
25 Rosenthal 1998.
26 "(...) and spirits must be invited to dance the bodies of descendants in possession-trance". Vannier and Montgomery 2016, p. 125.
27 Wendl 1999.
28 Hill 2018, p. ii and p. 142.
29 Weiß 2019.
30 Abiodun 2014, p. 319.
31 Wardell et al. 1989.
32 The term *Wakandafication*, coined by Jade Bentil (@jadebentil), is used to mark and discuss certain pictorial practices in which artists would use parts of Africa's material culture and certain cultural and/or pictorial practices of African descent, to construct a somewhat monolithic idea of Africa. Recent works that have been discussed very controversially in these contexts would be, for example, the film *Black Panther* (2018) or the visual album *Black is King* (2020) by Beyoncé et al.
33 Christopher Voncujovi. Interview. By Niklas Wolf. April 2019.
34 Taussig 1993, p. xv.
35 Rush 2010.
36 Coleman 2010, p. 495.
37 Gell 1998, p. viii.
38 Zillinger 2013, p. 44.
39 Rush 2010.
40 Turner 1964.
41 Emezi 2018.
42 Senghor 2009.
43 Being a short film by itself, *Diasporadical Trilogìa* contains videos for the tracks *JuJu Girl*, *Shine*, and *Running* from the Album *Diasporadical* (2016).
44 *Diasporadical Trilogìa*. Blitz Bazawule 2016. Film. 04.23.
45 The Yorùbá Òrìṣà of the sea, iconographically identical to depictions of Mami Wata.
46 A terminology that corresponds to magic-realism, a style of African literature of the 20th and 21st centuries, represented, for example, by Ben Okri. In *The Famished Road* (1991), Okri describes the powerful intersections between the real world and that of the spirits, in which material and immaterial entities equally coexist.
47 Meyer 1999, p. 69.
48 And could thus be read as an extension of WEB Du Bois idea of the Double Consciousness and as an artistic manifestation of the Triple Consciousness

Theory, which addresses the systematic, racist, but also sexist discrimination of BIPoC women. Welang 2018 and King 1988.
49 Diawara 2010, p. 161.
50 Cole and Ross 1977.
51 Howard et al. 2016.
52 Andrews 2019, p. 83.
53 Grossi 2020.
54 www.larryachiampong.co.uk/list-of-artworks/pan-african-flag-for-the-relic-travellers-alliance> Web. 9 July 2020.
55 The Electric Vodou Sound of Val-Inc | BESE Meets, 07.08.2019, *YouTube*. Web. 25 March 2021.
56 UPA live sessions: Val Jeanty (Val Inc) 11.01.2020, *YouTube*. Web. 25 March 2021.
57 Price 2002.
58 Houseman 2001.
59 Pressley-Sanon 2013.
60 Mamishie Rasta. Interview. By Niklas Wolf. March 2019.
61 Haraway 1988.
62 Samida et al. 2014, p. 169.
63 Harman 2018.
64 Skepoet2. "Marginalia on Radical Thinking. An interview with Graham Harman". *Symptomatic Commentary. Notes, Interviews, and Commentary on Art, Education, Poetics, and Culture*. 22 September 2014. Web. 20 March 2021.
65 Harman 2016.

References

Abiodun, Rowland. *Yoruba Art and Language, Seeking the African in African Art*. New York: Cambridge UP, 2014.
Adjei, Sela Kodjo. *Philosophy of Art in Ewe Vodu Religion*. University of Ghana, Legon. PhD dissertation, 2019.
Andrews, Curtis Terry David. *Vodu Is a Human to Me: Society, Song, and Drums in the Torgbui Apetorku Shrine of Dagbamete, Ghana*. Vancouver: University of British Columbia, 2019.
Aronson, Lisa. "Ewe Ceramics as the Visualization of Vodun". *African Arts*, vol. 40, no. 1, 2007, pp. 80–85.
Barthes, Roland. *Mythen des Alltags. Vollständige Ausgabe. Aus dem Französischen von Horst Brühmann*. Berlin: Suhrkamp, 2010.
Brubaker, Rodgers, and Cooper, Frederick. "Beyond 'Identity' ". *Theory and Society*, vol. 29, no. 1, 2000, pp. 1–47.
Basu, Paul, ed. *The Inbetweenness of Things. Materializing Mediation and Movement between Worlds*. London/New York: Bloomsbury, 2017.
Cole, Herbert M., and Doran H. Ross. *The Arts of Ghana*. Los Angeles: University of California, 1977.
Coleman, E. Gabriella. "Ethnographic Approaches to Digital Media". *Annual Review of Anthropology*, vol. 39, 2010, pp. 487–505.
Desmangles, Leslie G. "Replacing the Term, Voodoo' with, Vodou'. A Proposal". *Journal of Haitian Studies*, vol. 18, no. 2, 2012, pp. 26–33. Web.

Diawara, Manthia. *Neues afrikanisches Kino*. München: Prestel, 2010.
Drewal, Henry John. "Performing the Other: Mami Wata Worship in Africa". *TDR*, vol. 32, no. 2, 1988, pp. 160–185.
Emezi, Akwaeke. *Freshwater*. New York: Black Cat, 2018.
Frank, Barbara. "Permitted and prohibited Wealth: Commodity-possessing Spirits, Economic Morals, and the Goddess Mami Wata in West Africa". *Ethnology*, vol. 34, no. 4, 1995, pp. 331–346.
Gell, Alfred. *Art and Agency. An Anthropological Theory*. Oxford: Oxford UP, 1998.
Grossi, Angelantonio. "Religion on Lockdown/on the Articulation of Vodu, Media and Science". *Religious Matters in an Entangled World*. 15 April 2020. Utrecht University.
Hahn, Hans Peter, and Neumann, Friedemann, ed. *Dinge als Herausforderung. Kontexte, Umgangsweisen und Umwertungen von Objekten*. Bielefeld: Transcript, 2018.
Haraway, Donna. "Situated Knowledges: The Science Question in Feminism and the Privilege of Partial Perspective". *Feminist Studies*, vol. 14, no. 3, 1988, pp. 575–599.
Harman, Graham. *Immaterialism: Objects and Social Theory*. Cambridge: Polity Press, 2016.
———. *Object-Oriented Ontology: A New Theory of Everything*. London: Penguin Random House, 2018.
Hill, Elyan Jeanine. *Spirited Choreographies: Ritual, Identity, and History-Making in Ewe* https://escholarship.org/uc/item/5p68k9mj#metricsPerformance. California: UCLA, 2018.
Houseman, Michael. "Was ist ein Ritual". *Altäre. Kunst zum Niederknien*. Ed. Jean-Hubert Martin, Ostfildern-Ruit: Hatje-Cantz, 2001, pp. 48–51.
Howard, Ebenezer Kofi, et al. "The Aesthetic and Philosophical Values of Asante Linguist Staff Symbols in Textile Design". *International Journal of Innovative Research and Development*, vol. 5, no. 8, 2016. pp. 225–237.
King, Deborah K. "Multiple Jeopardy, Multiple Consciousness: The Context of a Black Feminist Ideology". *Signs*, vol. 14, no. 1, 1988, pp. 42–72.
MacGaffey, Wyatt. "Astonishment and Stickiness in Kongo Art: A Theoretical Advance". *RES: Anthropology and Aesthetics*, no. 39, 2001, pp. 137–150.
Meyer, Birgit. *Translating the Devil. Religion and Modernity amongst the Ewe in Ghana*. Edinburgh: University of Edinburgh, 1999.
Mitchell, W.J.T. *What Do Pictures Want? The Life and Loves of Images*. Chicago: University of Chicago Press, 2006.
Pratt, Mary Louise. "Arts of the Contact Zone". *Profession*, 1991, pp. 33–40, 34.
Pressley-Sanon, Toni. "Exile, Return, Ouidah, and Haiti: Vodun's Workings on the Art of Edouard Duval-Carrié". *African Arts*, vol. 46, no. 3, 2013, pp. 40–53.
Price, Sally. *Primitive Art in Civilized Places: Second Edition*. Chicago: University of Chicago Press, 2002.
Rosenthal, Judy. *Possession, Ecstasy, and Law in Ewe Voodoo*. Charlottesville/London: UP of Virginia, 1998.
Rush, Dana. "Eternal Potential. Chromolithographs in Vodunland". *African Arts*, vol. 32, no. 4, 1999, pp. 61–69.
———. "Ephemerality and the "Unfinished" in Vodun Aesthetics". *African Arts*, vol. 43, no. 1, 2010, pp. 60–75.

———. "In Remembrance of Slavery: Tchamba Vodun Arts". *African Arts*, vol. 44, no. 1, 2011, pp. 40–51.

Samida, Stefanie, Manfred K. H. Eggert, and Hans Peter Hahn, ed. *Handbuch Materielle Kultur. Bedeutungen, Konzepte, Disziplinen*. Stuttgart: J.B. Metzler, 2014.

Senghor, Léopold Sédar. "The Foundations of "Africanité," or "Négritude" and "Arabité". *Critical Interventions, Journal of African Art History and Visual Culture*, vol. 3, no. 1, 2009, pp. 166–169.

Taussig, Michael. *Mimesis and Alterity. A Particular History of the Senses*. New York/London: Routledge, 1993.

Turner, Victor W. "Betwixt and Between. The Liminal Period in Rites de Passage". Symposium on New Approaches to the Study of Religion. Proceedings of the 1964 Annual Spring Meeting of the American Ethnological. Ed. June Helm, Seattle: University of Washington Press, 1964, pp. 4–20.

Vannier, Christian, and Eric James Montgomery. "Sacred Slaves: Tchamba Vodu in Southern Togo". *Journal of Africana Religions*, vol. 4, no. 1, 2016, pp. 104–127.

Vernant, Jean-Pierre, and Zeitlin, Froma I. ed. *Mortals and Immortals: Collected Essays*. Princeton: Princeton UP, 1991.

Wardell, Allen, et al. *Yoruba. Nine Centuries of African Art and Thought*. New York: Harry N. Abrams, 1989.

Weiß, Matthias. "Gottesmutter oder Muttergöttin, schwarz oder weiß? Oder: Warum sich Beyoncé Pregnant with Twins als Plädoyer für Verflechtungs-Kunst-Geschichten lesen lässt". *Kritische Berichte*, vol. 1, 2019, pp. 45–57.

Welang, Nahum. "Triple Consciousness: The Reimagination of Black Female Identities in Contemporary American Culture". *Open Cultural Studies*, Band 2, Heft 1, 2018, pp. 296–306. Web.

Wendl, Tobias. "Slavery, Spirit Possession and Ritual Consciousness. The Tchamba Cult among the Mina of Togo". *Spirit Possession. Modernity Power in Africa*. Heike Behrend and Ute Luig (Eds.). Oxford: James Curry, 1999, pp. 111–124.

Zillinger, Martin. Die Trance, das Blut, die Kamera. *Trance-Medien und Neue Medien im marokkanischen Sufismus*. Bielefeld: Transcript, 2013.

Zsolnay, Ilona. "Ištar, "Goddess of War, Pacifier of Kings": An Analysis of Ištar's Martial Role in the Maledictory Sections of the Assyrian Royal Inscriptions". Kogan, L., et al. *Language in the Ancient Near East. Proceedings of the 53e Rencontre Assyriologique Internationale: Vol. 1*. Indiana: Eisenbrauns, 2010, pp. 389–402.

9 Ndambirkus and Ndaokus
Asmat Skulls in Transit

Jan Joris Visser

Introduction

In a secret memo, June 20, 1955, the Dutch Minister of Foreign Affairs was asked to make a propaganda movie showing the progress in the work of the Dutch "civilization" policy in New Guinea.

> Now that it appears that Indonesia will once again put West New Guinea on the roll at the 10th General Assembly of the United Nations, I feel I must raise the question of whether it is desirable or necessary to intensify the information of the American public about West New Guinea and if so, to what extent.[1]

The Dutch feared that with pressure from the United Nations (UN), they would lose control of their claim on West New Guinea after the independence of Indonesia. To convey their hard work and good intention, they needed a clear statement of how they were responsible for turning the savage Papuans into "proper" citizens. They asked the Administrative Officer, Bert van der Voort, to prepare for the arrival of a film crew. His task was to show the clichés of the "stone age cannibals" in Ajam, a village already under extensive Dutch control. The people there were asked to re-enact festivities that were forcibly forbidden for a generation, and to show Ndaokus "headhunted" skulls that had been prohibited by Dutch law. When the film crew arrived, they did not find the village they were looking for, with no signs of headhunters or savages. The disappointed film crew decided to recreate the existing image they were sent to film. Canoes were freshly painted, and confiscated skulls from the central administrative office in Agats, stored at the police bureau, were taken to Ajam. The people in the village were asked to remove all western clothing and, in amazement, watched the Dutch crew paint the recuperated old skulls with dog blood and red paint.[2] The human remains that were confiscated were part of the program to increase control over Dutch New Guinea. Part of this program were the medical campaigns in the 1950s to reduce the worldwide prevalence of Yaws, *Frambesia tropica*, from 50 to 150 million to fewer than 2.5 million. A simple shot of penicillin

DOI: 10.4324/9781003282334-12

was administered, and the effect was noticeable in days. Some Dutch doctors had been sent to West Papua just after WWII to redeem themselves for collaborating with the Nazis. Dr. Visser (not related), a specialist in Tropical Disease, travelled in the regions that were already under long Dutch control, where the possession of skulls was strictly forbidden, and to regions that had not yet been affected by the repressive Dutch regime. Travelling among the Asmat with his wife and baby, he received hundreds of artefacts from the people he treated as compensation for his work, ranging from shields and ethnographic items and an ancestral skull. These objects were given as a long-term loan to the Rijksmuseum voor Volkenkunde in Leiden, founded in 1837, and joined with the Tropenmuseum in Amsterdam and the Africa Museum in Berg en Dal as the National Museum of World Cultures. The museum has been actively researching the collection and updating the legal status by extensive provenance research. They found this collection of Dr. Visser to be legally in the possession of the family as a long-term loan, but not of enough interest to keep, either as a donation or a purchase. Dr. Visser's daughter Jacqueline, photographed with her mother in 1957, was contacted by the RMW to receive her father's collection in 2019. She did not expect to receive two containers of Asmat ethnographic material, including one adorned ancestral skull. Living in a small apartment south of Rotterdam, her house was not large enough to receive pallets with 5- metre-long spears, dance costumes, shields, and an ancestral skull or Ndambirkus ancestral skull. Thus, this particular Ndambirkus came on an open market, an opaque

Figure 9.1 Dr. Visser Md. "Receiving a Ndambirkus ancestral skull".
© Visser family photo, 1957.

Figure 9.2 "Checking confiscated skulls".Photographer: Cees van Kessel (msc) Object code BD/216/199 © Stichting Papua Erfgoed.

platform of curios dealers and collectors. As a sought-after symbol by curiosity collectors, Asmat skulls are seen as tangible remnants of the "last headhunters". This romanticized narrative started in the early 20th century through books and travel stories. Hundreds of Asmat skulls are being offered online, mostly fake or faked, adorned with non-indigenous feathers, the wrong wax, too many red Abrus seeds, or the wrong jaw binding. It is astonishing how many collectors and dealers are willing to manipulate a human skull to look like an Asmat skull.[3] This manipulation and creation of Ndambirkus skulls is exponential; of the 300–400 I have seen in the last few years, only a few are authentic in special collectors' groups on Facebook trading in human remains.[4] Presently, these human skulls are for sale online, via shops, and through special Facebook collector groups.

Asmat

Called the We-mana-we, or "people eaters" by their neighbouring Kamoro, the Asmat symbolism revolves around headhunting, parallel to the link between their people and the trees. Not only do they identify themselves as made from wood, but also they believe that their heads are fruit, feet are roots, and arms are branches. They also use wood to make ancestral figures, drums, and substitute skulls, preferably from the sweet-smelling wild Nutmeg tree. They believe that most deaths, excluding fragile members of the community like infants and seniors, are caused by enemies. These "killed" ancestors have to be remembered, often in the form of carved figures and shields, as a promise for future revenge. Headhunting as a concept is an integral part of the protection of the community. One of the first to write on the Asmat and Kamoro is father Zegwaard, a Dutch missionary:

> Among the important factors are (1) the cosmology of the Asmat (or rather, the influence of cosmic events on their lives), but this has now lost much of its significance; (2) the economic demand, sago-gathering and its cult; (3) fear of the spirits, expressed in the ritual of expelling the spirits as a characteristic feature of both large and small festivities; and (4) the need of prestige on the part of the male population, the desire for fame and the urge to impress the women of the village ... ... Almost every larger festivity or public ritual presupposes a headhunting raid. The festivities occur at regular, short intervals and generally last for several months. Often the festivities are organized at the same time or with a short interval in the various neighboring villages. The main festivities are: (a) the celebration at the building of a new bachelor's house, (b) the festivities on the occasion of the carving and the erection of an ancestor pole, and (c) the weaving of masks, followed by a solemn mask dance. On any of these celebrations the spirits of the dead are supposed to come back to the community of the living.[5]

The Asmat have a special relationship with skulls and two of the most recognizable ones are the Ndaokus and the Ndambirkus. The easily identifiable ancestral skulls from Asmat have adorned many books that boast travels to the "Last Cannibals".[6] As part of a western trend to look for the quirky and exotic, the Asmat was portrayed as "stone age cannibals" in hundreds of travel books. And the ornately ancestral skulls with their fine beads and feather works, strings of Job`s tears (Coix lacryma-jobi) were a much sought-after souvenir. Many have ended up in museums and collections in the West. As a symbol of the "Savage headhunter", these ancestral heads have been used in films, documentaries for book covers to feed on a western sense of the "exotic and bizarre", excluding the explanation of the complex functions of these human remains in Asmat society. Most skulls are a mix of origins and styles; very few are original Ndambirkus, and even if they are, they have often been modified to look like the "classic" image of the feather-crowned examples. Most seem to be European skulls, dressed up with Job's tear chains, eye sockets filled with wax, red seeds in the eyes, so-called abrus beans (abrus pecatorius), and elaborate feathers crowns. Some original Ndambirkus have a nasal ornament called a "bipane", just like the ones Asmat warriors usually wear through their pierced septums.[7] These "bipane" are made of bamboo, bone, or carved curves of a seashell divided into two parts, with the ends curved inward into spirals and connected with resin. The red seeds are originally "abrus beans" (abrus precatorius), which are toxic because of the presence of abrin. Ingestion of a single seed, well chewed, can be fatal to both adults and children. Ingesting intact seeds may result in no clinical findings, as they can pass undigested through the gastrointestinal tract because of their hard shell. Symptoms are identical to those of ricin, except abrin is more toxic by almost two orders of magnitude; the fatal dose of abrin is approximately 1/75 that of the fatal dose of ricin.

The ability of men to protect the village is essential for a sense of safety. To emphasize their strength, they rely on bragging rights. The tangible proof of a successful headhunting expedition is the Ndaoku skulls. These skulls are recognizable by a hole in the temple to remove brain matter on the side, and they mostly have the lower jaw missing. Supposedly to humiliate the slain enemy, the jawbone was removed and given to the women of the village as a necklace or trinket.

The Ndaokus seem to be important as a token of strength by the person(s) who took the head, but seems to diminish, perhaps losing strength over time or in passing them on to subsequent generations. Very few are found in museums, they were not traded or given away like the Ndambirkus but kept together in bundles in the men's communal houses. They are part of the complex storytelling of bravery, the capacity of the men to protect the village, having a repertoire of feats of bravery, strength, and wit. The skulls are used during ceremonies to emphasize strength and virility, often placed in front of the lower abdomen to transfer the Ndaokus power. Many later sculptures of both male and female ancestors show a sculpted head just above or in front of the sex.

Besides these two types of skulls, the Asmat carve substitute skulls in wood, like other people in New Guinea. These were originally perhaps indistinguishable in their functioning from actual skulls and could perhaps be considered human remains. My question is, if an artefact is chosen to incorporate an ancestral spirit, who can say that human remains are a more important vessel for their practices? These substitute skulls are found already in the earliest collections of the early 20th century of Asmat objects. After the Dutch repression of headhunting raids and accompanying festivals, there is no increase noticeable in the collections of substitute skulls. There seems to be no indication that later substitute skulls replaced the actual skulls to perform in rituals in a similar fashion, sublimating the act of headhunting with a story linked to a carved head. The Dutch forced stop seems to have ended the ritual related to headhunting, except for a few reported raids in the 1960s. Besides that, there are "tourist" substitute skulls on the market, made for sale.[8]

The separation of restitution of cultural heritage and the repatriation of human remains is a western construct and, in the West, we recognize the rights of the personal representatives of the dead to possession of the corpse or its remains for decent disposal. The return of Maori heads from French national museums provoked controversy before repatriation took place in 2012.[9] Restitution to New Zealand required a special parliamentary decision notably because "their value as objects trumped their condition of being human remains".

The trend to return human remains is clear; according to Malte Jettugis, the repatriation of skulls from Germany to Namibia from 2011 onwards took place without any legislation being implemented. Though still subject to controversy, the return of human remains apparently takes place in increasingly shorter intervals. Only recently, as Zimbabwe increased pressure on the United Kingdom to repatriate the remains of supposed veterans of the First Chimurenga, the British Natural History Museum felt obliged to respond instantly.[10] But how to separate substitute skulls, Ndambirkus ancestral skulls or Ndaokus as different, as either forms of Human Remains or Cultural Heritage? Can we treat them differently when attempting restitution or repatriation?

Restitution or Repatriation

Human remains in ethnographic collections are like Schrödinger's cat; until the observer has done the DNA test, it remains in two states. On the one hand they are Tangible Cultural Heritage and on the other they are Human remains. The moment that DNA test can prove the origin, the remains can be repatriated. The big question is of course, is it ethical to drill in these skulls to obtain this information? The German approach, like the Tübingens group project "Prekäre Provenienz – Menschliche Überreste aus dem kolonialen Erbe Afrikas vor 1919 in wissenschaftlichen Sammlungen Baden-Württembergs"[11] is to do extensive provenance research and not touch the objects. The human remains are foremost treated with dignity and respect, and the idea of performing more tests goes against their ethical guidelines. Their priority is to preserve the integrity of the object, not unlike a reliquary. This approach is confirmed with the handover of remains from Hawaii at the Übersee Museum in Bremen. Edward Halealoha Ayau leads Hawaii's efforts to recover heritage from abroad, he states: "In our culture, exposing iwi to light is considered highly offensive[...]Removing them, subjecting them to examination, putting them on display – those are all examples of exposure".[12]

As an advisor to the Belgian HOME project (Human Remains Origin(s) Multidisciplinary Evaluation), I found that the Belgian scientists were eager to do DNA tests to get clarity. The HOME project started in 2019, after the Brussels Parliament voted a resolution for the repatriation of human remains and the return of cultural objects collected during the colonial period. Researchers from seven institutions aim to answer ethical questions and provide a basis for applications for the return of non-Belgian human remains in Belgium. This does not mean there are no ethical guidelines, rather, the opposite. Their priority is just on repatriation.

As important elements to their cultural heritage, the skulls should be a testimony of Asmat culture. At present, there are no formal demands for restitution or repatriation, neither from the Indonesian government, nor from individuals or groups in Papua New Guinea. A demand from the Asmat themselves would likely be contrary to their present beliefs in the functioning of human remains to the present. But I expect a future generation to ask for a more respectful treatment of their human remains. In a broader movement of the small Asmat diaspora or perhaps in cooperation with the Australian Government's Indigenous Repatriation, chaired by Papuan Ned David from the Torres Straits.[13] There are European initiatives like the Exeter's Royal Albert Memorial Museum (RAMM) with the Designation Development Fund on researching human remains, researching the possibility of repatriation of Papuan skulls from the Sepik and Fly River and New Hebrides. The RAMM is:

> Proactive in returning human remains since its first act in returning human remains to New Zealand in 1996. It continues to acknowledge that many of these remains hold no value to science and recognizes that holding remains in its collections is a practice deeply offensive to originating communities. Where possible, human remains should return to their place of origin for the purpose of reburial.

The UN have already added a recent report in July 2020 (A/HRC/45/35)[14] to the general protection of human remains and cultural heritage as is initiated by the Human Rights Council in 2007:

> the Expert Mechanism on the Rights of Indigenous Peoples examines good practices and lessons learned regarding efforts to achieve the ends of the United Nations Declaration on the Rights of Indigenous Peoples, focusing on the repatriation of ceremonial objects, human remains and intangible cultural heritage

The report is filled with broad generalizations on burial practices of indigenous peoples:

> Like many others, typically honour their dead with funerals and other ceremonies. Indigenous spiritual teachings require that the dead must remain at rest and undisturbed in their burial places; intergenerational respect for these places is often maintained through ceremonial practices honouring those who have passed away.

The importance is always to ask the people themselves what they prefer and not let a false sense of "cleaning the slate" have an overzealous return for unwanted human remains. The result of the Dutch dispossession of human remains that functioned in Asmat societies will never be fully understood. What has been the effect of taking away not only part of the object that confirmed the "bragging rights" of Asmat men, but also the ancestral Ndambirkus skulls that were part of their cultural heritage? As a historic event, this is part of the 20th-century entangled relationship between the

Dutch and the Asmat and a defining token of the created stories to legitimize the control of the people, not only in New Guinea, but also with many indigenous groups that were usurped for political and economic purpose.

I am not a legal expert, but I understand the problem of ownership, neither traditional or international legal concepts nor the framework for both institutes as well as the art trade fit dealings with these contested cultural heritage objects. An interesting approach from Evelien Campfens is to create heritage titles:

> It is based on a (verifiable) continuing cultural link that entitles people with rights defined in terms of access and control, not in terms of absolute and exclusive ownership. Although we are used to defining relations between objects and people by way of exclusive ownership rights, this exclusivity does not fit cultural property.[15]

Campfens focuses on the different interest groups, which means an object in a legal dispute can be given a heritage title to grant access to former owners or creators who are tied to the objects based on a historic cultural link.

Ethics

In line with Walter Benjamin's "aura" of authenticity, Ken Hillis rightfully states that the West "fetishizes the exteriorization of memory onto objects" (Hillis, 2006: 170).[16] We often imbue human remains with a sense of taboo. In the original context, the function of human remains is as diverse as the cultures they come from. There is no single approach to dealing with the human remains in western collections, only that they must be approached with close collaboration with the people they came from. Even "neutral" scientific data like DNA analysis to determine if there are direct relatives might be an unnecessary interference.

Europe is dealing with their Colonial Heritage on a grand scale for the first time. And we use European sentiments when dealing with Human remains. Human remains were mostly either used for medical or (pseudo) scientific research or given a religious connotation by the Church. One of the great protagonists for respectful treatment of human remains is William Cobbett, co-authoring The Anatomy Act 1832 (2 & 3 Will. IV c.75)[17] of the United Kingdom that gave specific licence only to doctors, teachers of anatomy, and bona fide medical students to dissect donated bodies. It was enacted in response to public revulsion at the illegal trade in corpses. So, there was an ethical framework against grave robbery, even though that did not stop the trade in Maori Mokomokai (Toi Mokos), sometimes made "sur commande" and shipped to London. Cobbett made it perfectly clear: "Why, who is science for? Not for poor people. Then if it is necessary for science, let them have the bodies of the rich, for whose benefit science is cultivated".[18]

Meanwhile, the largest dealer in human remains in Europe has been the Catholic Church. Relics were an essential part in Catholic Church orthodoxy since the Second Council of Nicaea in 787, when church authorities made it mandatory that every church should have a relic on the altar, controlling and monopolising the reliquary market. Even though it goes against the first two commandments of the Decalogue of venerating objects, the church, for financial and political reasons, created a special exception for relics; "the body of the Blessed and of the Saints, destined for the resurrection, has been on earth the living temple of the Holy Spirit and the instrument of their holiness, recognized by the Apostolic See through beatification and canonization".[19] This has shaped our western sense of veneration of Human remains, even if most other societies do not share our perspective.

In the 20th century, this feeling of unease resulted in a scientific frame to deal with human remains that were collected by pseudo-scientific researchers in the 19th century. For scientific remains, there is the Vermillion Accord on the treatment of Human Remains,[20] adopted in 1989 at World Archeological Congress Inter-Congress, South Dakota, the United States, and in extension the Tamaki Makau-rau Accord,[21] a more specific agreement on the display of sacred objects and adopted in January 2006 by the Council of the World Archaeological Congress at its inter-congress in Osaka, Japan. Both agreements emphasize the need to involve the community and that permission should be obtained from these affected communities and, by definition,

> [h]uman remains include any organic remains and associated material. Sacred objects are those that are of special significance to a community. Display means the presentation in any media or form of human remains and sacred objects, whether on a single occasion or on an ongoing basis, including conference presentations or publications.[22]

Returning to the question of what to do with human remains from the Asmat, can we anticipate future returns? And if so, how can we let an unbridled trade of human remains go on whilst we know the complexity of those coming repatriations?

Conclusion

Many European countries are dealing with their colonial histories and their extensive institutional collections. As much as human remains seem to feel like the culmination of the disappropriation of indigenous cultures, they are but a small part of the collections and a relatively small part of the responsibility to understand the entangled histories.

Returning ancestral skulls to the Asmat might be something the West is eager to do. It would likely not be appreciated by the people themselves. Not only were some skulls given as a diplomatic transfer or even used as "spies" to transfer information. It might even be an insult to return Ndaokus. More importantly, a return could interfere with existing and continuing practices, already under great stress. The Dutch, and later the Indonesian Government, have overtaken the Asmat and other people in Papua New Guinea by military force and fused small groups into larger communities for control. A 1962 US-sponsored agreement between Jakarta and the Dutch to transfer the region to a temporary UN authority was ignored and Indonesian security forces effectively invaded. The occupying forces, both Dutch and Indonesian, have changed family structure and lineage systems amongst these Papuans, forcing them into these larger compounds. The United Nations Convention for the Protection of Cultural Property in the Event of Armed Conflict of 1954 calls on States to take special measures to protect cultural property and to avoid misappropriating or damaging such property during times of armed conflict or occupation. But even though the 1954 The Hague convention is the first multilateral treaty dedicated exclusively to the protection of cultural heritage during an armed conflict, the UNDRIP remains a better approach. In the future, if there is an indication of possible return, it is essential to follow the UNDRIP proposition, "to enable the access and/or repatriation of ceremonial objects and human remains in their possession through fair, transparent and effective mechanisms developed in conjunction with the indigenous peoples concerned".[23]

Cooperation with the indigenous people in West Papua is difficult since there are no clear representatives. The Organisasi Papua Merdeka (Free Papua Movement) is composed of different interest groups without a central head.[24] It is likely that, like the Moluccan representatives in both Indonesia and the Netherlands, they will have a more defined structure in the near future, with a possibility to negotiate on behalf of the people in western Papua.

Repatriation must be considered as a part of the restitution process, starting with the acknowledgement of historic injustice. The need to send back human remains is still mostly initiated by western institutions and is generally a laudable gesture of reconciliation. The return of human remains should nevertheless not be a part of future negotiations of restitution or reparations with the indigenous people or the countries of origin. Human remains cannot be a part of a "horse-trading" used in bargaining and negotiations but should be a step toward understanding how complex and extensive the entanglements of histories are in the colonial period. Presently, the western institutes hold the objects and documents that are essential for future provenance research. Until they are fully disclosed and accessible by researchers of the people themselves and the States where the remains originated from, both should be treated with transparency, reverence, and caution.[25]

Meanwhile, the market of online human remains is growing exponentially.[26] The internet gives an international platform to what used to be a few quirky collectors, now a possibility to join in large numbers. Facebook groups like "Authentic Tribal Skulls" and Catawiki give a new option to purchase human remains, especially newly forged decorated skulls, easily. This means that human remains from different populations are manipulated to look like they have another origin, obfuscating the origin of these remains. There is a need for a clear framework to deal with these ancestral skulls respectfully, no matter their origin, and to liberate them from being used as a continuation of the stigmas that focus on headhunting as "exotic". This framework is important to present dealings, and also to anticipate future requests of repatriation, to create a safe space for the human remains in limbo.

Notes

1 "Voorlichting over Ned.Nw.Guinea in de Ver.Staten" brief nr. 190942/2411", June 20, 1955, Algemeen Rijksarchief Den Haag.
2 "Report from Netherlands New Guinea. Propaganda film voor de Engelstalige wereld over Nieuw-Guinea", 1956, RVD (NAA-archief).
3 Huffer, Damien Graham, Shawn "The Insta-Dead: The rhetoric of the human remains trade on Instagram", Internet Archaeology, 10.11141/ia.45.5, 45 (2017). Also see Hillis, Ken (2006) "Auctioning the authentic: eBay, narrative effect, and the superfluidity of memory", in Ken Hillis, Michael Petit and Nathan Epley (eds) Everyday eBay: Culture, Collecting, and Desire, pp. 167–185. London.
4 Tanah Merah, in the Asmat region, was known for the penal camp (concentration camp 1928–1942). Undesirable individuals, prominent Indonesians who later held an important place in the new Indonesia after 1945, have been imprisoned here like Dr. Mohammad Hatta 1st Vice President of the Republic of Indonesia and Soetan Shahrir Min. President. https://repository.overheid.nl/frbr/sgd/19281929/0000293773/1/pdf/SGD_19281929_0001806.pdf
5 Gerard Zegwaard, "Headhunting Practices of the Asmat of Netherlands New Guinea" American Anthropologist, New Series, Vol. 61, No. 6, 1959, pp. 1020–1041.
6 Bjerre, Jens De laatste kannibalen in Nieuw Guinea, Amsterdam 1957.
  Veenstra, Johanna "Een blanke vrouw onder de kannibalen" J H Kok 1928.
7 Dirk Smidt, *Asmat Art: Woodcarvings of Southwest New Guinea* (1999).
8 http://tribalartasia.com/Tribal%20Art%20Asia%20Human%20Skulls/Tribal-Art-Human-Skulls.html
9 "La France restitue 20 têtes maories à la Nouvelle-Zélande".
  www.culture.gouv.fr/Nous-connaitre/Decouvrir-le-ministere/Histoire-du-ministere/Ressources-documentaires/Discours-de-ministres/Discours-de-minist res-depuis-1998/Frederic-Mitterrand-2009-2012/Articles-2009-2012/La-Fra nce-restitue-20-tetes-maories-a-la-Nouvelle-Zelande
10 Malte Jaguttis "Colonialism and its Objects. Remarks on the Framework for Repatriation and Restitution under Public International law" (2014).
11 Tubingen University "3 Wege-Strategie für die Erfassung und digitale Veröffentlichung von Sammlungsgut aus kolonialen Kontexten in Deutschland" March 2019 www.cp3c.de/3-Wege-Strategie/
12 Catherine Hickley, "Native Hawaiians Collect Ancestors' Skulls from European Museums" *New York Times*, February 10, 2022.

13 Gareth Harris, "Issue of repatriation back on the agenda" December 2, 2013 www.museumsassociation.org/museums-journal/news/2013/12/02122013-repatriation-back-on-agenda/
14 United Nations Human Rights "Repatriation of ceremonial objects, human remains and intangible cultural heritage under the United Nations Declaration on the Rights of Indigenous Peoples – Report of the Expert Mechanism on the Rights of Indigenous Peoples" A/HRC/45/35.
15 Campfens, E. Whose Cultural Objects? Introducing Heritage Title for Cross-Border Cultural Property Claims. Netherlands International Law Review, Vol. 67, 2020, p. 258. https://doi.org/10.1007/s40802-020-00174-3
16 Hills and Petit, 2006, pp. 167–85.
17 Cobbett, William "Eleven Lectures on the French and Belgian Revolutions", 1832, Vol. 3.
18 Cobbett, William "Eleven Lectures on the French and Belgian Revolutions", 1832, Vol. 3, page 13.
19 Congregation for Divine Worship and the Discipline of the Sacraments, Notificazione circa la concessione di culto in occasione del pellegrinaggio di reliquie insigni di Beati, prot. N. 717/15 of January 27, 2016; Apostolic Constitution Pastor Bonus, art. 69.
20 "The Vermillion Accord on Human Remains Adopted at WAC Inter-Congress", South Dakota 1989.
21 "The Tamaki Makau-rau Accord on the Display of Human Remains and Sacred Objects" adopted WAC Inter-Congress, Osaka, Japan 2005.
22 Fforde, Cressida "Tamaki Makau-Rau Accord on the Display of Human Remains and Sacred Objects (2005)" Springer, 2014. pp. 7209–7210.
23 (UN 2007, art. 12, 1), United Nations Declaration on the Rights of Indigenous Peoples Figure 2007 article 12, 1 www.un.org/esa/socdev/unpfii/documents/DRIPS_en.pdf
24 The Working Group on Indigenous Populations, Fifth Session, August 1987 Geneva https://irp.fas.org/world/para/docs/merdeka.htm
25 Förster, Larissa "These Skulls are not Enough – The Repatriation of Namibian Human Remains from Berlin to Windhoek in 2011", Dark matter November 18, 2013.
26 Christine Halling and Ryan M. Seidemann, "They Sell Skulls Online?!" A Review of Internet Sales of Human Skulls on eBay and the Laws in Place to Restrict Sales. *Journal of Forensic Studies* (2016).

References

Bjerre, Jens. *De Laatste Kannibalen in Nieuw Guinea*. California: Scheltens & Giltay, 1957.
Campfens, Evelien. "Whose Cultural Objects? Introducing Heritage Title for Cross-Border Cultural Property Claims." *Netherlands International Law Review*, vol. 67, no. 2, 2020, pp. 257–295.
Cobbett, William. *Eleven Lectures on the French and Belgian Revolutions, and English Boroughmongering*. London: W. Strange, 21, Paternoster Row, 1832.
"Directional memorandum for film coverage of Netherlands New Guinea", *Algemeen Rijksarchief*. Den Haag June 20, 1955.

Fforde, Cressida. "Tamaki Makau-Rau Accord on the Display of Human Remains and Sacred Objects (2005)." *Encyclopedia of Global Archaeology*, 2014, pp. 7209–7213. https://archaeologicalethics.org/book/tamaki-makau-rau-accord-on-the-display-of-human-remains-and-sacred-objects-2005-reference-work/

Free Papua Movement – Organisasi Papua Merdeka. "Statement Concerning the Right of Self-Determination of the West Papuan People." United Nations: The Working Group on Indigenous Populations", Fifth Session, Geneva. August 1987. https://irp.fas.org/world/para/docs/merdeka.htm

Förster, Larissa "These Skulls are not Enough – The Repatriation of Namibian Human Remains from Berlin to Windhoek in 2011", In *Dark Matter: In the Ruins of Imperial Culture*, November 18, 2013.

Halling, Christine L., and Ryan M. Seidemann. "They Sell Skulls Online?! A Review of Internet Sales of Human Skulls on eBay and the Laws in Place to Restrict Sales." *Journal of Forensic Sciences*, vol. 61, no. 5, 2016, pp. 1322–1326.

Harris, Gareth. "Issue of Repatriation Back on the Agenda." *Museums Association*, August 14, 2013. www.museumsassociation.org/museums-journal/news/2013/12/02122013-repatriation-back-on-agenda/#

Hickley, Catherine "Native Hawaiians Collect Ancestors' Skulls from European Museums" *New York Times*, February 10, 2022.

Hillis, Ken. "Auctioning the authentic: eBay, narrative effect, and the superfluidity of memory", in Ken Hillis, Michael Petit and Nathan Epley (Eds.). *Everyday eBay: Culture, Collecting, and Desire*, London: Routledge. 2006. pp. 167–185.

———., Petit, Michael. *Everyday eBay: Culture, Collecting, and Desire*. London: Routledge. 2006. pp. 167–185.

Huffer, Damien, and Shawn Graham "The Insta-Dead: The Rhetoric of the Human Remains Trade on Instagram." *Internet Archaeology*, vol.45, no. 4, 2017, https://doi.org/10.11141/ia.45.5

Jaguttis, Malte. "Colonialism and Its Objects. Remarks on the Framework for Repatriation and Restitution under Public International Law." *Küstliche Tatsachen*, 2014. http://artificialfacts.de/colonialism-and-its-objects-remarks-on-the-framework-for-repatriation-and-restitution-under-public-international-law1/

Kontaktstelle für Sammlungsgut aus kolonialen Kontexten in Deutschland. "3 Wege-Strategie Für Die Erfassung Und Digitale Veröffentlichung Von Sammlungsgut Aus Kolonialen Kontexten in Deutschland." *Kontaktstelle Für Sammlungsgut Aus Kolonialen Kontexten in Deutschland*, February 20, 2020. www.cp3c.de/3-Wege-Strategie/

"La France restitue 20 têtes maories à la Nouvelle-Zélande" www.culture.gouv.fr/Nous-connaitre/Decouvrir-le-ministere/Histoire-du-ministere/Ressources-documentaires/Discours-de-ministres/Discours-de-ministres-depuis-1998/Frederic-Mitterrand-2009-2012/Articles-2009-2012/La-France-restitue-20-tetes-maories-a-la-Nouvelle-Zelande

"Notificazione circa La Concessione Di Culto in Occasione Del Pellegrinaggio Di Reliquie Insigni Di Beati. *Congregation for Divine Worship and the Discipline of the Sacraments*. prot. N. 717/15 of January 27, 2016. www.vatican.va/roman_curia/congregations/ccdds/index.htm

"Report from Netherlands New Guinea. Propaganda film voor de Engelstalige wereld over Nieuw-Guinea", 1956, RVD (NAA-archief). https://repository.overheid.nl/frbr/sgd/19281929/0000293773/1/pdf/SGD_19281929_0001806.pdf

Smidt Dirk. *Asmat Art: Woodcarvings of Southwest New Guinea.* Singapore: Periplus, 1999.

"The Vermillion Accord on Human Remains", adopted at the World Archeological Congress". Vermillion, South Dakota, 1989.

"The Tamaki Makau-rau Accord on the Display of Human Remains and Sacred Objects", adopted World Archeological Congress, Osaka, Japan, 2005.

United Nations. "United Nations Declaration on the Rights of Indigenous Peoples." Article 12.1, 2007. www.un.org/esa/socdev/unpfii/documents/DRIPS_en.pdf?0.05145342793718122

United Nations. "Repatriation of Ceremonial Objects, Human Remains and Intangible Cultural Heritage under the United Nations Declaration on the Rights of Indigenous Peoples." *United Nations*, United Nations, https://digitallibrary.un.org/record/3876274?ln=en

Van Der, Zee Pauline, et al. *BISJ-Poles: Sculptures from the Rain Forest.* Amsterdam: KIT Publishers, 2007.

Veenstra, Johanna, and D. K. Wielenga. *Een Blanke Vrouw Onder De Kannibalen: Christus-Prediking in Den Soedan.* Netherlands: J.H. Kok, 1928.

Zegwaard, Gerard A. "Headhunting Practices of the Asmat of Netherlands New Guinea." *American Anthropologist*, vol. 61, no. 6, 1959, pp. 1020–1041, https://doi.org/10.1525/aa.1959.61.6.02a00080

10 On the Art of Forging Gods

Techniques, Forces and Materials in an Afro-Brazilian Religion[1]

Lucas Marques

Introduction

In the transition from the nineteenth to the twentieth century, Raymundo Nina Rodrigues, considered as one of the founders of Brazilian anthropology, was intrigued by the fact that, for the black population in Bahia, such as for the people in West Africa, stones, trees or iron objects, when consecrated, were worshiped as being gods. He states that "any iron object can be worshiped as Ogum, as long as it has been consecrated" (Rodrigues 1935, 43–44). A little thunderstone, in turn, can be the materialization of the *orixá* Xangô, what he called "the clearest manifestation of Bahian litholatry" (14). To this double perplexity – that the gods must be created throughout a series of ritual relations and that they could be things – Nina Rodrigues attributed the name "fetishist animism". Based on a racist and evolutionist perspective, he claims that the term marked "a very curious phase of animism, in which its deities already shared the anthropomorphic qualities of polytheistic deities, but they still preserved the outer forms of primitive fetishism" (173). The term, thus, indicated a supposed "mental confusion of the primitive thought", which did not separate the planes of immanence and transcendence, the material from the spiritual.

After more than a century of Nina Rodrigues' work, one can say that this perplexity remained alive among scholars of religions of African origin in Brazil. Of course, since then, things (and their gods) have never stopped populating the pages of ethnographies about these religions, but most of the time, they only appeared tangentially or subsumed to other dimensions, be they social, political or economic. Things and gods thus remained as separate and irreconcilable realms. It was only recently, as Goldman (2009) recalls, that "a new interest in the material objects of Candomblé has provoked a return to the topics formerly grouped under the confused and certainly accusatory rubric of fetishism" (115). Thus, authors such as Latour (2010), Sansi (2005), Halloy (2013) and Goldman (2009) returned to the theme in order to build new and inspiring perspectives on the relationship between people, things and gods in Candomblé.[2] This essay follows a similar path, but with a slightly different focus. While most of the analyses emphasize

DOI: 10.4324/9781003282334-13

religious objects as "already made" (on the materiality of things), my aim here, inspired by Ingold's (2011) proposal, focuses on the processes that give birth to things and gods in Candomblé. In doing so, I seek to demonstrate how technique and ontology (or technique and life) cannot be thought of separately in this universe, where gods and materials are made and kept alive through a constant ritual and technical work.

To explore this theme, I draw on fieldwork research[3] carried out between 2012 and 2015 in the workshop of José Adário dos Santos, better known as "Zé Diabo". In this workshop, located in the Historic Centre of Salvador, Bahia, Zé Diabo had been working for over 50 years producing iron artefacts known as "*ferramentas de orixá*" (Orixá tools). These artefacts belong to African-derived religions, such as Candomblé and Umbanda, and after a series of technical and ritual gestures become the entities themselves materialized. In Candomblé, these entities are called Orixás, deities who mediate the relation between God (*Olodumaré*) and humans.[4]

In this chapter, I propose to follow the different stages of making an artefact of the Orixá Exu, from the moment the entity reveals itself, going through the process of sketching the artefact, forging the iron pieces and connecting them by welding, until the moment the artefact is delivered and goes to a candomblé house (*terreiro*). By following the "operational chain"[5] of manufacturing an Orixá tool, I seek not just to include the spirits in the analysis but also to demonstrate the very inseparability between spirit and matter in this universe. For that, it will be necessary to take seriously a certain theory of forces that permeates Zé Diabo's workshop. A theory that links humans, materials and gods around particular forces that are ritually manipulated.

The Jabá of Ogum

Located at Ladeira da Conceição da Praia, number 26, where sex workers, blacksmiths and marble workers share the famous sidewalks that inspired Jorge Amado's novels, the "Nação José" workshop is one of the oldest in the region. It was there, in 1958, that José began to learn the craft of the blacksmiths of Orixás when he was only 11 years old. At that time, he was an apprentice in the workshop of his mentor, Martiniano Prates. They made custom iron gates, *agogôs*[6] and Orixá tools that were sold at the former *Mercado Modelo*, a traditional market in Salvador. Later, José managed to open his own workshop, exclusively to produce Orixá tools and sacred Afro-Brazilian instruments, such as *agogôs*.

At the age of 75, Zé Diabo is considered by the people of Candomblé as one of the most traditional blacksmiths of Orixás in Bahia. His process of technical work with metals accompanied his learnings in Candomblé. Initiated in the religion when he was still a child by his maternal grandmother, Barbara do Sacramento, Zé Diabo is also a respected *babalorixá* (Candomblé priest). That is the reason his clientele considers him to be someone who "knows how to do things", or, as Raul Lody (1983) puts it, someone who fulfils "the precepts to be able to do it right, as the custom dictates, as required by the religious tradition" (19). In 1968, Robert Farris Thompson, during a trip to Bahia, attested that: "[José Adário] Dos Santos follows firm Yoruba canons of expression while at the same time designating modern tools of iron as extensions of Ogún's realm" (Thompson 1987, 57).

Each tool produced by Zé Diabo is unique, made in order to mediate the particular relation between the person and their Orixá. Due to its uniqueness, each artefact goes through a specific creation process. From the beginning, the blacksmith must intuit the shape and characteristics of each Orixá, creatively exploring the possibilities that the iron offers and the traditional forms of each entity. Beyond just making an artefact, the blacksmith must be knowledgeable about which technical choices are appropriate to establish certain specific relations between matter, the gods, the initiates and the craftsman himself. These choices involve, among other things, the raw material, colour, shapes, textures and, mainly, the ways of making dedicated to each Orixá.[7]

In Candomblé, as Roger Bastide (2001) pointed out, each part of the universe belongs to an Orixá. Inspired by Lévy-Bruhl's ideas, Bastide called this phenomenon the "participation principle". According to him, the Yoruban philosophy – and, therefore, the philosophy of Candomblé – acts through a "crystallization of a set of participations between humans, things and orixás" (70). The mythical Yoruba division present in the spiritual plane (the *Orun*) expands to everything that exists in the material plane (the *Aiye*). Thus, each Orixá has a set of materials that express it and through which it materializes in the world.

In this system, iron belongs to the Orixá Ogum, patron of agricultural knowledge and, above all, the divine artisan who dominates metals. Ogum is the blacksmith Orixá, lord of wars and technologies. He is the second Orixá of the pantheon of the Afro-Brazilian gods, preceded by Exu, to which he is closely linked. All production must pass through the path of Ogum. He is known as the one who opens paths and is referred to as the lord of the roads. Zé Diabo states that "Ogum is everything. Everything has to have Ogum. Every tool carries Ogum, the jaba of Ogum. There is nothing you can do without him."[8] Despite being consecrated to the Orixás Oxalufã and Omolu, Zé Diabo has a very close relationship with Ogum, since it is he who governs the entire technical process of the blacksmith. Thus, in order to work with iron, he must follow the *path* of Ogum, paying obeisance to this Orixá. This means that Zé Diabo only manufactures tools for those Orixás who "*work with iron*", that is, deities with iron as their raw material. In general, they are hunter and warrior Orixás, such as Exu, Ogum, Oxóssi, Obaluaiê, Ossain, Tempo and Oxumarê. Working with other materials would require dealing with other strengths and abilities, following other paths. As Zé Diabo asserts, "*I was born to work the iron, in the rough. I was raised like that. It was Ogum who made me this way*".

188 *Lucas Marques*

Technique, as conceptualized by Leroi-Gourhan (1993), is a mode of relation that favours the genesis of both the artefact and the human (and, in this case, also the gods). Returning to Zé Diabo's words, it is through the technique – and the forces that inhabit it – that the blacksmith himself is built. The technique guides the energies that the blacksmith must contend with. Through the interaction with iron, Zé Diabo builds himself as a blacksmith and strengthens his relationship with Ogum. This is what he calls the *jabá of* Ogum: the blacksmith's work, but also the technique and the energies (which, in Candomblé, are called *axé*) that flow into the iron.

Every piece of iron has the energy of Ogum. However, some irons are considered to be stronger or more alive than others. Rusted irons, for example, are more powerful, because they carry more energy (*axé*) of the Orixá. Especially those coming from specific artefacts linked to Ogum, such as highway screws, anchors for sailing ships, nails, knives, swords, chains or even automotive engines, turnstiles, irons of old buildings and so on. These materials are considered *raw*, as they have a concentrated force of the Orixá and often do not even need to be worked by the blacksmith. According to Zé, the Orixá tools were produced mainly with these materials in the past. Nowadays, however, Zé Diabo usually buys the material from used metal deposits (junkyards) or even in specialized hardware and metal stores. Nevertheless, he carefully chooses each material, depending on the tool he will produce and according to specific thickness,

Figure 10.1 Zé Diabo in his workshop welding agogôs.
Source: author, 2013.

shape and texture. Each material has a different density, ductility, resilience, weight and melting point, the characteristics that must be taken into account when working with the forge – and which, as mentioned earlier, cannot be disconnected from the Orixá's own strength. Even though these irons do not have the same strength as raw material, it is through the work of the blacksmith that such irons acquire more strength, becoming more alive. The *jabá of Ogum*, an intensity of the Orixa's strength, is imbued in the material through Ogum's characteristic work, the forge. Therefore, the work of Zé Diabo in his workshop consists of channelling certain energies through the various transformations that irons go through – from the raw material to a *terreiro*. When the Orixá tool leaves the workshop, it undergoes new making rituals that will link this god artefact to an initiate in the religion. In order to follow this process, I move on to describe the making of an Exu Orixá tool.

A Request from Exu

It was an ordinary Thursday at Zé Diabo's workshop. The sound of metals reigned, the noise of sawdust, the welding, the hammering on the anvil. Space and time were defined by the senses. In the workshop, it was necessary to listen to the sound of metals, the iron screaming and pulsing at the touch of the hammer. Each action – forging, soldering, assembling, painting and drying – had its own time, space and rhythm. These rhythms were interrupted only when someone arrived at the workshop or when we went out at the end of the day to have a beer at Evandro's bar next door.

That was the case when, on that Thursday, a black lady hurried up the stairs to speak to Zé Diabo. The lady, Dona Dalva, carried a small piece of torn paper with some disconnected doodles. In the middle of them, there was a drawing of Exu holding a key and a trident. She handed the paper to Zé Diabo, who promptly opened it and examined it at length. Dona Dalva then explained that she had dreamed of her Exu, and, as soon as she woke up, she had intuitively drawn it on a piece of paper. "*It was Exu who requested*", she said, "*he wants to be made this way*". Studying the paper, Zé Diabo asked her a few questions in order to discover the *quality*[9] of the deity and what the iron would "accept" from the sketch. He asked, for example, if the line on his head was a hat and if his head would have to be uncovered or not. In addition, he said that the key should be attached to Exu's foot by a chain because he is the only one who has the power to open and close doors. Finally, he said that the key and trident had to be made with a 3/8 iron;[10] otherwise, the tool would not last long. Dona Dalva agreed and said she would need the tool for the following week, as the deity was demanding to be made. Zé Diabo then settled a price for the order, and she gave him an advance.

After the conversation, Zé Diabo redrew her scribbles on another piece of old paper, creating new lines where the hat, the horns, the key and the trident were highlighted. With a measuring tape in hand, he imagined the proportions of the artefact. Despite referring to the artefact that would be produced, the drawing did not seem to be a reliable reproduction of what would be the final format of the tool. In other words, it was not a "project" of the artefact – in the modern sense of design (Flusser 2013) – but a form of engagement between Zé and the entity itself in which he senses its forms and proportions through a tensioned dialogue. Communication that takes into account both the desires of the Orixá and the forms and transformations that the iron matter itself is capable of *accepting*. As he says: "*everything has to have its size, its place in the world. If you have drawn something wrong, it is useless, the iron will not obey, it will not want to be made that way*". The actions of the Orixá and the iron cannot be thought of as two different things. The materiality of iron itself is the Orixá and vice versa.

Of all the tools manufactured by Zé Diabo, the Exus are the only ones that can appear in an anthropomorphic format, having a well-defined body and face. Exu, regarded as the first in the pantheon of the Yoruban gods, is the closest entity to humans in Candomblé, the messenger between the Orun and the Aiye. As a kind of trickster, he is prone to inversions and games. He is also the Orixá of malice and sexuality, often identified by a huge phallus (*ogó*). The street and crossroads are his domain. Finally, Exu is the Orixá of movement, the very dynamics of action and transformation, the principle of multiplicity (Elbein dos Santos 1977).

In general, the Exu tools can be made from clay, stone, wood or, as is more common in the Candomblé of Bahia, in wrought iron sculptures. These sculptures usually present two distinct patterns. The first, termed by Zé Diabo as "figures", are sculpted in ideogram formats, in a combination of crosses, tridents, spears, arrows, swords and other props that express the transformative nature of the Orixá, akin to the "*pontos riscados*" of Umbanda or the "*firmas*" of the Cuban Palo Monte.[11] The latter, called "*Exu dolls*", "*slaves*" or even "*devils*", are manufactured in anthropomorphic formats, having eyes, mouth, nose and ears, but also horns, tails, knives and an exposed sexual organ, in addition to carrying tridents, knives, keys and other mundane elements.

As one of its many versions indicates, Exu is often associated with the figure of the devil. It is, in fact, because of this association that Zé Diabo earned his nickname. When he took the figurines of Exu to be sold at the old Mercado Modelo, people began to call him Zé Diabo, associating him with the entity. This association, however (like everything concerning Exu), is only partial and often reflects prejudice against these religions. As Mariano Carneiro da Cunha (1983) points out, the incorporation of elements such as horns, tridents and tails in Exu statuettes relates more to a recreation of elements already present in African contexts than to the association with the Christian demon. Furthermore, as Jim Wafer (1991) recalls, the "confusion" between Exu and the devil reveals Exu's corruption, seen from the Christian conception of evil, and the devil's reinterpretation when seen by Candomblé.

Thus, at the same time that Exu was demonized, the Christian demon himself also became a little bit of the Orixá. Exu is the very figure of the double, of reversion. He may or may not be the devil through his multiple variations. Close to humans, Exu shares stories of his multiple human forms, carrying mundane elements to intercede in favour of those allied with him. This is the case, for example, of Dona Dalva's Exu, called *"tranca-rua"* (street lock). In one of his hands, he carried a key with him so that he could open or lock the paths and doors. This key is manipulated in different ways: it may come out of Exu's hand, it may be locked with a padlock, it may be at the feet of the deity and so on, depending on the ritual and the desired purposes. To manipulate the shapes of the Orixá tools is to activate the very forces through which they are able to act in the world. Thus, the materials and insignia that each entity carries not only "represent" the deity but are fundamental to updating certain relations, allowing the deity to *work*. As Sansi (2007) suggests, artefacts in Candomblé should be thought of as *sacred-concrete* objects, "not simply an abstract symbol of an Orixá but the concrete memory of a relationship between the Orixá and the devotee" (39).

Forging Gods

Four days had passed since Dona Dalva's request, and Zé Diabo had not yet started to manufacture the tool. The sketch was fading on the workshop wall, mixed with papers, beads and rubble. The delivery was scheduled for Tuesday, and so, on that Monday morning, Zé Diabo took the drawing off the wall to start making the Exu. It is with this Orixá that, whenever possible, Zé Diabo usually begins his work, following the classificatory order of the Orixás as they appear in the *xirê*, a sequence in which the Orixás are revered or invoked during the services intended for them. He always starts with Exu, the first Orixá, and then moves on to Ogum, Oxóssi and so on, depending on the demand of the moment. In addition, he seeks to be connected with the various forces that permeate the workshop, carrying out a series of care and preparation rituals before starting to work. Thus, he asks for permission from the divinities that govern his craft (especially Exu and Ogum). He prays an Our Father and a Hail Mary and lights a candle for the Catholic saints arranged on a small altar in the background.

With the drawing in hand, Zé Diabo begins to choose the materials that will be used for the preparation of the Exu, taking into account their sizes, thicknesses and textures. Amid cigars and old pieces of iron, he takes a thick and heavy iron tube of approximately 40 cm, which will form the head, neck and trunk of the entity. He also measures and saws some plates and iron bars of different thicknesses in different sizes. Here, a new way of relations between the blacksmith, the material and the gods are established. At this stage of preparation of the materials, he starts a more intense dialogue with the iron and the various utensils of the workshop. There is a need to be sensitive to the possibilities offered by each material: the iron bars are stubborn; the plates are dangerous; the saw may want to break; hammers are deceiving and so on. This sensitivity, however, is above all practical, insofar as it requires an impression of a specific gestural rhythm on the matter in a synergistic interaction between the blacksmith, the materials and the gods. This complex synergy will permeate all the work in the workshop and will be fundamental to the process of individuation of the Orixá tool, as will become clearer in the next production stage, the forge.

Forging is undoubtedly the most important part of Orixá tool making. It is what characterizes the work and the very constitution of the blacksmith. In addition, through forging, the energies of the deities are channelled into the artefact, gestating it.[12] Before going to the fire – an activity that he performs only once a day, usually in the morning – Zé Diabo fulfils a series of specific rituals, necessary to leave him with a "good head" for the job. During the activity, he rarely says anything. All one hears is the sound of the bellows and the machine, the fire burning and the successive blows of the hammer on the anvil: "*If you talk too much, your judgment will go away*", he says. Between the strokes of hammering and waiting for the bars to heat up, Zé Diabo always smokes a cigar. Its smoke mixes with the smoke from the furnace that heats the metals. Tobacco, according to him, allows the gods to "*open his head*", leaving him with a good *orí* (head, in Yorubá) to work.

The forge requires a certain brutality from the blacksmith, a certain strength in the technical gesture of striking and bending the iron. At the same time, it also demands a specific sensibility for the rhythms and synergies between the different movements. All elements must constantly be attuned. The fire must be controlled by means of the wind from the bellows and the right amount of coal, based on an unconscious calculation between the rhythm of work and the burning of the fuel. The iron must be heated until it reaches a certain temperature, which is perceived from the redness of the material, sufficient to become malleable, but not so much as to melt. It is at that moment that Zé Diabo, with the help of the tongs (one of the extensions of the blacksmith's arm), removes the iron from the fire and places it on the anvil, striking it with a heavy hammer (another body extension), with fast and extremely accurate movements. Each gesture requires a certain rhythm and prints a specific shape to the material, which is "folded" several times until it reaches the desired shape.

In addition to the materiality of metals, the blacksmith's gestural interactions must take into account the spiritual energies that pulsate in each activity that he engages. Thus, he must deal with the specific energies of each deity: Ogum, lord of iron and forge; Exu, Orixá of transformation; Xangô, who has the power of fire; Oxum, lady of the waters; Iansã, owner of the wind and so on. Through this synergistic rhythmic complex comprising fire, hammer, bellows, the blacksmith's technical ability and the force of the deities, iron gradually becomes something else, an Orixá tool.

After forging, the artefact is "assembled", that is, its various parts are put together by means of the weld. If during the preparation and forging, the

On the Art of Forging Gods 193

dialogue of the blacksmith with the material and with the Orixás is more gestural than spoken, then, at the stage of assembling, the dialogue becomes more verbal, even artful. As the irons are beaten, sawn and assembled, they acquire an ontological status as an Orixá tool. At this stage, Exu, the trickster Orixá, provokes the blacksmith, inciting him to make mistakes or making his work more difficult. Such as breaking the saw, making him get burnt in the weld, disappearing the materials, escaping the lathe bar and so on. Exu always demands a high standard response, either in the form of a more "rude" and spoken dialogue with the entity-artefact, or in the form of a more "firm" bodily engagement of the blacksmith.

Finally, the assembled artefact is sanded and painted with a thin layer of varnish. This task is usually attributed to his son, José, or to me, due to the fact that, during the fieldwork, I ended up becoming a kind of helper and apprentice to Zé Diabo.[13] With the use of tools such as hammers and pliers, the activity involves removing the excess impurities caused by the weld, to *"make the devil look like a human"*, as Zé Diabo says. At the end of this stage, in the afternoon, the Exu tool is placed to dry under the sun, always looking outside – so that the entity protects the workshop. At that moment, the tool takes on a very particular ontological status; while it remains an artefact (or, as Zé would say, *"just a piece of wrought iron"*), it is no longer just a piece of iron, because it carries the *jabá of Ogum*, the vital energy (*axé*) of that Orixá. As it becomes increasingly divine, the Exu tool also

Figure 10.2 Exus and Ogum in Zé Diabo's workshop.
Source: author, 2013.

becomes more human. That is why, at this stage, Zé Diabo would usually put a lit cigar in Exu's mouth, or even insert a lottery game in one of his horns, as Exu is a fan of gambling and usually brings luck to those who ally with him. The tool, in some way, is already Exu. As I heard several times from Zé Diabo's clients: "*the tool leaves the workshop already alive*". This "life", however, is a life that will still go through many other processes of making, being crossed by other modes of existence.

Forging Relations

The following morning, Dona Dalva appeared accompanied by an *ogã*[14] of her *terreiro* to get the Exu tool. She sat down and talked with Zé Diabo while discreetly settling her due. After leaving the workshop, the Orixá tool went to a Candomblé *terreiro*, where it will be *made* again. In composition with other elements, the artefact will form the *assentamento* (settlement) of the Orixá, believed to be the materialization of the deity on earth. Once it is *made*, this settlement will become a constituent part of the person, an energetic and bodily extension of the person–Orixá relational complex, something close to what Alfred Gell (1998) called a "distributed person". The *assentamento* must be constantly fed, receiving sacrifices, offerings, food, being washed with herbs and other substances such as olive oil, palm oil or honey, actively participate in the dynamics of exchange relations that will strengthen the relationship between the person and their Orixá (Rabelo 2014). The series of relations transform the materials and the forces that compose them. Over time, irons corrode, stones darken, clay may break, leaves may decompose, trees might die, as well as people or even gods can disappear from this plane.[15] This is related to the *axé* cycle itself, which may increase, decrease, dissipate, concentrate and so on, depending on the ritual activities (Elbein dos Santos 1977).

Since this process of composition of forces is linked to the very potential of the material, the "biography" of the artefact[16] is fundamental to activate certain relations in a process that crosses different modes of existence.[17] For example, the older and more worn an *assentamento* is, the more strength it will have, as it is a sign that it has received more offerings. As sacrificial blood has been spilled more often on it, its existence is more consolidated. Zé Diabo's Ogum, for example, is one of his strongest and most important Orixá tools. It was *settled* more than 40 years ago, at the time that he opened his own workshop. It is an imposing *assentamento*, not so much because of its size, but because of the marks it has accumulated during its existence. The irons that make up the tool are completely worn out, rusted and corroded, a sign of the climate action, and also of the countless offerings it has already received, the libations of olive oil, blood, salt, honey, *cachaça* and so on. Zé Diabo is proud of the ageing tool, and, in some way, the wear and tear of materials are signs of the strength of this relationship. As Zé Diabo declared:

This Ogum has been with me since I arrived at the workshop, and it will continue with me until I leave this world. Because it was not made with those weak irons that are used today, it has strength; it was made with a strong iron, such as those of a ship. That is why, although it gets corroded, it resists, it will not break easily.

Therefore, the existence of Ogum cannot be separated from the very materiality of iron: it is through wearing, the actions that corrode and modify it, that the person-Orixá-material relationship is made.

This system of channelling, modulation and maintenance of forces could be translated as a kind of "ecology". In this ecology, *axé* can be considered a force that ontologically precedes the very distinction between people and things. The production rituals, therefore, aim to individuate these forces. But this individuation, to use a term proposed by Simondon (2002), is never complete, requiring a constant work of maintenance and composition. In other words, if everything in Candomblé is "alive", then this life is only possible if it is inserted in the very fabric that constitutes it, in this mutual engagement between forces and flows.

At first, the ecological approach proposed by Tim Ingold (2011) helps us to think about all this relational "mesh" that involves forces and flows in Candomblé, drawing attention to the processes of formation of "things" to their itineraries and transformations. Ingold proposes to reverse the emphasis on the materiality of things to the properties of materials and their processes of formation, rejecting the notion of object to insert things in the flow of life. However, it is important to note that if we follow the way people, things and gods are made in Candomblé, it becomes apparent that these religious practices offer their own concept of life. In Candomblé, everything is alive and permeated with *axé*. Things, gods and people, however, have different degrees of existence. They exist "more" or "less", according to the different intensities of force that run through them. A stone, for example, could be an *otá* (i.e. a special stone that carries the presence of the god), a powerful stone or just an ordinary rock that even so possesses the energy of the Orixá (see Sansi 2005). As Bastide (2001) states, it is not a logical identification but "a whole range of degrees of participation, from simple associations to identifications" (257). Thus, between "being" and "not-being", there is an infinite number of possibilities of modulations that make things different. If everything exists, some things must still be done. This, I believe, is Candomblé's great existential challenge, in a world where everything is (already) alive, how is it possible to make life, manipulate forces and compose worlds?

Conclusion, or the Art of Making

If we take up and expand the notion of "participation" present in Bastide's work, one can say, as Goldman (2007) proposes, that Candomblé has a kind of "basic monism", a force (*axé*) that constitutes "everything in the universe according to a process of differentiation and individuation" (116). According to the author, this force exists in excess, in a "virtual" plane that is "updated" through ritual manipulation. Each being is constituted as "a kind of crystallization or molarization resulting from the modulating flow of ashe, which starting out as a general and homogeneous force continuously gets more diversified and more concrete" (ibid., 110). Based on the fact that *axé* can be thought of as a force that crosses everything that exists and can exist in the universe in different modulations, Goldman (2009) suggests that Candomblé provides an "alternative theory of the creation process" (128–129). This process is less like the Western conception of creation, which operates through the addition of elements (an example is the artistic process of painting), and more like the artistic process of sculpture, which operates by means of polishing and updating virtualities that, however, already existed as realities.[18] Goldman's argument allows us to explore a certain notion of making in the world of Candomblé. An idea that does not explain the process of making within a Western hylomorphic model, separating form from matter, being from becoming. Making, in Candomblé, should be thought of less as creation and more as a process of composition and individuation of a series of forces that already exist excessively in the world. To use a term recently proposed by the philosopher Yuk Hui (2017), it is another "cosmotechnic" at stake here, another way of conceiving technique, cosmos and the relation between them.[19]

Following the making of an Orixá tool, it is clear that it is through Zé Diabo's gestures, rhythms and movements, that is, through his technique, that the strength of the Orixá – the *jabá of Ogum* – is actualized in the materials. But, to deal with these gestures, the blacksmith must take into account the materials' own "desires", the way they "ask" to be made. Hence, as we have seen, the process of transforming iron into an Orixá tool, more than merely technical, involves the channelling of forces (of axé) on that material through technical gestures and rhythmic movements. By participating in this synergy of movements and forces, Zé Diabo puts a little of himself into the tool, charging the material with his work, his energy and that of the Orixá to which he is connected.

Although worked by the blacksmith, the iron is and is not a "simple piece of iron". It has always possessed the force of Ogum, yet, it still needs to be continually made, manufactured. Thus, the vague notions of "animism" or "fetishism", so cherished by Western perceptions of otherness, do not do justice to the complex systems of channelling and composition of forces present in Candomblé, where things, gods and people go through different processes of individuation through a balance that is always unstable and demands constant care and manipulation.[20] As Goldman (2009) states, the fact that in Candomblé, everything already exists in excess does not mean that there is nothing to be done; quite the contrary: it is because the energies are in excess in the world that they need to be manipulated, made, manufactured.

"Axé, as Robert Farris Thompson (1984) brilliantly defined it, is the "power-to-make-things-happen."[21] In a world filled with *axé*, there is always something to be made, some energy to compose, some ritual that allows you certain things, some requirement of obligation. Making is creating passages in a world full of forces: channelling certain energies towards certain objectives, forming existential territories composed of different things. These passages will always have certain effects, which will have to be dealt with in the course of life. So, we could think of Candomblé as an art of composing and decomposing lives, modulating the forces that permeate different beings. After all, this is the true art practiced by Zé Diabo: an art of creating life, of channelling forces that allow things (gods, artefacts, people) to happen.

Notes

1 The research was funded by the Conselho Nacional de Desenvolvimento Científico e Tecnológico (CNPq) and Fundação de Apoio a Pesquisa do Rio de Janeiro (Faperj) in Brazil. I would like to thank Zainabu Jallo for the fruitful dialogue and for the opportunity to contribute to this volume. I am eternally grateful to Zé Diabo for teaching me everything that I know about the fascinating world of Candomblé. I also thank Marcio Goldman, Edgar Rodrigues Barbosa Neto and Luisa Elvira Belaunde for commenting on the research of which this text is a part, as advisors and evaluators, respectively. Luisa kindly read and made corrections to this text, for which I am very thankful. Finally, my special thanks go to Maria Garcia, who had the generosity and patience to help me translate this article.
2 It is worth remembering that this new interest came in the midst of broader discussions in anthropology, such as the so-called material turn, the "new animism" and the "ontological turn" (see Henare, Holbraad, and Wastell 2007).
3 The research was funded by CNPq and Faperj and resulted in my dissertation thesis (see Marques 2016).
4 Although in Candomblé there is a supreme God, called Olodumaré, this God is inaccessible to humans and there is no specific ritual dedicated to Him. Thus, the Orixás (particles of the supreme force) are responsible for mediating the relation between the celestial and the mundane planes, the *Orun* and the *Aiye*.
5 The idea of the operational chain (*chaîne opératoire*) was initially formulated by Leroi-Gourhan (1993) and is conceived as a method, allied to a theoretical framework, committed to understanding the nature and role of technical activities in human societies, describing the chain of actions on the matter (Schlanger 2005).
6 *Agogôs* are tonal bells used in Candomblé ceremonies.
7 See Silva (2008).
8 All Zé Diabo's quotes were recorded from a fieldwork carried out between 2012 and 2015.
9 The quality (*qualidade*) is a kind of variation, or individuation of an Orixá. For example, Ogum Xoroquê is one of the qualities (or *caminos* in Cuban Santería)

of Ogum. Tranca Rua is one of the qualities of Exu, something that individualizes it, presenting specific characteristics.
10 It is a cylindrical and solid iron bar, approximately 0.56 kg/m and about 9.5 mm in diameter.
11 For the Kongo Graphic writing in the Cuban Palo Monte, see Martínez-Ruiz 2013.
12 It is interesting to notice some similarities between this process and those described in ethnographies on metallurgy in African context, like in Childs and Killick (1993) and Dieterlen (1964). In many of these narratives, the fabrication of metal artefacts is compared to human pregnancy, connecting the furnace to the womb.
13 More than just observing, during the fieldwork I started to actively participate in the daily work at the workshop, helping Zé Diabo in the different stages of the production of artefacts. Over time, Zé also started to invite me to spaces that went beyond the limits of the workshop, as in the various rituals performed in the Candomblé terreiros with which he had some kind of connection. So, my learning process involved both a technical apprenticeship with metals and an apprenticeship in Candomblé. In the workshop, I had to learn to listen to the iron and to respond to its demands, understanding that iron was not "just a piece of iron." On the learning process in Candomblé and in Zé Diabo's workshop, see Marques 2021.
14 The *ogã* is a male honorific role in Candomblé that is responsible for a series of tasks, such as playing the *atabaques* (Candomblé drums), carrying out the animal sacrifices and performing the mediation between the *terreiro* and the public sphere.
15 In a fundamental article, Karin Barber (1981) discusses how for African Yorubá People it is the attention given to the deities that maintain and keep their existence. In Yoruba thought, humans make their own gods, since the power of the Orisà depends on the attention that is devoted to them.
16 See Kopytoff (1986).
17 Some of the Orixá tools produced by Zé Diabo end up in museums and art exhibitions in different places of the world, such as the Museu Afro Brasil in São Paulo, the Fowler Museum in California and in the Museu Afro-Brasileiro in Salvador. In some sort of a detour from its sacred path, these artefacts are transformed into "ethnic objects" and enter the art circuit. This carries a series of cosmopolitical effects that take place at the crossroads between art, museums and candomblé (as explored by the work of Sansi 2005), tensioning the very notion of art, museum and even life. I pretend to explore these tensions in another opportunity.
18 The vocabulary is inspired by the concepts of virtual and actual elaborated by Gilles Deleuze (2002). Both virtual and actual exist as realities, but the latter is a concretization of the former, that still exist in virtuality.
19 I intend to outline what would be a Candomblé cosmotechnic in further work.
20 For the notion of metastable balance of technical objects, see Simondon (2002). For the author, individuation refers to ontogenic processes that are not limited to the unity of being (characterized by the notion of individual). The process of becoming does not exhaust the "pre-individual" reality of being – a reality that is characterized by its own genesis. Such a perspective allows us to think of being not as an already constituted unit (or an identity), but as a continuous

and tensioned process of individuation that is maintained through a metastable system (or a transductive unit). In the case of Candomblé, a process that requires constant ritual work.
21 Or, inspired by Latour's notion of factish, the power-to-make-things-make (see Latour 2010).

References

Barber, Karin. "How Man Makes God in West Africa: Yoruba Attitudes Towards the "Orisa". *Africa: Journal of the International African Institute*, vol. 51, no. 3, 1981, pp. 724–745.
Bastide, Roger. *O Candomblé Da Bahia: Rito Nagô*. São Paulo: Companhia das Letras, 2001.
Childs, S. Terry, and David Killick. "Indigenous African Metallurgy: Nature and Culture." *Annual Review of Anthropology*, vol. 22, 1993. pp. 317–337.
Cunha, Mariano Carneiro da. "Arte Afro-Brasileira." *História geral da arte no Brasil*, vol. 2. São Paulo: Instituto Walter Moreira Salles, 1983. pp. 973–1033.
Deleuze, Gilles. "The Actual and the Virtual." *Dialogues II*. Rev. ed. Trans. Eliot Ross Albert. New York and Chichester: Columbia UP, 2002. pp. 148–152.
Dieterlen, Germaine. "Contribution à L'étude des Forgerons En Afrique Occidentale." *École pratique des hautes études, Section des sciences religieuses*, 1964. pp. 3–28.
Elbein dos Santos, Juana. *Os Nagô E a Morte*. Petrópolis: Ed. Vozes, 1977.
Flusser, Vilém. *Shape of Things: A Philosophy of Design*. London: Reaktion Books, 2013.
Gell, Alfred. *Art and agency: an Anthropological Theory*. Oxford: Clarendon Press, 1998
Goldman, Marcio "An Afro-Brazilian Theory of the Creative Process: An Essay in Anthropological Symmetrization." *Social Analysis*, vol. 53, no. 9, 2009, pp. 108–129.
———. "How to Learn in an Afro-Brazilian Spirit Possession Religion." *Learning Religion: Anthropological Approaches*, no. 17, 2007, pp. 103–119.
———. "Jeanne Favret-Saada, os afetos, a etnografia." São Paulo: Cadernos de. Campo vol. 13, no.13, 2005: 149-153
Halloy, A. "Objects, Bodies and Gods." In: *Making Spirits: Materiality and Transcendence in Contemporary Religions*. Diana Espirito Santo and Nico Tassi (eds.). London: I.B. Tauris, 2013. pp. 133–158.
Henare, Amiria, Martin Holbraad, and Sari Wastell (eds.). *Thinking Through Things: Theorising Artefacts Ethnographically*. London: Routledge, 2007.
Hui, Yuk. "Cosmotechnics as Cosmopolitics." *E-flux Journal*, no. 86, 2017. Web.
Ingold, Tim. *Being Alive: Essays on Movement, Knowledge and Description*. London: Routledge, 2011.
Kopytoff, Igor. "The Cultural Biography of Things: Commoditization as Process." *The Social Life of Things: Commodities in Cultural Perspective*. Arjun Appadurai (ed.). Cambridge: Cambridge University Press, 1986, pp. 64–91.
Latour, Bruno. *On the Modern Cult of the Factish Gods*. Duke University Press, 2010.
Leroi-Gourhan, André. *Gesture and Speech*. Cambridge: MIT Press, 1993.
Lody, Raul. "Oxé de Xangô: Um Estudo de Caso Da Cultura Material Afro-Brasileira." *Afro-Ásia*, vol. 14, 1983, pp.15–21

Marques, Lucas. "Forjando Orixás: Técnicas E Objetos Na Ferramentaria de Santo Da Bahia." *Série Antropologia*, vol. 452, 2016, pp. 1–188.

———. "Learning to Learn in Candomblé: Notes on Paths, Knowledge, and the 'Education of Distraction'". *Religion*, vol. 52, no. 1, 2021, doi:10.1080/0048721X.2021.2011087.

Martínez-Ruiz, Barbaro. *Kongo Graphic Writing and Other Narratives of the Sign*. Philadelphia: Temple University Press, 2013.

Rabelo, Miriam. *Enredos, Feituras E Modos de Cuidado: Dimensões Da Vida E Da Convivência No Candomblé*. Bahia: Edufba, 2014.

Rodrigues, Raymundo Nina. *O animismo fetichista dos negros bahianos*. Civilização Brasileira, s. a., 1935.

———. *Os Africanos No Brasil*. Rio de Janeiro: Centro Edelstein, 2010.

Sansi, Roger. "The Hidden Life of Stones: Historicity, Materiality and the Value of Candomblé Objects in Bahia." *Journal of Material Culture*, vol. 10, no. 2, 2005, pp. 139–156.

———. *Fetishes and Monuments: Afro-Brazilian Art and Culture in the Twentieth Century*. New York: Berghahn Books, 2007.

Schlanger, Nathan. "The Chaîne Opératoire". In: Colin Renfrew and Paul Bahn (Eds.). *Archaeology – Key Concepts*. London: Routledge, 2015.

Silva, Vagner Gonçalves da. "Arte Religiosa Afro-Brasileira: As Múltiplas Estéticas Da Devoção Brasileira." *Debates do NER: Nucleo de Estudos da Religião da UFRGS*, vol. 1, no. 13, 2008, pp. 97–114.

Simondon, Gilbert. *L'individuation à la lumière des notions de forme et d'information*. Grenoble: Éditions Jérôme Millon, 2002.

Thompson, Robert Farris. *Flash of the Spirit: African & Afro-American Art & Philosophy*. New York: Vintage Books, 1984.

Wafer, Jim. *The Taste of Blood: Spirit Possession in Brazilian Candomblé*. Philadelphia: University of Pennsylvania Press, 1991.

Index

Achimpong, L. 161
actor-network-theory 3, 165
Adinkra 155
al guitara 139–40, 144, 147
antiquarianism 1, 15, 103, 114
Apollinaire, G. 64
Appadurai, A. 5, 48, 73, 75, 79
àṣẹ 156
Asmat 10, 171–80
Assentamento 194
Axé 193, 195, 196

Babalorixá 186
Bamako 65–6, 68–9, 71, 74
Bastide, R. 187
Basu, P. 4, 5, 69
Bazawule, S. 158
Benin 150–1; Benin City 28–9
Benjamin, W. 55, 178
Bennett, J. 2, 4
Bergdamara 80
Bhabha, H. 139, 142, 145, 147
Bourgeot A. 139–4
Braidotti, R. 2
British Museum 102–4, 107–15, 176
Bühler, A. 26

Cameroon 41, 43, 48, 51–2
Candomblé 10, 159, 185–99
Carneiro da Cunha, M. 190
Caspar, F. 27
Chômeur 139–40, 144–5
Christoph, H. 162–3
Ci Wara 62, 64, 71
Claudot-Hawad, H. 140–5
Clifford, J. 6, 34, 44, 69
colonial 4, 5, 7–8, 10, 19–24, 27, 29, 31, 41–2, 44–5, 48–9, 54–7, 78–91, 104, 121, 123, 129, 141–2, 147, 150–61, 163, 166–80; administration 23, 68; colonial heritage 91–2; liabilities 17; colonization, tragic process of 23
Congo 29, 43, 61
Cook, J. 7–8, 100, 104, 115
cosmology 48, 52–3, 156, 174
cultural haemorrhaging 7
cultural turn: cultural heritage 176; cultural turns 2

Damaraland 84
de bahia, Salvador 10, 159, 186
decolonisation 19; decoloniality 20
De Martino, E. 52
Derain, A. 64
desert blues 139–40, 147
diaspora 43, 74, 159, 177; diasporas 150, 156–7; objects of 64
Diasporadical Trilogîa 158–9
Douglas, M. 2
Dutch 87, 10, 104, 134–5, 171–2, 174–5, 177–80
Duval-Carrié, E. 163

ecology 195
Elbein dos Santos, J. 190, 194
ethics 10, 178
ethnographical 30, 74, 128, 133
Exu 10, 187–94

Fabricus, J. C. 110
Farka Touré, A. 144
Farris Thompson, R. 187
Faulkner, W. 115
fetishist animism 185
fetishistic 3; fetishism 196
Förster, L. 69
Foumban 41

202　Index

Frambesia tropica 171
Frankfurt 54, 60–1, 66–7
Frobenius, L. 8, 60–77

Gell, A. 2, 152, 165, 194
Ghana 6, 90, 150–5, 158–60
Grimme, G. 48
Guillaume, H. 139–44
Gweagal 100, 105, 106, 115

Hahn, H. 61, 73, 151
Hahotoe 156–7
Haraway, D. 165
Harman, G. 3, 154, 165
Hawai'i 101, 106
headhunters 171, 173; headhunting 10, 173–81
Herero 80, 82, 84, 89
heritage 4–5, 41, 43, 48, 52–3, 71, 85, 91–2; cultural heritage 43, 70, 74, 102, 114, 151, 155, 157, 161, 175–7, 180; cultural heritage objects 178; heritage-making 44
Hicks, D. 2
Hildesheim 163, 165
Hinduism 150, 151, 154, 157
Hoe 111–13, 115
human remains 7, 10, 25, 27, 129, 171, 173–81; human skulls 31
Humboldt Forum 42
hybridity 43, 139, 142, 147

Ibeji 156–7, 159
Imperial Germany 120–2, 131
Ingold, T. 6, 186, 195
Ishumar 9, 139–45, 147
Ištar 153–4

jabá of Ogum 186–96
Joest, W. 9, 119–35

Kalashnikov 9, 139–40, 143–4
Karingana wa karingana 54
Keita, D. 69–74
kel tamasheq 142
Königliches Museum für Völkerkunde 88, 122
Kopytoff, I. 64
Kratz, C. 47

Latour, B. 3, 43, 165
Legba 162
Leroi-Gourhan, A. 188

Lévi-Strauss, C. 2, 15
Lévy-Bruhl, L.187
Libya 140–1, 143
liquid modernity 53
Lody, R. 187

Malé, Salia 69–70
Mali 7–8, 33, 60–3, 65–7, 69–74, 140, 143
Mambrol, N. 142
Mamishi Rasta 152–5, 157, 165
Mami Wata 152, 157, 159, 160, 162–4
Mana 105
Maori 26–8, 102, 108–9, 111, 114, 175, 178
Marcel, M. 2, 5
medals 9, 121, 125–6, 132–5
migrant materialities 4, 5
Miller, D. 3, 15
Miller, F. 107
Miller, J. F. 107, 112
Mitchell, W. J. T. 154, 165
mobility 6
musealization 64, 151, 162
museology 17

Namibia 42, 52, 80, 82–3, 86, 89–91
Naturvölker 82, 85, 87–8, 93
Ndambirkus 10, 171–7
Ndaokus 10, 171–6, 179
New Guinea 10, 30, 109, 121, 171, 175–8, 180
New Materialism 2
Nigeria 43, 90
nomadic 9, 139–46; *lumpen-nomad* 141
nonhuman 1; non-human 1, 2, 160, 165

Obaluaiê 187
Ogum 185–9, 191–8
Ondyise 84, 91
ontogenetic 6
ontological 2, 165, 186, 193, 195; flat ontology 3; object-oriented-ontology 165; ontology 3, 10, 186; OOO 165
Order of Albrecht 124, 128
òrìṣà 156
Orixá 185–98
Ossain 187
Otavi 80–1, 83
otherness 46, 85, 91, 163, 196
Ovambo 80
Oxóssi 187
Oxumarê 187

Papua New Guinea 176, 180
Paravicini, E. 26
Parkinson, S. 111, 112
Pasolini, P. P. 48, 55
Peffer, J. 5, 64
Penny, G. 78, 120
petitio principii 139–40, 145
phenomenology 3
Phillips, Ruth 5, 42, 56
presentification 48, 52, 152
provenance 4–5, 7–8, 63, 72, 98–100, 119, 154–5, 157, 172, 176, 180
Prussia 124, 127; Prussian 121–2, 127, 130, 132–3

restitution 26–7, 29, 33, 60, 70, 99–100, 135, 175–6, 180
Rijksmuseum voor Volkenkunde 172
ritual 26, 52, 65, 70–2, 154, 156, 158, 162, 164, 174–5, 185–6, 191, 196–7; ritual objects 30, 62–5; rituals 155, 175, 189, 191–2, 195
Rodrigues, Raymundo N. 185
Rurutu 102, 104–5, 109
Rütimeyer, L. 23, 28

Sahara 140–1, 145–6
Sarasin, F. 30, 36
Sarasin, Paul 30
Sarr, F. 60
Savoy, B. 60
Schlagintweit, H. 121, 129
Schlagintweit, R. 121, 129
Serrurier, L. 119–20
Sidibé, S. 69, 71–4
skulls 10, 26, 27, 31; Asmat Skulls 171–6
Sloane, H. 6

Society Islands 104–9
Sogoni Koun 62–3
Sri Lanka 30–2

Tagelmust 142
Tahiti 104–6, 108, 111, 114
Tchamba, Tchamba-Vodun 155, 157
terreiro 186, 189, 194, 198
teshumara 139–40, 142–5, 149–8
Thilenius, G. 63
Tierra del Fuego 102, 104–9
Togo 61, 150–1, 155, 160
Touareg 139–47
Traoré, B. 144
Traoré, N. 66–8

Umlauff 28, 30, 89
United Nations 171, 177, 180

Vodun 148–66
Volkswagen 9, 139, 146
von Bode, W. 132, 137

Webster, W. D. 28
Wedaarachchige, D. P. 31–2
We-mana-we 173
Weule, Karle 63
Winneba 151

Xangô 185, 192

Yorùbá 156, 159; Yoruba 168, 187, 190, 192; Yorubá 98

Zé Diabo 186–98
Zeller, R. 81–2, 87
Zillinger, M. 158
Zimmerman, A. 120–1
Zuni 33–4

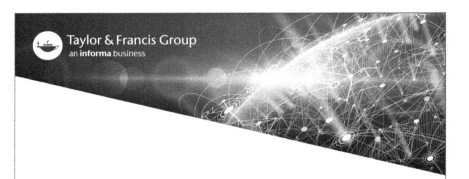

Milton Keynes UK
Ingram Content Group UK Ltd.
UKHW020221260924
448819UK00017B/300